John Burnside

CONTEMPORARY CRITICAL PERSPECTIVES

Series Editors: Jeannette Baxter, Peter Childs,
Sebastian Groes, and Kaye Mitchell

Guides in the *Contemporary Critical Perspectives* series provide companions to reading and studying major contemporary authors. They include new critical essays combining textual readings, cultural analysis, and discussion of key critical and theoretical issues in a clear, accessible style. Each guide also includes a preface by a major contemporary writer, a new interview with the author, discussion of film and TV adaptation, and guidance on further reading.

Titles in the series include:

Ali Smith edited by Monica Germana and Emily Horton
Andrea Levy edited by Jeannette Baxter and David James
Hilary Mantel edited by Eileen Pollard and Ginette Carpenter
Ian McEwan (2nd Edition) edited by Sebastian Groes
J. G. Ballard edited by Jeannette Baxter
Julian Barnes edited by Sebastian Groes and Peter Childs
Kazuo Ishiguro edited by Sean Matthews and Sebastian Groes
Salman Rushdie edited by Robert Eaglestone and Martin McQuillan
Sarah Waters edited by Kaye Mitchell
Don DeLillo edited by Katherine Da Cunha Lewin and Kiron Ward
John Burnside edited by Ben Davies

John Burnside

EDITED BY
BEN DAVIES

BLOOMSBURY ACADEMIC
LONDON · NEW YORK · OXFORD · NEW DELHI · SYDNEY

BLOOMSBURY ACADEMIC
Bloomsbury Publishing Plc
50 Bedford Square, London, WC1B 3DP, UK
1385 Broadway, New York, NY 10018, USA
29 Earlsfort Terrace, Dublin 2, Ireland

BLOOMSBURY, BLOOMSBURY ACADEMIC and the Diana logo are trademarks of
Bloomsbury Publishing Plc

First published in Great Britain 2020
This paperback edition published in 2021

Copyright © Ben Davies and contributors, 2020

Ben Davies and contributors have asserted their right under the Copyright, Designs and
Patents Act, 1988, to be identified as Author of this work.

The third party copyrighted material displayed in the pages of this book
are done so on the basis of fair dealing for the purposes of criticism and
review in accordance with international copyright laws, and is not intended
to infringe upon the ownership rights of the original owners.

For legal purposes the Acknowledgements on p. xii constitute an extension
of this copyright page.

Cover design: Eleanor Rose
Cover image © Getty Images

All rights reserved. No part of this publication may be reproduced or
transmitted in any form or by any means, electronic or mechanical,
including photocopying, recording, or any information storage or retrieval
system, without prior permission in writing from the publishers.

Bloomsbury Publishing Plc does not have any control over, or responsibility for,
any third-party websites referred to or in this book. All internet addresses
given in this book were correct at the time of going to press. The author
and publisher regret any inconvenience caused if addresses have changed
or sites have ceased to exist, but can accept no responsibility for
any such changes.

A catalogue record for this book is available from the British Library.

A catalog record for this book is available from the Library of Congress.

ISBN: HB: 978-1-3500-3697-0
PB: 978-1-3502-3744-5
ePDF: 978-1-3500-3699-4
eBook: 978-1-3500-3698-7

Series: Contemporary Critical Perspectives

Typeset by Integra Software Services Pvt. Ltd.

To find out more about our authors and books visit www.bloomsbury.com
and sign up for our newsletters.

Contents

Series Editors' Preface vii
Foreword: Starting Hares (Nicholas Royle) viii
Acknowledgements xii
Contributors xiv
Chronology of John Burnside's Life xvii

By Way of an Introduction: John Burnside, Writer
   Ben Davies 1

1. John Burnside's Metaphysical World: From *The Dumb House* to *A Summer of Drowning*
   Peter Childs 13

2. John Burnside's Numinous Poetry
   Jan Wilm 25

3. 'A Temporary, Sometimes Fleeting Thing': Home in John Burnside's Poetry
   Monika Szuba 39

4. Violent Dwellings and Vulnerable Creatures in *Burning Elvis* and *Something Like Happy*
   Alexandra Campbell 53

5. 'This Learned Set of Limits and Blames': Masculinity, Law and Authority in the Work of John Burnside
   Ruth Cain 67

6 Consequences of Pastoral: The Dialectic of History and Ecology in *The Light Trap*
Tom Bristow 81

7 Walking the Tightrope: Félix Guattari's *Three Ecologies* and John Burnside's *Glister*
Phill Pass 97

8 'A Kindred Shape': Hauntings, Spectres and the Poetics of Return in John Burnside's Verse
David Borthwick 109

9 'It Was Suddenly Hard Winter': John Burnside's Crossings
Julian Wolfreys 121

The Space at the Back of the Mind: An Interview with John Burnside
Ben Davies 133

Notes 143
Further Reading 147
Index 162

Series Editors' Preface

The readership for contemporary fiction has never been greater. The explosion of reading groups and literary blogs, of university courses and school curricula, and even the apparent rude health of the literary marketplace indicate an ever-growing appetite for new work, for writing which responds to the complex, changing and challenging times in which we live. At the same time, readers seem ever more eager to engage in conversations about their reading, to devour the review pages, to pack the sessions at literary festivals and author events. Reading is an increasingly social activity, as we seek to share and refine our experience of the book, to clarify and extend our understanding.

It is this tremendous enthusiasm for contemporary fiction to which the Contemporary Critical Perspectives series responds. Our ambition is to offer readers of current fiction a comprehensive critical account of each author's work, presenting original, specially commissioned analyses of all aspects of their career, from a variety of different angles and approaches, as well as directions towards further reading and research.

Our brief to the contributors is to be scholarly, to draw on the latest thinking about narrative, or philosophy, or psychology, indeed whatever seemed to them most significant in drawing out the meanings and force of the texts in question, but also to focus closely on the words on the page, the stories and scenarios and forms which all of us meet first when we open a book. We insisted that these essays be accessible to that mythical beast, the Common Reader, who might just as readily be spotted at the Lowdham Book Festival as in a college seminar. In this way, we hope to have presented critical assessments of our writers in such a way as to contribute something to both of those environments, and also to have done something to bring together the most important qualities of each of them.

Jeannette Baxter, Peter Childs, Sebastian Groes and Kaye Mitchell

Foreword: Starting Hares

Nicholas Royle

How to start talking about the voluminous and remarkable work of John Burnside? Answer: with something small, like a poem, in a spirit of anarchism. As he concludes his Preface to *On Henry Miller* (2018): 'What we need, each of us, is to become our own anarchists - which is to say, to unlearn our conditioning and refuse to be led, thus transforming ourselves into free-thinking, self-governing spirits.' Few contemporary writers evoke as sharply as Burnside does the challenges and difficulties of such anarchy. How can we unlearn? How might we transform ourselves? What is free thinking?

The poetic is key. It is his key. Take 'A Dead Hare, in the Driveway at Over Kellie, 15th October 2015', a poem in part about finding one's key ('the house key/spilling from my fingers in the dark'). The poet (the 'I' of the poem's storm), evidently drunk, comes home in a taxi late at night to find, near his front door, a dead hare 'almost unscathed': 'I stooped down/and ran my fingers through the empty pelt.' The taxi driver gets out, apparently also to have a look. It's not clear how the creature has died. Then the poem shifts, for its final two verses, to the following day:

> By morning, the fur had creased
> and shriveled, and the outcurve of the eye
> was nothing but a smudge
> of glaze and pulp, the limbs
> extended, still, as if they could recall
> the joy of bounding through the summer grass,
> still formal, while its substance leached away
> and left behind a corpse, abridged, unspooled,
> all tenderness surrendered to the rain
> so quietly, it made me want to stop
> and let the spell come over me, a brief

> rehearsal of the self shrugged off or pared
> away, another body shining through
> as skin and bone, perhaps, but with its light
> intact, the tawny camber of the soul
> protracted, till the chance of something new
> seemed possible, if only for an hour.

Feelings of, and for, non-human animals abound – not just in Burnside's poems but throughout his novels and other works. It's about the encounter: as he puts it, 'every time a human being encounters an animal, or a bird, he learns something new, or remembers something old that he had forgotten'.

In calling the body of this hare 'a corpse', the poem quietly affirms its linguistic strangeness, along with an expansiveness of time and a non-anthropocentric liberty. The word 'corpse' is today conventionally used only of humans, but it was not always so; death is the leveller, for hare and human alike. There is no 'I' in these two verses, only a single reference to a passive 'me'. 'Let the spell come over me': such openness to being taken over, to the possibilities of possession and magical thinking, is a sort of Burnside signature. Everywhere in his poetry, novels and memoirs, we can find the pleasure and danger of 'the spell': it is the condition of storytelling and (a different but also striking concern in his work) story-listening. There is a 'rehearsal of the self shrugged off': in this word *rehearsal* we are invited to think of the impossible – at once a practice performance (for when each one of us, hare or human, dies) and a narration or recounting (each time, each 'tawny camber', is unique). The brief drama may be a fiction, but the image of 'another body shining through' remains.

Burnside is fascinated by questions of time and scale (hence in part the critical attention to his work in the context of deep ecology): the poetry enacts this in its form and syntax. The ruinous work of rain occupies the first of these verses, yet that governing word comes only at the end, and even then is only a momentary stay ('all tenderness surrendered to the rain/so quietly, it made me want to stop'). In a seventeen-line sentence of Wordsworthian expansiveness and intricacy, the poem insists – despite time's creasing and shrivelling and smudging – on a sense of extended joy ('the limbs/extended, still, as if they could recall/the joy of bounding... '), in such a way that the 'body' of the final stanza becomes a mysterious metamorphosis of the 'dead hare' and 'self shrugged off' and 'something new'. The poem affirms an imaginative transformation, 'another body shining through' – not as some religious revelation but more in the etiolated mode of Robert Browning's 'Two in the Campagna' ('Then the good minute goes'), or Thomas Hardy's peripheral 'moments of vision', or Wallace Stevens's 'blazoned' interludes: 'From this the poem springs: that we live in a place/That is not our own and, much more, not ourselves/And hard it is in spite of blazoned days.'

Which is not to say that religion has not left its mark on Burnside: in his impish, perverse, Poe-like way he keeps the Catholic imagination disturbingly alive. As he writes in the memoir *A Lie about My Father*:

> If there is an afterlife, for me it will be limbo, the one truly great Catholic invention: a no man's land of mystery and haunting music, with nobody good or holy around to be compared to – *they* will all be in heaven – just the interesting outsiders, the unbaptised and the pagan, and the faultless sceptics God cannot quite find it in Himself to send to hell.

This 'no man's land of mystery and haunting music' Burnside has made his oeuvre. The novels reverberate with the music of others. He is a deeply literary writer – echoes and invocations, refrains and adaptations swirl about his work: Lucretius, Dante, Shakespeare, Wordsworth, Poe, Melville, Rimbaud, Conrad, Lawrence, Woolf, e.e. cummings, Salinger and so many others. He will talk, for instance in *Waking up in Toytown*, about 'that *certain slant of light* sensation' and leave it to readers to pick up the eerie heft of Emily Dickinson. And a critical monograph could be written about musical references in Burnside's books – from pagan and classical through to Neil Young, Brian Eno and beyond. But his work has a singular, 'outsider' music of its own, a music that becomes more haunting as we become attuned to how one poem or one novel is layered on another, but also as we hear (and cannot un-hear) the innumerable resonances and correspondences between his poetry and fiction, on the one hand, and his memoirs and autobiographical writings, on the other.

An entire essay might be given over to exploring the play of a single word, such as, say, 'glister', as it appears – fleetingly, charmingly – in the fine poem 'Haar' ('the glister of handmade toffees'), and then reappears – pervasively, horrifyingly – in the eponymous novel. The word has a rich history, perhaps best known through the proverbial 'All that glisters is not gold'. David Hume, in 1759, remarks that 'The false glister catches the eye, and leaves no room ... for the durable beauties of solid sense and lively passion'. As a noun, 'glister' is an archaism – but it is one that Burnside brings back to life and, in *Glister*, turns into a sparkling, haunting and claustrophobic world akin to Stephen King's *The Shining*. Mixing the nastiness of *The Wasp Factory* with the succulence of Wallace Stevens, *Glister* confronts us with murder, all glinting and showy in 'a *bower*, like those elaborate structures that some exotic birds make, when they want to attract a mate'. Burnside's novels — consistently focusing on uncomfortable strangeness and duplicity, domestic estrangement, the weird in the wild, the inhuman in the human – remind us that 'uncanny' is originally a Scottish word. But while his fiction has affinities with a 'Scottish Uncanny' – with writers such as Hogg, Stevenson, George Douglas Brown, Iain Banks,

Muriel Spark and A. L. Kennedy – it also refuses categories and resists pigeon-holing, nationalistic or generic.

Burnside could have killed his father. Perhaps every human male adult can identify with that sentiment. But Burnside really could, nearly did; he rehearses these patricidal aspirations and designs in the memoir about his alcoholic, abusive father. His memoirs detail experiences of physical threat and violence, as well as a psychological and spiritual resistance to 'the normal', which readers cannot then forget or set aside when turning to the novels and poems. In one passage of *A Lie about My Father* Burnside recalls a childhood holiday in Blackpool, in 1965. He was sitting in the sun on the wall outside the guest house when,

> out of nowhere, a boy appeared, a small, pale-faced boy with straw-coloured hair, laughing and saying something I couldn't hear. Momentarily, I was looking at him, trying to make out what he was saying – and then I was falling: backwards at first, then turning, twisting, my hands coming up over my face, my head darkening…

To be pushed and fall backwards into a basement: this is the sort of violent abruptness we become wary of encountering at any moment in Burnside's work.

The writing is sometimes shocking, often disturbing and at moments joyous and uplifting. And invariably what is most affecting is its attentiveness to a sense of the poetic, even in the glibbest phrase or idiom. It can also be, at moments, very funny. There is, for example, the moment when he recalls a question often asked of schoolchildren, 'one of those questions that always begin with *And*. "And what do you want to be when you grow up?"' John, the poor, psychologically if not physically abused, frightened boy growing up in a council house in Cowdenbeath, always replies 'without a moment's hesitation: "An Italian."' Burnside's work unnervingly illustrates D. H. Lawrence's observation that 'Nothing is wonderful unless it is dangerous.' In his life and in his writings, he likes becoming lost. And he encourages us to see that we need to get lost too.

Acknowledgements

I would like to thank all those who took part in the John Burnside Symposium held at the University of Portsmouth in November 2014; the papers and discussion inspired this present volume. For its support, both financial and collegial, I would like to thank the Centre for Studies in Literature at the University of Portsmouth. Thanks are also due to Jo West of the now sadly closed Blackwell's in Portsmouth for supporting the John Burnside Symposium, as well as many other events over many years. At Bloomsbury, I would like to thank David Avital, Clara Herberg and Lucy Brown. I would also like to thank Peter Childs and Sebastian Groes for their support with this project. Most of all, I would like to thank John Burnside for his public reading at the Portsmouth symposium, for answering numerous questions and for willingly being interviewed – in general, for being supportive and accommodating throughout this project.

The authors, editor and publisher are grateful to be able to quote from the following works: *The Asylum Dance* by John Burnside published by Jonathan Cape. Reproduced by permission of The Random House Group Ltd. ©2009; *Myth of the Twin* by John Burnside published by Jonathan Cape. Reproduced by permission of The Random House Group Ltd. ©1994; *A Normal Skin* by John Burnside published by Jonathan Cape. Reproduced by permission of The Random House Group Ltd. ©1997; *Still Life with Feeding Snake* by John Burnside published by Jonathan Cape. Reproduced by permission of The Random House Group Ltd. ©2017; *Swimming in the Flood* by John Burnside published by Jonathan Cape. Reproduced by permission of The Random House Group Ltd. ©1995; *The Good Neighbour* by John Burnside published by Jonathan Cape. Reprinted by permission of The Random House Group Limited. © 2005; *The Light Trap* by John Burnside published by Jonathan Cape. Reprinted by permission of The Random House Group Limited. © 2002. We are also grateful to Rogers, Coleridge & White Ltd UK to be able to quote from the following works by John Burnside under fair dealing: *The Hunt in the Forest* (2009) published by Jonathan Cape; *All One Breath* (2014) published by Jonathan Cape; *Black Cat Bone* (2011) published by Jonathan Cape; *Gift Songs* (2007) published by Jonathan Cape. Likewise, we are also grateful to United Agents to be able to quote from *Still Life with Feeding Snake* (2017) published by Jonathan Cape under fair usage. For granting permission to include Julian Wolfreys' chapter in this volume, thanks are due to Jean-Michel Ganteau, director of *Études britanniques contemporaines*; it was originally published as an essay: Julian Wolfreys (2015), 'It Was Suddenly Hard Winter': John Burnside's Crossings, *Études britanniques contemporaines*, 48: http://journals.openedition.org/ebc/2192; DOI: 10.4000/ebc.2192. Should other permissions be found wanting, the editor wishes to express his utmost apologies. He will gladly include them in any future editions of this volume.

Ben Davies
Southsea, November 2018

Contributors

Tom Bristow is International Junior Research Fellow in English Studies, Durham University; Research Fellow at Institute of English Studies, University of London; Honorary Fellow, Centre of Excellence for the History of Emotions at the University of Western Australia. He is the author of *The Anthropocene Lyric: An Affective Geography of Poetry, Person, Planet, Place* (Palgrave, 2015), co-editor of *The Cultural History of Climate Change* (Routledge, 2016) and editor-in-chief of *Philosophy Activism Nature*. Articles combining Tom's interest in the arts and sciences have been published in *Angelaki, Australian Literary Studies, Environmental Humanities, Green Letters, Philology Quarterly* and *Scottish Literary Review* amongst others.

David Borthwick lectures in literature and environmental humanities at the University of Glasgow's School of Interdisciplinary Studies. He is Programme Convenor for the MLitt programme in Environment, Culture and Communication. His research focuses on UK ecopoetry, the poetics of walking and the future of place.

Ruth Cain is Senior Lecturer in Law at the University of Kent, UK. She works across disciplines, usually, but not always, at the intersection points of law, literature and cultural studies. She has written variously on mental health, parenting, psychoanalysis and the study of neoliberal doctrines of 'well-being' and health. Her current projects include a study of the online culture around high-conflict divorces, research into the well-being and mental health impact of precarious work and the self-measurement of mental (ill) health. She has for some time been working on a monograph on neoliberal 'elite' parenting culture entitled *Privatising Motherhood: Confession and Anxiety in Neoliberal Parenting*.

Alexandra Campbell is Early Career Fellow in English Literature at the University of Edinburgh. Her research emerges at the intersection of several critical discourses, including critical ocean studies, the environmental humanities and world literature perspectives. She is particularly interested in ecologies and poetries of the sea and is currently working on her first monograph, provisionally titled 'Hydropoetics: Atlantic Modernity, World Ecology and the Techno-Ocean', which examines the cultural and historical parameters of oceanic resource exploitation in contemporary North Atlantic writing, focusing on discourses of extraction, disposal and transmission at sea. Her published and forthcoming articles appear in *The Journal of Postcolonial Writing*, *Humanities*, *Études Écossaises* and *Anglistik*, and she has contributed a book chapter in the Palgrave edited collection *The Politics of Space and Place in Scottish Literature*.

Peter Childs is Professor of Modern and Contemporary English Literature at Newman University, Birmingham, UK. The author or editor of over twenty books, he is well known internationally as a leading critic of contemporary British literature and culture as well as postcolonial writing. He has published widely on literature post-1900 and on such writers as E. M. Forster, Ian McEwan, Julian Barnes and Paul Scott in particular. His books include *Contemporary Novelists: British Fiction since 1970* (Palgrave, 2005, 2012), *Aesthetics and Ethics in Twenty-First Century British Novels* (Bloomsbury, 2013) and *Modernism and the Post-Colonial* (Continuum, 2007).

Ben Davies is Senior Lecturer in English Literature at the University of Portsmouth. His research focuses on contemporary literature, philosophy, literary theory, narratology, time and sexuality studies. He is the author of *Sex, Time, and Space: Exceptional Intercourse* (Palgrave, 2016) and the co-editor of *Sex, Gender and Time in Fiction and Culture* (Palgrave, 2011). He has also published essays in a number of edited collections, as well as articles in *Critique: Studies in Contemporary Fiction* and *Textual Practice*.

Phill Pass has taught at the University of St Andrews. He is the author of *The Language of Self: Strategies of Subjectivity in the Novels of Don DeLillo* (Peter Lang, 2014) and has published in *Forum for Modern Language Studies* and *Agenda*. He is a previous recipient of the Dan Cruickshank Memorial Fund Scholarship.

Nicholas Royle is Professor of English at the University of Sussex. His books include *Telepathy and Literature: Essays on the Reading Mind* (1991), *E. M. Forster* (2000), *Jacques Derrida* (2003), *The Uncanny* (2003), *How to Read Shakespeare* (2005), *Veering: A Theory of Literature* (2011), *An Introduction to Literature, Criticism and Theory* (Fifth edition, 2016, co-authored with Andrew Bennett), and *Hélène Cixous: Dreamer, Realist, Analyst, Writing* (2020). He has also published two novels, *Quilt* (2010) and *An English Guide to Birdwatching* (2017). He is currently completing a book entitled *Mother: A Memoir*.

Monika Szuba is Lecturer in English Literature at the University of Gdańsk, Poland. Her research is mostly concerned with twentieth- and twenty-first-century Scottish and English poetry and prose, with a particular interest in ecocriticism informed by phenomenology. She is the author of *Contemporary*

Scottish Poetry and the Natural World: Burnside, Jamie, Robertson and White (Edinburgh University Press, 2019); editor of *Boundless Scotland: Space in Scottish Fiction* (Wydawnictwo Uniwersytetu Gdańskiego, 2015); and co-editor with Julian Wolfreys of *The Poetics of Space and Place in Scottish Literature* (Palgrave, 2019) and *Reading Victorian Literature: Essays in Honour of J. Hillis Miller* (Edinburgh University Press, 2019).

Jan Wilm is a writer, translator, and critic. He is the author of *The Slow Philosophy of J. M. Coetzee* (Bloomsbury, 2016) and the co-editor of *Samuel Beckett und die deutsche Literatur* (Transcript, 2013) and *Beyond the Ancient Quarrel: Literature, Philosophy, and J. M. Coetzee* (Oxford University Press, 2017). His first novel, *Winterjahrbuch* (Schöffling & Co.), was published in German in 2019. He has translated books by Maggie Nelson and Andrew O'Hagan into German. His book reviews have appeared in the *Frankfurter Allgemeine Zeitung*, the *Neue Zürcher Zeitung*, the *Times Literary Supplement* and the *Los Angeles Review of Books*.

Julian Wolfreys was, most recently, Professor of English Literature and Director of the Centre for Studies in Literature, at the University of Portsmouth. The author and editor of numerous studies of nineteenth- and twentieth-century literature and literary theory, his most recent publications are *Haunted Selves, Haunting Places in English Literature and Culture 1800-Present* (Palgrave, 2018) and, as co-editor with Monika Szuba, *The Poetics of Space and Place in Scottish Literature* (Palgrave, 2019).

Chronology of John Burnside's Life

1955	Born in Dunfermline on 19th March to 'Tommy' and Theresa Burnside. Burnside family live in Cowdenbeath, first in a King Street tenement and then in a prefab on Blackburn Drive.
1961	Burnside family move to Birmingham for several weeks, before returning to Cowdenbeath.
1965	Burnside family move to Corby, Northamptonshire.
1973–1976	Attends Cambridgeshire College of Arts and Technology, graduating with a BA(Hons) in English and European Thought and Literature.
1976–1994	Employed in numerous jobs, before working in computer systems analysis for a decade. During this period, admitted twice to Fulbourn Mental Hospital.
1988	Publication of first volume of poetry, *The Hoop*, which wins a Scottish Arts Council Book Award.
1991	Publication of second poetry collection, *Common Knowledge*, which wins a Scottish Arts Council Book Award.
1992	Publication of *Feast Days*, which wins the Geoffrey Faber Memorial Prize.
1994	Returns to Fife and becomes a freelance writer. Publication of *The Myth of the Twin*.
1995	Publication of *Swimming in the Flood*.
1995–1997	Becomes Scottish Arts Council Writer in Residence at the University of Dundee.
1997	Publication of *A Normal Skin* and publication of first novel, *The Dumb House: A Chamber Novel*.

1999	Becomes Lecturer in Creative Writing at the University of St Andrews. Elected a Fellow of the Royal Society of Literature. Publication of *The Mercy Boys*, which receives an Encore Award.
2000	Publication of *The Asylum Dance* and first short story collection, *Burning Elvis*. *The Asylum Dance* is shortlisted for the T. S. Eliot Prize and the Forward Poetry Prize, wins the Whitbread Poetry Award.
2001	Publication of *The Locust Room*. Release of television miniseries *Dice*, written with A. L. Kennedy.
2002	Publication of *The Light Trap*, which is shortlisted for the Saltire Society Scottish Book of the Year Award and the T. S. Eliot Prize.
2003	Publication of *Living Nowhere*.
2004	Publication of *Wild Reckoning: An Anthology Provoked by Rachel Carson's Silent Spring*, edited with Maurice Riordan.
2005	Publication of *The Good Neighbour*, which is shortlisted for the Forward Poetry Prize.
2006	Publication of *Selected Poems* and first memoir, *A Lie about My Father*, which wins the Saltire Society Scottish Book of the Year Award and the Sundial/SAC Non-Fiction Book of the Year Award.
2007	Publication of *Gift Songs* and *The Devil's Footprints: A Romance*.
2008	Receives Cholmondeley Award for poetry. Publication of *Glister*.
2009	Awarded the Prix Litteraire Europeen Madeleine Zepter for the French translation of *A Lie about My Father*, *Un mensonge sur mon pere*. Publication of *The Hunt in the Forest*.
2010	Publication of second memoir, *Waking up in Toytown*.
2011	Becomes Professor in Creative Writing at the University of St Andrews. Receives the Petrarca-Preis for poetry. Publication of *Black Cat Bone* and *A Summer of Drowning*. *A Summer of Drowning* shortlisted for the Costa Book Awards. *A Lie about My Father* wins the Corine International Literature Prize. *Waking up in Toytown* shortlisted for PEN/Ackerley Award. *Black Cat Bone* wins the Forward Poetry Prize and the T. S. Eliot Prize.

2012	Awarded the Spycher: Literaturpreis Leuk for poetry. Wins the Eccles British Library Writers in Residence Award; residency begins in January 2013.
2013	Publication of *Something Like Happy*.
2014	Appointed as a judge for the 2015 Man Booker Prize. *Something Like Happy* wins the Edge Hill Short Story Prize. Publication of *All One Breath* and third memoir, *I Put a Spell on You*.
2014–2015	Writer in Residence at DAAD (Deutscher Akademischer Austauschdienst), Berlin.
2016	Becomes a Fellow of the Royal Society of Edinburgh.
2017	Publication of *Still Life with Feeding Snake*, *Ashland & Vine* and *Havergey*.
2018	Radio play 'Coldhaven' wins *The Hörspielpreis der Kriegsblinden* (War Blinded Audio Play Prize). Publication of *On Henry Miller: Or, How to Be an Anarchist*.

By Way of an Introduction: John Burnside, Writer

Ben Davies

'John Burnside' is neither 'just' a poet nor 'just' a novelist; he is a writer. His writing includes prose fiction and (non)-fiction, poetry, critical essays, journalism, a television screenplay and more. As with the way in which many of Burnside's writings offer the reader a glimpse of something only to take it away, unveiling and veiling it simultaneously – for instance, the mysterious *huldra* in *A Summer of Drowning* (2012) or the mouse that is both 'impossible' and 'definitely there' in 'Slut's Hair' (Burnside 2013: 42) – 'John Burnside' is not something that is simply there, or present. He is, as it were, a type of Rubin vase: for some, a poet; for others, a novelist; for some, an essayist; for others still, Burnside *is* a writer who writes across genres. The texts that fall under the name 'John Burnside' interrelate and can, indeed, be seen as one overall text with its various folds, twists and creases. This wider text involves order and disorder, the illogical and the irrational – ways of seeing and thinking that, though different, are not altogether separate from more 'rational', trusted, traditional forms of epistemology and dwelling or *being-in-the-world*. Given his prolific output across numerous forms (including nine novels, fourteen collections of poetry, three memoirs and two short story collections to date) and the way in which his writing often asks its reader to see and think differently about the world, 'John Burnside' can be seen as a writer-thinker, a type of poet-intellectual. Burnside is a 'poet' in the broadest of senses, a thinker-maker involved in the act and process of creation (*poiesis*), and his overall text provokes thought, particularly about the world in which we, human animals, live.

Not necessarily a household name or a publicly known contemporary 'author' in the same way as, say, Zadie Smith or Ian McEwan are (see the interview in this volume), Burnside has been critically recognized and rewarded for his writing, receiving numerous prizes and accolades (see Bracke 2014: 437–8). For poetry, these awards include the Scottish Arts Council Book Award (*The Hoop* and *Common Knowledge*), the Geoffrey Faber Memorial Prize (*Feast Days*), the Whitbread Poetry Award (*The Asylum Dance*), the Forward Poetry Prize and the T. S. Eliot Prize (*Black Cat Bone*). Prizes for his prose works include the Encore Award (*The Mercy Boys*), the Saltire Society Scottish Book of the Year Award, the Sundial/SAC Non-Fiction Book of the Year Award, the Corine International Literature Prize and the Prix Litteraire Europeen Madeleine Zepter (*A Lie about My Father*). For his writing more generally, Burnside has also received the Spycher: Leuk Literturpreis and the Petrarca-Preis. He is also a Fellow of both the Royal Society of Literature (elected in 1999) and the Royal Society of Edinburgh (elected in 2016).

As a counterpart to this critical acclaim and recognition, however, John Burnside's writings also include 'failures', or at least what he himself sees as failures. For instance, he describes his first collection of poetry, *The Hoop* (1988), as 'a car crash', and he has labelled the three novels that follow his debut novel *The Dumb House* (1997) – *The Mercy Boys* (1999), *The Locust Room* (2001) and *Living Nowhere* (2003) – 'disastrous' (Crown 2011: paras 11, 13). Such a sense of failure is, however, not merely something in and of the past, the retrospective self-assessment of a more mature and successful writer. In the preface to *On Henry Miller* (2018), Burnside confesses: 'I was stuck. The book was almost finished, and I was trying to make a decent fist of liking it … but I was failing miserably' (2018a: ix). More than single, specific instances of failure, Burnside also sees failure as part of the writerly mode of being. Defending Henry Miller's desire to receive the Nobel Prize for Literature, Burnside explains: 'what [people] perhaps fail to appreciate is just how hard it is, for the literary writer, to live with the constant suspicion of inevitable failure that comes with the job' (143). The inkling, anticipation and wariness of failure: a fundamental part of literary writing – of being a writer. Of course, Burnside's judgements about his own works are personal, subjective assessments, and the reader can accept or dismiss them as she wishes. However, such observations and appraisals at least offer a sense of what it may mean to say that a text 'fails'. For Burnside specifically, failure partly derives from the difference between the imagined or envisioned and the written: 'there's no doubt', he says, 'that that original image that you had in your head is not matched by the thing that gets put on the paper at the end. So, it's a sense of partial failure, at least, if not complete failure' (see Interview).

Alongside these reflections on the theoretical differences between the imagined or ideal poem and the written or the 'actual' poem, the notion of failure also allows Burnside's readers to think about his writing in different ways. For instance, Burnside's discussion of his struggle with *On Henry Miller* provides a glimpse of his thinking and writing process: 'in the end, I had to write this book in order to find out why I wanted to write this book. Then, of course, I had to throw it all away and start again' (2018a: xxviii). This insight into writing-as-thinking, as a form of exploration itself, this openness to failure – of effort, deletion, rethinking and rewriting – acknowledges and unveils the imprecision, impermanence and potential failure inherent in all writing, which, as the word 'essay' at least embodies (see Dillon 2017), can only ever be a form of trying and trial; writing and thought are at best provisional attempts. As Burnside writes in 'Strong Words' (2000), the poetic, the philosophical and the provisional are, for him, mutually imbricated: 'I was first drawn to poetry as an instrument and a discipline, a means by which I might discover what I knew about myself and the world; thus, from the beginning, I felt that my own work was always and necessarily provisional, and so, philosophical' (259). Provisionality and the risk of failure are characteristic of Burnside's thought and his philosophic, writerly, poetic project, as he continually attempts to think in ways that are different from, and challenge, conventional, rational modes of thought and knowledge. He purposely pursues forms of irrationality, and he celebrates getting lost, moving away from accepted ideas and received opinion, so as to open up different ways of seeing, thinking and being. For instance, in his second memoir, *Waking up in Toytown* (2010), Burnside asks: 'Who wants to be safe? Who wants to be sane? Who wants to be *normal*?' (216). In his third memoir, *I Put a Spell on You* (2014), a text of 'digressions' in which he reflects upon numerous and varied subjects, Burnside specifically explores the '*thrawn*', that which is '*twisted, crooked, distorted, misshapen, deformed, awry, turned in a wrong direction*'; the '*perverse, obstinate, contrary, cross-grained intractable, not amenable*' (38). The *thrawn* are the wild forms of life that can provoke and beget ways of thinking, seeing and living that are not conventional, sanctioned or part of the 'Authorised Version' (*passim*) of societal existence.

In his explorations of alternative ways of dwelling, Burnside often turns to modes of thought and living that challenge mainstream thinking and so-called 'objectivity' (2018a: xxvi). An essential dimension of such thinking for Burnside is 'Daoist-Anarchism', which ultimately requires one 'to live according to one's inherent nature' (20). To live in such a way, we must, Burnside emphasizes, 'unlearn our conditioning and refuse to be led, thus transforming ourselves into free-thinking, self-governing spirits and, if we are fortunate indeed, to become one with the Way' (xxx), that is, with 'the Dao, the Universal Order, Nature, and so on, though none of these terms are adequate' (83). As Burnside explains, one cannot describe, seek out or understand the 'Way'; rather, he learned that 'if you accepted the natural order and simply observed it ... then you could apprehend that order *in its workings*' (83). For Burnside, then, the 'Way' is, and opens up, a way of 'seeing' and 'knowing' that is different from many prevailing forms of epistemology and 'scientific' knowledge. Correlatively, as part of his 'quest' (see Burnside 2003: 9; 2017b) to articulate different ways of being and thinking, Burnside also emphatically and consistently opposes the opposition between science and art. For instance, he (and Maurice Riordan) describes 'ecology' as a 'delineation of a *Logos* of dwelling, a *Logos* that is neither exclusively "science" nor "art", but side-steps such definitions in an attempt to understand, in the fullest sense, what it means to dwell in the world as humans' (Burnside and Riordan 2004: 21). As a way to explore and understand how humans dwell, Burnside's writings are, then, not simply part of the contemporary 'culture industry'; rather, they are part of an intellectual, creative act and mode of thought; they are texts that ask the reader to see and think differently, particularly about our 'creaturely' existence, our dwelling and *being-in-the-world*. For Burnside, being in 'accord' with the earth and all other living things, recognizing our own 'creatureliness' and being part of the natural way, is the only way to live as humans if we are not to continue damaging the earth (see Burnside 2006b: 93). As he writes in the essay 'Samiland: The Finnmarksvidda' (2018), which moves between and across the material, the imaginary and the aural, it is essential to recognize, as did the ancient Sami, 'that we are neither great, nor worthless, but creatures under the sun, like the bear and the elk, the halibut and the seal, the reindeer crossing the great plain and the Artic poppy that turns on its delicately engineered stem to follow the sun in its path through the sky' (2018b: 28).

A further set of oppositional terms Burnside's writing challenges, and which provoke us to think carefully about his work, are 'truth' and 'falsehood'. Approaching Burnside's texts as those of a living writer and, importantly, one who has written memoirs, 'life writing', 'autofiction' – whatever label one wishes to use – can make the desire to read the writer into and from the work especially seductive. However, Burnside's writings warn against any simple equation between life and writing, writing and life. In the note that precedes *Waking up in Toytown*, for example, Burnside provides a common disclaimer, telling the reader: 'This book is as factually accurate as memory allows.' He further addresses the vicissitudes of memory in the text itself, admitting, for instance: 'I don't know why I am remembering all this so clearly. There are other, better narratives from that time locked away in my head, rich seams of silver and anthracite, veins of gold and mica that would be so much more gratifying to unearth – but I can't get through, I can't find a way into that glittering substratum' (2010: 104). Alongside such fairly standard provisos and explorations about the fallibility of memory, Burnside's first memoir, *A Lie* about *My Father* (2006), approaches the nexus of life, truth, lies, narrative and fiction in a more complex and intricate way. The very title immediately warns (or reminds) the reader to be cautious, and the note he provides ahead of the narrative is much more intricate than the one that precedes *Toytown*, advising: 'This book is best treated as a work of fiction. If he were here to discuss it, my father would agree, I'm sure, that it's as true to say that I never had a father as it is to say that he never had a son' (2006a). The reader is not told that this is a work of fiction: the note provides only a recommendation, *at best*. Consequently, the authorial note is less authoritative than the status and function of this standard paratextual apparatus may imply. Moreover, the question of 'truth' is not settled; rather, it is kept open, made more ambiguous, with the logic being at least double: Is Burnside's statement true? Is it false or negatively true and therefore affirmative? Ultimately, the note offers a type of riddle or paradox, left open and unanswered, potentially unanswerable.

This riddle-like uncertainty permeates Burnside's first memoir, both as a general mood and as a subject for exploration. As Burnside's reflection on his first stay in a mental hospital shows, for example, he explores the intricate relationship between truth, lies and narrative:

> This story is a lie about madness: it's bound to be a lie, because nothing I say about that first visit to Fulbourn could be true. A lie, or a story, which amounts to the same thing, if what I say differs in any way from my medical records: records I have seen and marvelled at, for their sheer – *what?* Stupidity? (2006a: 255)

Lies and stories are equivalent, yet supposed guarantors of truth, the medical records, are undermined due to a sense of their 'stupidity'; as an institutionalized form of legal-psychiatric discourse, Burnside implies, these records do not tell the truth, the whole truth or, perhaps, even anything like the truth as he experienced or remembers it. As Burnside's text shows (or reminds us at least), truth and falsehood are not diametrically opposed; rather, they are intertwined, part of a relationship that becomes even more complex in the realm of writing. Indeed, Burnside's narrative of and on truth, lies and stories resonates emphatically at the present moment given the current interest in so-called 'post-truth' (Oxford Dictionaries Word of the Year 2016), as it directly draws attention to notions of truth and narrative constructions. As if distantly echoing Nietzsche's analysis of accepted lies and unaccepted truths in 'On Truth and Lying in a Non-Moral Sense' (1873), Burnside explores lying's many forms and its various effects. He recalls, for instance, school history as being 'just an excuse in facts, an avoidance of obvious errors, rather than any attempt to get at the truth. It was also an exercise in power' (2006a: 102). Moreover, Burnside makes a distinction between sanctioned, conventional lies and those that have an epiphanic or revelatory effect in his day-to-day life, explaining: 'Part of this daytime enterprise is the tissue of lies by which I construct a visible self. Sometimes the lies are authorised, the textbook lies of citizenship and masculinity and employment we are all obliged to tell. Occasionally, they are the lies that reveal the unofficial version of the self, the truth of being' (2006a: 309). Through such explorations, Burnside's memoir has both a particular present, *à la mode* force and a significance beyond any current, faddish relevance. Indeed, Burnside's first memoir may aim to get at a truth, for him and possibly for the reader as well, but it also positions itself as lie. Moreover, it problematizes generic categories, creating a text that is part-novel, part-memoir, and it thereby offers a particularly rich text through which to think about longstanding (as well as current) ideas concerning truth, lying, fiction and narrative (see also Menn 2018).

Without explicit recourse to the theoretical curve that includes Wimsatt and Beardsley, Barthes, Foucault *et al.*, Burnside's own writings, then, emphasize that there is no simple relation to be discovered between his life and his writing (even his 'life writing'). Consequently, it may be more productive to think about Burnside's texts as a type of space; space is, after all, a recurring concern throughout his writing. Moreover, in *A Lie about My Father*, Burnside partly unveils the mysterious, intangible space of creation, 'at the back of [his] mind, where stories unfold according to their own logic – not common sense, not wisdom, not folly, but story logic, destiny, character, whatever we choose to call it' (2006a: 225). In the interview in this volume, Burnside elaborates on this particular space in more detail, explaining:

> at the back of your mind, you've got a big pool and you drop lines down into it and then fish things out of the subconscious. You've also got a kind of big headland or something behind the back of your head, which goes out the back of your head, and into the world, and so forth, and into memory, and history, into the woods, in a sense.[1]

For Burnside, creation comes from a type of space, which he renders in terms of other types of space – as well as the pool, the headland and the woods, this space is made up of harbours, forests, orchards and meadows (Interview); it is space doubled or even squared. Interesting in themselves for their glimpse of a certain way of thinking about creation and the space of creativity and *poiesis*, these unveilings also remind the reader that reading is, in part at least, always to take up and dwell with/in the space of an other. Significantly, Burnside reveals that such indetermination is, moreover, part of his creative space, explaining: 'it isn't just my head, as it were, it's whatever that drops back into, in terms of, you know, folk memory, or members of a tribe' (Interview). The space of creativity is not entirely internal; nor does it belong to a single self or subject. Reading Burnside in particular, this space is especially resonant, as much of his thought focuses on space, ecology, dwelling and *being-in-the-world*; his writings also feature many spaces that involve the darker, more disturbing aspects of human life, such as the basement in *The Dumb House*, for example. More recently, *Ashland & Vine* (2017) specifically emphasizes the important relationship between space and storytelling. In this narrative about narrative, Jean Culver's kitchen becomes – along with the Sacred Grounds coffee shop – a space of creation, a space in which she tells her story to alcoholic Kate Lambert as a means of care, 'exchanging stories for sober days, like some latter-day Scheherazade' (2017a: 332). Significantly, this space is itself described as being other than simply internal and sealed, with Kate reflecting on her first visit that 'the kitchen was a wide, high space and, with all the windows open, it didn't seem to belong entirely with the house, as if its true allegiances were to the garden' (17). As with the description of Burnside's creative space, Culver's storytelling space 'drops back' into, and seems to belong to, the external world, thereby also diminishing any simplistic borders or divisions. Moreover, the kitchen as a site for storytelling may also be a certain externalization or mirroring of one of the spaces where Burnside's own creativity sometimes takes place; offering a glimpse of his writing life in 'My Working Day' (2017), he discloses: 'Often, the bewildered victim of a gamut of sleep disorders that, so far, have defied medical science, I can be found in our kitchen at three in the morning, pen in one hand, a cup of valerian tea in the other' (2017b: 4).

None of this, of course, is to say that the reader should make a simple equation between Burnside's description of a mental, creative space and his texts; indeed, this introduction has argued against any such straightforward biographical reading or one-dimensional analysis of Burnside's work. However, the imagery of Burnside's creative space can help to remind us that reading is a form of dwelling, of being alone and together with an other simultaneously. Images, metaphors and ideas of space, and dwelling in and with a text, also help move the reader and critic away from the biographical. Indeed, this mental/textual space can be seen as another facet of 'Burnside's' poetic ecology, another aspect of its textual unfolding. Approaching Burnside's work with such images and ideas in mind may encourage the reader to think about the text as a space and not simply as the means of the representation of space. Metonymically, such metaphors ask us to consider how reading can inform our thinking and *being-in-the-world*, as dwelling also involves complex relations between the internal and the external, the spaces we occupy and the spaces that we, as humans, are.

In the preface to *On Henry Miller*, Burnside invokes a different type of spatial metaphor, explaining that this study of the American writer comes at 'a particular juncture of [his] own life' (2018a: xxiv). As he elaborates in the interview in this volume, this juncture was marked by ill health, a sense of diminished purpose, and feeling delimited by people labelling him a poet only. Importantly, his sense of being at a juncture is, Burnside says in the interview, not simply historical. Indeed, his desire to write in a more politically engaged way may only just be beginning, he says. The idea of the juncture and its related senses and images provide the reader with a further spatial (and temporal) metaphor through which to think about 'John Burnside'. The juncture marks a space of joining – the past to the present and the future, as well as past, present and future work. 'Juncture' also signals a time of crisis. This collection seems particularly timely, then, offering the first volume on Burnside's writing across all its forms and genres.[2] Moreover, this introduction is being written at the same time as the Intergovernmental Panel on Climate Change (IPCC) released its 2018 report on the effects of global warming and the urgency with which we need to reduce CO_2 emissions (see www.ipcc.ch/report/sr15/). Given Burnside's ecological thought and writing, and his long-standing concern with dwelling and forms of 'creaturely' existence, his work seems especially pressing and important at this particular moment, this 'eco-juncture'. The metaphor of 'juncture' also underscores the way in which this volume does not offer some sort of exhaustive or authoritative overview – as if it that were ever possible. Instead, the chapters in this book open up an exploration of texts that are grouped together under the signature 'John Burnside'; they enter into dialogue with previous scholarship and keep such dialogue open for and to the future. Correlatively, the chapters do not fix John Burnside as a poet, a novelist, a memoirist or an essayist; collectively, they cover his writing in its many forms, keeping designation, fixity and taxonomy at most provisional. This volume can itself, then, be seen to offer a type of juncture, an opening up and joining together, of what has been written by and on John Burnside, and what will be written by and on him in the future to come.

At the opening of this juncture, Peter Childs's essay provides a way into the writings of John Burnside through its consideration of Burnside's 'metaphysical world'. Focusing on the interrelationships between the physical and the metaphysical across Burnside's oeuvre, and in particular the fiction from *The Dumb House* to *A Summer of Drowning*, this chapter analyses the many binaries and dualities that occur in Burnside's work, such as twins and doubles, the signifier and signified, science and imagination. Childs's chapter provides an intricate reading of the animistic, Gnostic and alchemical elements of Burnside's writing, proposing that they offer a form of knowledge and revelation via the senses rather than the conscious mind, which ultimately exposes us to our undisclosed selves and makes possible transformation or healing. Jan Wilm's chapter also focuses on the spiritual and religious dimensions of Burnside's work, ranging across his Judeo-Christian, Buddhist, Hindu and pagan influences and references. His reading of Burnside's poetry, from *Swimming in the Flood* (1995) to *Black Cat Bone* (2011), and its heightened effects analyses the interrelationships between the sacred and the profane, the material and the spiritual. For Wilm, Burnside's poetics of ambiguity and indeterminacy create a numinous effect. Specifically addressing Burnside's frequent conjuring up of ghosts and spirits, Wilm argues that these common, yet wondrous, figures offer alternative forms of epistemology, creating and presenting the numinous. Moreover, such figures are part of the way in which, Wilm contends, Burnside's poetry brings about a 'secularization of the numinous'.

Keeping with poetry, Monika Szuba's chapter analyses a central concern throughout Burnside's work – dwelling. Reading across collections from *The Light Trap* (2002) to *Still Life with Feeding Snake* (2017) together with Heidegger's theoretical work on dwelling, for example, Szuba argues that Burnside's poetry reveals the necessity to locate oneself and find a home, however temporary any dwelling place may be; finding a home is, for Burnside, an ongoing quest. In her analysis, Szuba focuses in particular on the relationship between dwelling and language, and the problematic of naming. She argues that Burnside's poetry deploys various naming strategies as a way to order the world, even if such ordering is plural and provisional. Burnside's emphasis on the role of language in dwelling, Szuba argues, opens up the world to us and us to the world. In her chapter, Alexandra Campbell also focuses on the homely and the domestic but turns instead to Burnside's unsettled and unsettling domestic spaces. She explores the cruelty and violence that run throughout Burnside's prose works and analyses the ways in which homes are both threatening and under threat in his two short story collections, *Burning Elvis* (2000) and *Something Like Happy*. For Campbell, Burnside's violent dwellings have urgent, pressing ecological implications, bound up with notions of responsibility, kinship and vulnerability. Violence is, she argues, presented by Burnside as part of an ethics of vulnerability and a possibility of renewal and grace; exposure and vulnerability present the possibility for renewed forms of human 'creaturely' being and rejuvenated ecological relations with others. In keeping with the darker elements of Burnside's work, Ruth Cain analyses the undersides and unwritten laws of his poetry, fiction and memoirs. Positioning Burnside as a political commentator on today's global moment and its related ethics, Cain specifically focuses on the interrelationships in Burnside's work between masculinity, gender and class. She demonstrates that Burnside's writings work to unravel fixed generalizations concerning class and gender and open them up to more intricate and complex readings. Through a close analysis of *I Put a Spell on You*, Cain argues that Burnside writes against the neoliberal 'Authorised Version' of life and offers an alternative in the form of the 'thrawn', which, she proposes, is as an example of the Lacanian Real. In her insightful political reading, Cain also explores the gender and ethical contradictions entailed in the idea of the 'thrawn' and the complicated relationship between Burnside's representations of 'sociopathic masculinity' and the more anarchic-utopian elements of his writing. For Cain, Burnside is a challenging and complex writer, whose work ultimately offers an intricate and uneasy examination of contemporary life.

The following two chapters both focus predominantly on single works by Burnside. In his chapter, Tom Bristow offers a sustained analysis of Burnside's eighth volume of poetry, *The Light Trap*. Arguing for the volume's importance in Burnside's oeuvre, Bristow specifically focuses on the way in which *The Light Trap* partakes in, and also develops, the traditions of pastoral and elegy. Specifically, Bristow argues, the volume's tripartite structure reflects Burnside's dialectical thinking, which involves mental imagining, perceptions of space and social practice, as opposed to the simpler oppositional figurations often encountered in pastoral. Correlatively, Bristow argues, this volume moves beyond the traditional elegiac sense of loss, presenting instead forms of decreation in which humans are seen as either being at one with nature or as having been absorbed into the landscape. *The Light Trap*, Bristow argues, deconstructs the ecology/history binary and offers a rendering of home in exile, opening up forms of communal animal life. Also focusing on ecology, Phill Pass likewise keeps his attention on one work, Burnside's novel *Glister* (2008). Specifically, Pass reads *Glister* alongside Félix Guattari's *The Three Ecologies* (1989) to argue that Burnside's novel emphasizes the need for radical ecological transformation, which can only be achieved in the Anthropocene if we attend to personal subjectivity, society and technology together; both Guattari and Burnside, Pass argues, demonstrate that incrementalist environmentalism does not work. In this forceful reading, Pass ultimately argues that *Glister* offers not an answer to our current environmental degradation but demonstrates, ecopolitically and ecopoetically, the need for radical change if we are to sustain some form of viable communal life.

The final two chapters visit Burnside's haunting, spectral concerns and, correlatively, the unsettling quality of reading his work. In his chapter, David Borthwick focuses on spectral figures and the supernatural across Burnside's poetry, from *The Myth of the Twin* (1994) to *Still Life with Feeding Snake*, as a way to think through ideas of cultural inheritance and personal identity. For him, Burnside's spectres are not ghosts in the traditional sense but are, rather, forms of Derridean hauntology. Looked for and welcomed, rather than feared by Burnside's speakers and characters, these spectral 'presences' challenge and disrupt perception, rationality and linear time; they open up *kairotic* moments of creative rupture and thereby serve as emblems of political possibility.

Correlatively, Borthwick argues that Burnside's texts also perform hauntings of their own, forming an overall palimpsest of spectral revisitations, which challenges linearity and the idea of free-standing poems or poem sequences. Consequently, Borthwick proposes that reading Burnside can be unsettling; it requires continuous engagement and never-ending negotiation. In the volume's final chapter, Julian Wolfreys analyses the haunted nature of Being in Burnside's work, focusing on novels such as *Glister* and *The Devil's Footprints* (2007), as well as poems from *The Hunt in the Forest* (2009) and *Black Cat Bone*. Reading figures of crossing, he argues that Burnside frequently gets something 'across' to the reader without them realizing it; Burnside's writings infiltrate and cross into the reader. Through moments of suspension (*epoché*), Wolfreys proposes, Burnside's writings make the reader self-aware of her Being, albeit haunted by the other and loss. Correlatively, Burnside the novelist and Burnside the poet come together through moments of narrative suspension, which are, at the same time, moments of poetic rupture. Interwoven with this analysis, Wolfreys argues that reading Burnside is something never accomplished; we cross over and into his texts but never know or consume them. Coming at the end of this edited collection, ideas of *beginning-to-read*, textual haunting and continual negotiation importantly open up, once more, questions about how we read the writer – poet, novelist, memoirist, essayist, political commentator – 'John Burnside'. Indeed, the chapters that make up this volume offer various ways into the writings of 'John Burnside', together forming part of an unsettled and continuing encounter.

Introduction: **By Way of an Introduction: John Burnside, Writer**, Ben Davies

Bracke, A. (2014), 'Solitaries, Outcasts and Doubles: The Fictional Oeuvre of John Burnside', *English Studies*, 95 (4): 421–40.

Burnside, J. (2000), 'Strong Words', in W. N. Herbert and M. Hollis (eds), *Strong Words: Modern Poets on Modern Poetry*, 259–61, Tarset: Bloodaxe.

Burnside, J. (2003), *Otro Mundo Es Posible: Poetry, Dissidence and Reality TV*, Edinburgh: Scottish Book Trust, Dundee Contemporary Arts and the Scottish Poetry Library.

Burnside, J. (2006a), *A Lie about My Father*, London: Jonathan Cape.

Burnside, J. (2006b), 'A Science of Belonging: Poetry as Ecology', in R. Crawford (ed.), *Contemporary Poetry and Contemporary Science*, 91–106, Oxford and New York: Oxford University Press.

Burnside, J. (2010), *Waking up in Toytown*, London: Jonathan Cape.

Burnside, J. (2013), *Something Like Happy*, London: Jonathan Cape.

Burnside, J. (2014), *I Put a Spell on You: Several Digressions on Love and Glamour*, London: Jonathan Cape.

Burnside, J. (2017a), *Ashland & Vine*, London: Jonathan Cape.
Burnside, J. (2017b), 'My Working Day: "Writing Is What I Steal from the Usual Flow of Things"', *The Guardian*, 4 February: 4. Available online: https://www.theguardian.com/books/2017/feb/04/john-burnside-writing-day-ashland-and-vine (accessed 7 August 2018).
Burnside, J. (2018a), *On Henry Miller: Or, How to Be an Anarchist*. Princeton and Oxford: Princeton University Press.
Burnside, J. (2018b), 'Samiland: The Finnmarksvidda', in M. Smalley (ed.), *Cornerstones: Subterranean Writings – From Dartmoor to the Arctic Circle*, 22–8, Toller Fratrum: Little Toller Books.
Burnside, J. and M. Riordan (2004), 'Introduction', in J. Burnside and M. Riordan (eds), *Wild Reckoning: An Anthology Provoked by Rachel Carson's Silent Spring*, 13–21, London: Calouste Gulbenkian Foundation.
Crown, S. (2011), 'John Burnside: A Life in Writing', *The Guardian*, 26 August. Available online: https://www.theguardian.com/culture/2011/aug/26/john-burnside-life-in-writing (accessed 30 July 2018).
Dillon, B. (2017), *Essayism*, London: Fitzcarraldo.
McCarthy, P., ed. (2011), *Dwelling Places: An Appreciation of John Burnside* [Special issue], *Agenda*, 45 (4)–46 (1).
Menn, R. (2018), 'Unpicked and Remade: Creative Imperatives in John Burnside's Autofictions', in H. Dix (ed.), *Autofiction in English*, 163–77, Basingstoke and New York: Palgrave Macmillan.

1

John Burnside's Metaphysical World: From *The Dumb House* to *A Summer of Drowning*

Peter Childs

In his essay 'Iona: A Quest for the Pagan' (2000), Burnside says he believes in an 'underlying pattern that informs the universe' and a 'fundamental self' discerned occasionally by 'those who have transcended the contingent person', and that he 'experienced this authentic ground of being by some process of self-forgetting' (2000b: 22). In Burnside's blending of animism and Gnosticism, knowledge comes through physicality, with sensory perception more than the conscious mind providing understanding.

In his second volume of memoirs, *Waking up in Toytown* (2010), Burnside also notes, not for the first time, that:

> When I *was* a full-scale lunatic, I suffered from a condition called apophenia. This condition, this unease, was described by Klaus Conrad, the schizophrenia specialist who coined the term, as *the unmotivated seeing of connections*, coupled with the *specific experience of an abnormal meaningfulness*. In other words, seeing things that weren't there ... For normal folk, this connective faculty allows them to make sense of the world, to find a modest local and hopefully *shared* order by which to live. For the apophenic, it means a wild and unrelenting search for the one vast order that transcends all others, a hypernarrative, an afterlife ... I still suffer from this condition, though only very occasionally. (2010: 5–6)

Burnside's writing seems to be fuelled by these twin perspectives: a belief in an 'underlying pattern that informs the universe', and a 'fundamental self', but also a knowledge that such beliefs are coloured by his apophenic sensibility, an 'unmotivated seeing of connections' that to different degrees underpins how his principal characters 'make sense of the world'. It may be this condition that spurs an unrelenting search in his writing for the connective tissue of a hypernarrative, but, if so, Burnside's distinctive receptivity also contributes significantly to the uniqueness of his poetry and fiction.

For example, in the essay 'Strong Words' (2000), Burnside makes clear the basis for his heightened perception of connectedness and for the openness to the non-human world found in his writing. He says we are 'part of a rich and complex narrative', that we are human but more truthfully express ourselves as spirits, and as such 'we also live in eternity' (2000c: 260). In this chapter, I shall consequently sketch aspects to this responsiveness in Burnside's novels and then turn to a discussion of the influence of gnostic and alchemical ideas across his writing.

Fictions of Spiritual Connection

Burnside's first novel sets out distinctive twin perspectives, in characteristically brutal terms. Near the start of *The Dumb House* (1997), its protagonist, Luke, declares: 'Happiness, or fulfilment, or whatever else you choose to call it, seems to me to consist of a glimpse of the world as a patterned and limited whole' (Burnside 1998: 23). To find the essence of this pattern, Luke takes the approach to locating the soul of a hubristic scientist: 'I believed there would be a moment when the spirit ebbed ... I wanted to see what it was like when the life dissolved, leaving nothing but inert matter' (65). He adds that, 'Sometimes I managed to open a living body carefully enough to be able to see the heart beating ... I knew that, one day, I would discover its essence' (67).

Despite his psychopathology, Luke is informed by an intimation with which Burnside has sympathy. Luke feels connected to the earth and to some ancient, pagan existence, 'a manifold spirit, like the *genii cucullatii* I had read about in a book on pagan Britain: those dark creatures of the verges and borderlines the Romans had adopted as companions to Mercury ... if spirits existed, in any form, they would have to be like these: impersonal, neutral, rooted in the physical, utterly remote from human concerns' (85–6). We later learn that Luke's teacher, Miss Matheson, tried to explain to him in school that 'dissection is murder', and that the imperceptible 'soul' is also cut away in such an operation: 'as soon as you chose to dissect a living thing, you lost its essence, something bled away, something invisible' (184). Luke nonetheless believes that taking a scalpel to flesh can reveal 'some filament of preternatural warmth, some subtly of design' (184). In Luke's failure, Burnside underlines a conviction of material enquiry's inability to find this 'filament', akin to a statement of hardware's lack of potential to reveal anything meaningful of the software it enables.[1] Similarly, the material world is unable to apprehend the immaterial, so Burnside's many angels, ghosts, devils and preternatural others, such as the *huldra* in *A Summer of Drowning* (2011), are intimations of the essential precondition sought by Luke and that haunts existence.

Like Burnside, Luke is also attracted to the Tibetan Buddhist concept of *bardo*, an intermediary state 'to guide the soul through death' (Burnside 1998: 139), and one that reappears in Burnside's sixth novel *Glister* (2008). More complex in its conjectures on the ethereal and spectral than *The Dumb House*'s search for evidence of a soul, *Glister* plays repeatedly with the question of whether any putative spiritual essence is 'intrinsically good' or 'a creature that takes up residence in the human body like a parasite and feeds on it, a creature hungry for experience and power' (Burnside 2008: 236). Burnside's benign images of spirit draw repeatedly on the traditional symbol of the bird, but in *Glister* a darker cryptid figure is characteristically caught in the portrayal of the pupal Moth Man, which in part alludes to the supernatural bird creature supposedly sighted in West Virginia in the mid-1960s.[2] The Moth Man comes to be equated with the Angel of Death (Burnside 2008: 254), acting like a *bardo* figure to guide the spirit to another world, but Burnside also calls this figure 'the necessary angel', referencing Wallace Stevens's name for the imagination and subjective reality in 'Angel Surrounded by Paysans' (ll. 11–13), which closes Stevens's collection *The Auroras of Autumn* (1950). In the poem, a supernatural creature visits the inhabitants of a village to bring them to a renewed understanding of reality:

> I am the necessary angel of earth,
> Since, in my sight, you see the earth again,
> Cleared of its stiff and stubborn, man-locked set.

Thus, in keeping with Burnside's other quasi folk-tale novels, *Glister* mythologizes the transformation of an industrial landscape in a way that complements an apophenic understanding of connections between ineluctable and intuited realities, between the visible and the hidden. From one angle, this can be understood in terms of the mythopoeic imagination that informs Burnside's approach to prose as well as verse. For instance, in his Introduction to a selection of poetry by Stevens, Burnside espouses the view that 'Poetry is how we imagine the world' and, as such, is an 'ontological activity' inseparable from fundamental understandings of existence and being (Stevens 2008: vii–xiv).

In Burnside's third novel, *The Locust Room* (2001), Paul's housemate Steve has hallucinations of angels and ascensions while recovering in the Fulbourn hospital in Cambridgeshire. Echoing Burnside's portrayal of himself recovering in the rehabilitation clinic when *'Waking up in Toytown'* (2010: 1–11), Steve imagines looking in a mirror and seeing 'a small hole in nature, an emptiness, a loose stitch which, if pulled, might unravel the universe and show its underlying blackness, a blackness like decay, or like the small local darkness that falls each and every time an animal dies' (2002: 158). The final simile encapsulates a central message of the novel's specific interest in respect for the sanctity of lives steeped in silence, stealth and solitude. Throughout Burnside's writing, there is a Manichean dark side to this sensibility, here most clear in the Cambridge rapist, mindful of both himself and the assembly around him in a kind of double-consciousness.[3] He is said to be 'like that invisible presence the Arctic explorers described when they came home from being lost, walking for hours or days in the snow and the dark, with a single unseen companion' (148).

In Burnside's previous novel, *The Mercy Boys* (1999), Sconnie similarly believes 'there is a real world that we cannot see or directly experience unless we get outside ourselves, unless we forget who we are' (2000a: 55). A familiar character type in Burnside's writing of the troubled, questing male experiencing an apophenic perception of preternatural connections, Sconnie is finally victim to a Lawrentian sun-god sacrifice when he becomes prey to Nietzschean murderers, who are reminiscent of Luke in *The Dumb House* (see Lawrence, *The Plumed Serpent*, 1926, and 'The Woman who Rode Away', 1925; see also, Nietzsche, *Beyond Good and Evil*, 1886). Sconnie's own dreamlike epiphany of falling through space as he loses consciousness in a drink-and-drug haze is turned into nightmare as Burnside's brutal clown-dressed students ritualize their murder of Sconnie in terms of 'the priests who would open his veins and draw out his soul' (2000a: 212).

In contrast to Sconnie's dark interior sun-sacrifice, the narrative's more central character, Alan, concludes the novel by finding release far from society in the exterior light and space of water. He stands at the shore of the loch with 'a sense of the life that was waiting to touch him, not just at the surface of his skin, but ... as far as whatever it was the soul might be, buried in its house of flesh' (2000a: 259). While Sconnie dies with a certainty of the waste and banality of his killing, Alan embraces the weightlessness of slipping into water as the words 'Spirit and light' run through his mind (265). The close of *The Mercy Boys* suggests a transition into the intermediate *bardo* state accompanied by the dream-figure that opened the novel, when in this premonition of his own passing, Alan rescues a bird-like angel that he fears will die in the 'watery light of Magdalen Green' (7–8).

In *The Devil's Footprints* (2007), as in *Glister*, the negative of this winged image appears as Michael ponders the embodiment of 'fear': 'a man in the process of becoming a bird, or a bird that had started to become a man, hideously ugly, perhaps, but capable of inspiring pity' (2007: 34). Michael first imagines that the devil is a living creature 'somewhere between angel and beast, between Ariel and Caliban' (4). Only later does he recognize a spectral relation to the fear he himself experiences, when he says:

> I felt something rise to the surface of my skin, something old, a forgotten sensation of fear ... an apprehension that somehow predated my human existence ... All at once, I was aware of a chill, animal pleasure, a continuity between my own flesh and the shadows in the bushes. (134)

He decides at the end of the novel that 'before it became the devil, that spirit had been something else – an angel, Pan, the *genus cucilatus*, some wandering breath of wind or light that touched a man from time to time' (202). Such stories, linking human emotion to mythological presences, also have numerous traces in Burnside's preceding novel, *Living Nowhere* (2003), in which spectral manifestations are identified as markers of something that has been long lost to contemporary culture (110). At Jan's funeral, for example, Tommy wonders what it would be like 'if all the spirits returned – not just the people, but everything: the animals, the birds, the children dead in childbirth, the trees felled to make way for factories and roads. Think of the slow fade of those ghostly stains on the air, in the grass, in the earth' (183–4).

Gnosticism and Alchemy

Imagining the co-presence of everything that has existed is one vision of the underlying connective pattern Burnside's novels speculate upon, but as I suggested at the start, an important strand in Burnside's 'wild and unrelenting' perception of patterns is his interest in Gnosticism and its associations with alchemy. Burnside has said that for him poetry is 'a form of alchemy' (2000c: 259) and that he was drawn to Gnostic texts as a student:

> some of the Gnostic ideas are actually taken up in alchemy. By 'alchemy' I mean a magical process and I saw it then as a kind of metaphor: it seemed to me that changing metal into gold was quite straightforwardly a metaphor for taking incomplete and messed up human mind and spirit and trying to achieve a pleroma or fullness out of that. (Dósa 2003: 13)

The fundamental tenet of Gnosticism, which has had many traditions since its heyday in the second century, is that the route to the divine is through the revelation of knowledge and not through faith, and also that this gnosis is of a particular kind: a direct experiential awareness of the senses rather than a rational understanding in the mind (Martin 2006: 28). Elements of the Gnostic tradition that Burnside incorporates into his writing are numerous, and a list might feature the following examples: the conviction that a gnosis exists in every person not the few and can be awoken by insight (Rudolph 1983: 57); that this insight comes like poetry in an ordinary activity, often 'a sudden moment of clarity and silence into which something else makes its presence known' (Martin 2006: 30); an interest in dualisms or binaries, informed by the Gnostic view of two co-existing cosmological and anthropological levels; (Rudolph 1983: 57–67); an understanding of death and resurrection as not embodied but an awakening into a fundamental reality or true nature shielded by immersion in the distracting activities of near-constant social interaction (Pagels 1990: 42); a belief in the divine Mother as well as Father, a dyad embracing male and female elements (Pagels 1990: 71–2); and to an extent a fascination with the idea of the twin, which in Gnostic writing is found in the *Gospel of Thomas*, attributed to Jesus's twin brother (Pagels 1990: 47), and from which Burnside is wont to quote.

Burnside says he has no religion but has long been intrigued by spiritual writings and the concept of 'the soul' (Burnside 2000b: 22). Echoing the novel extracts I have cited, Burnside elucidates this by explaining that for him the soul is neither immortal nor personal but something experienced in moments of self-forgetting when the individual is detached from social consciousness, absorbed in activity and consequently removed into a more fundamental identity. It would be possible to align this with numerous philosophical theories, but Burnside argues that an 'underlying pattern that informs the universe ... cannot be described, only intuited' (22–3). This gnosis seems not to be adequately communicable in verbal language, which is why Burnside says that what is 'needed is an image' (23). Thus, his fiction foregrounds such symbols as *The Devil's Footprints* in the snow, the *Glister* ship in the chemical factory and the hawthorn tree in *Living Nowhere*. Chiming with the quotation above from *Living Nowhere*, Burnside also says these mythemes help him, as a poet and person, to appreciate 'a pagan sensibility which believed that everything – humans, animals, trees, stones – is connected in an almost sensual way to everything else' (2000b: 23–4). He suggests that this is what he finds, for example, 'walking along a beach on an island at the edge of the Atlantic' where 'you suddenly see yourself from outside, no isolated figure, but one woven into the continuum of human history' (25).

To put a name to this, on occasion Burnside makes reference to the New Testament word 'Pleroma', mentioned above by Burnside in the interview with Dòsa and also the title of one of his poems. The word is often translated from the Greek as 'fullness' but refers to the divine sphere, or existential truth, that Gnostics believed to subsist behind social reality, which is here akin to the shadow play of Plato's cave. In some ways most significantly, Gnosticism foregrounds the importance of the mythic dimension to stories, seeing them as poetic avenues to transformation, with little pretension to verisimilitude. Similarly, Burnside's fiction almost invariably follows this narrative trajectory, allegorizing a pilgrim's troubled progress towards pleroma in the form of greater understanding, insight or knowledge.

In terms of alchemy, Burnside is clearly attracted by the alchemists' interests in harmony and balance, but two aspects appear particularly significant. The first is his fascination as a poet with wordplay and its link to mythopoeic stories of the 'language of birds' (Martin 2003: 23, 29), considered by alchemists to be a secret key to perfect knowledge, and sometimes called 'green language' (also the subject of Salman Rushdie's all but forgotten first novel *Grimus*, 1975). The second is the theory in ancient and medieval philosophy that the four elements of earth, air, fire and water are the substantial constituents of the world. Aspects of the elements, for example, give names to the four sections of *Living Nowhere*, and Burnside's novels seem on occasion to incorporate the theory of transformation, in which each element can become another through the application of their fundamental properties of hotness, wetness, dryness and coldness.

Living Nowhere

To move to an exploration of the above in relation to Burnside's fiction, I'd like to follow his lead and start with an image. Appropriately, the original cover of *Living Nowhere* presents a dystopian picture of the mytheme of the tree of knowledge, central to many religions but also to Gnosticism and alchemy, in the form of a solitary enclosed thorn standing in a concreted car park with a green world lying behind in the darkness. This image appears to Burnside to be a stark metaphor for much contemporary human living and illustrates his comment that 'I have an argument with separating human beings from the natural world, as if we were somehow not natural' (Dósa 2003: 11).

In the novel, the first description of a hawthorn tree coincides with Alina's hallucinatory experience of pleroma:

> Standing alone at the far end of a gravel path, a low gnarled hawthorn tree kept filling with light from the passing traffic, then darkening again, as if it were breathing. Beyond that, the land was still: a cold silent emptiness. Alina had been trying not to notice how black it was, a deep black in the

green of the yew trees along the graveyard walks, a blackness, even, in the falling snow. She had imagined it would be something terrible, thinking about that blackness here among the dead; but then, all of a sudden, she was struck with a dark, vivid sense of it, of the black in the green of the sap, the black in the white of the snow, like something from a treatise in alchemy, black: nigredo, the true energy of the world that wasn't dark at all, or at least, wasn't malevolent, no matter how dangerous it seemed. (Burnside 2003: 15)

'Nigredo' here refers to the supposed uniform black matter with which all alchemical ingredients had to be cleansed (it is alluded to or named in several of the novels from *The Locust Room* through to the black ash at the close of *A Summer of Drowning*), but in analytical psychology, it has been adapted to describe a painful period of isolation during which the individual has a growing awareness of the Jungian archetype of the shadow, or unconscious links to primitive animal instincts (see Jung 1968). This concept is used repeatedly by Burnside as characters undergo various rites of passage: as he himself says, 'most of my stories are about young men who are suddenly faced with the fact that ... they haven't been paying attention to the world around them and it's time to change. In different ways at the end of each of those stories the characters are faced with the possibility of growth, which is a painful thing, but nevertheless an exciting, meaningful and authentic thing' (Dósa 2003: 21).

When applied to *Living Nowhere*, this comment describes the diegetic arc followed by Francis after his personal crisis, which is also the turning point of the novel and takes place at Jan's funeral near the low hawthorn tree that Alina imagines as being the entrance to pleroma through a return to the condition of *nigredo*. It is also, importantly, the site of Francis's mother's burial and the place to which he returns at the close of the novel: 'near a thorn tree at the end of a long gravel path, out by the edge of the cemetery' (Burnside 2003: 357). Francis is described as a 'stolen child' (308), who returns to Corby after his transformation, initiated at the thorn, and like Burnside's poetry (e.g. the sequence 'Urphänomen' in *Feast Days*, 1992), *Living Nowhere* is suffused with stories of metamorphoses, changelings and temptations to follow characters such as Orpheus or the Fairy King into other realms (Burnside 2003: 33, 41, 261) through what is called the 'glister of the living, energised world' (6).

The turning point of *Living Nowhere* also illustrates Burnside's interest in alchemical change: Francis describes how he spent Jan's funeral thinking that it was wrong to put him 'in a casket in the wet earth' when 'if I knew anything at all, it was that my soul belonged to fire' (232). He then recalls that Jan himself would have preferred a 'sky burial' akin to the Tibetan Buddhist practice of leaving the empty vessel of the corpse cut up for the birds (233). Francis describes how, thinking about this at the funeral, he moved towards the hawthorn tree at the far end of the path and disappeared through a gap in the hedge – described as a 'portal' of the kind 'animals use, deer coming in from the fields to browse the graveyard roses following a path they had used for generations, ignoring the lines of human settlement' (234). This complements repeated images of passing in Burnside's poetry, such as the animistic spirit beings who 'arrive through the hedge' in the poem 'Angel Eyes' from *The Myth of the Twin* (1994), but, in alchemical terms, Francis rejects the materiality of water and earth used in Christian Baptism and the Burial of the Dead. Instead, he chooses the dry elements of fire and air that convey him towards a feral existence outwith the above 'lines of human settlement'. Francis also explains the spiritual significance of the alchemical process to Jan and illuminates the Part's title of 'The Air of the Door', when he says 'we aren't born with souls, we become souls, and that becoming is a process of mixing, of one person becoming another, or becoming two, or disappearing into thin air' (2003: 246).

Prior to Francis's disappearance, the first two Parts of *Living Nowhere* are each separated into four sections, their different narrators espousing alternative views of reality, which resonate with the different properties of the four substances. For example, one of these narrators is Tommy, Francis's father, who begins from a contrasting elemental standpoint to his son. At Jan's funeral, Tommy also thinks of alchemical transformation as 'water and salt and carbon returning to the wet earth and becoming something else, something new. The thought – the thought of becoming the very thing that had replaced what had gone before – appealed to him' (183). Tommy grounds his belief in earth's equal ability to lead to nigredo alongside Jan and Francis's valorization of air and fire: 'everything decayed to those smallest particles, atoms and molecules, drops of water, grains of salt' (184). It is also notable that Tommy uses twice the word 'something', one of Burnside's 'preferred lexical choices' to avoid linguistic definition. Discussing Burnside's poetry, David Borthwick says that the word is used 'to suggest liminal states and emergent presences' that slip through the normal classifications of cultural space (2011: 93), which is, additionally, an apt way to describe Burnside's connotative images, used in preference to linguistic denotation.

Language and Lyricism

Despite this attraction to connotative representation, Burnside's medium is not painting, sculpture or photography, art forms chosen by several of his characters, but literary language. His lexical selections are consequently linked to the attempt at a transformative quest for nigredo in the distillation of vocabulary and imagery. In his interview with Dòsa, he argues:

> If you say that poetry is a kind of alchemical process, a process of revelation, you're talking about the purification of something which is seen as crude, mixed-up, something almost contaminated ... It seems to me that what the job of poetry might be in the 21st century is taking everyday experience, almost the banal, and rediscovering in it a kind of essential *life* – not necessarily beauty, but an essential authenticity or vitality. (Dósa 2003: 14)

Creating a parallel with Francis's disappearance in *Living Nowhere*, Burnside reaffirms this elsewhere when he speaks of poetry seeking a 'clarity of being that alchemists call pleroma. At its best, the lyric opens a door in the everyday and allows me to pass into the otherworld behind the taken-for-granted' (Burnside 2005: 61).

In similar terms, Burnside illuminates the ambiguity in the title of *Living Nowhere*:

> '*Il y a un autre monde, mais il est dans celui-là*,' ['There is another world, but it is in this one'] says Paul Eluard. To speak of another world has, historically, been to commit to an essentially mystical or religious agenda, and so to a province of wishful thinking ... but Eluard's remark points us in another direction altogether: the other world is here, now, but we pass it every day, we miss it ... Eluard's entirely secular programme was to uncover that *autre monde* – that nonfactual truth of being: the missed world and, by extension, the missed self who sees and imagines and is fully alive outside the bounds of socially engineered expectations – not by some rational process (or not as the term is usually understood) but by a kind of radical illumination, a re-attunement to the continuum of objects and weather and other lives that we inhabit. (Burnside 2005: 60)

Whether this other world is taken to be a symptom of apophenia, metaphysical irrationality or poetic metaphor, Burnside's works are inseparable from attempts to escape the banal through some kind of transformation, inspired by elemental nature, imagination, alcohol or LSD. *Living Nowhere* opens with Alina contemplating 'the glister of the living' spirit of everything as she imagines converting the poison of Corby 'into something good and true, the way an alchemist would transform base metal into gold' (2003: 6–7). In *A Lie about My Father* (2006), Burnside similarly talks about how for him, taking an acid trip connected him back to the sacred.

> LSD-25 is a sacrament; by which I mean, something that allows the celebrant to win back some participation in his environment ... acid did what the host failed to do ... It connected me back to the world, it re-attuned me to the subtler, deeper frequencies of the material. It made me see the possibility of wholeness, of what the alchemists called pleroma. (2006: 177–8)

Lastly, Burnside adopts a Gnostic view of quotidian – as opposed to banal – reality, in that he advocates revelation as a kind of turning away from socialized thinking through attention to imagination. This is a numinous understanding of not duality but the division between a Platonic reality and the shadow play of a life blinkered by dogmatism, materialism, consumerism and so on. The transformation from such passivity to an active understanding is a kind of alchemy for Burnside, repeatedly played out in metaphor, folktale and the uses of the sublime in his writings. It is also often evident in a mixing of genres that suggests an intersection of the pastoral tradition with scientific realism. He explains:

> I am using the term the quotidian to mean the actual unfolding of the world around us ... Set against that is the banal ... what we make of the quotidian when imagination fails: a condition that can arise from fatigue, dislocation, need, or simply as the result of 'socialisation'. The quotidian is the lyric poet's grail: the otherworld so carefully folded within the taken-for-granted as to be almost invisible. (Burnside 2005: 64)

As a novelist, Burnside writes about transformation derived from experience, but it is a poetic sensibility that underpins his philosophical conviction: 'this discipline of the imagination is the central human concern and, without it, there can be no compassion, no good judgement, no justice ... Without it, we live as mere persons, not as spirits, guided through life by road maps prepared for us' (60). Elaine Pagels, one of the foremost scholars of Gnosticism, writes that 'like circles of artists today, Gnostics considered original creative invention to be the mark of anyone who becomes spiritually alive' (1990: 48). Yet, what is distinctive in Burnside's numinous writing is the combination of his poetic sensibility with an interest in overcoming socialized alienation through imagination and sensory experience, producing a conviction that there is an apprehensible reality, and, however inexpressible it may be, the individual's socialized separation from that reality can be subject to transformation, or – in Burnside's terminology – healed.

Chapter One: **John Burnside's Metaphysical World**, Peter Childs

Borthwick, D. (2011), 'To Comfort Me with Nothing: John Burnside's Dissident Poetics', *Agenda*, 45 (4)–46 (1): 91–100.
Burnside, J. (1998), *The Dumb House*, London: Vintage.
Burnside, J. (2000a), *The Mercy Boys*, London: Vintage.
Burnside, J. (2000b), 'Iona: A Quest for the Pagan', *Southfields*, 6 (2): 21–5.

Burnside, J. (2000c), 'Strong Words', in W. N. Herbert and M. Hollis (eds), *Strong Words: Modern Poets on Modern Poetry*, 259–61, Tarset: Bloodaxe.
Burnside, J. (2002), *The Locust Room*, London: Vintage.
Burnside, J. (2003), *Living Nowhere*, London: Jonathan Cape.
Burnside, J. (2005), 'Travelling into the Quotidian: Some Notes on Allison Funk's "Heartland" Poems', *Poetry Review*, 95 (2): 59–70.
Burnside, J. (2006), *A Lie about My Father*, London: Jonathan Cape.
Burnside, J. (2007), *The Devil's Footprints*, London: Jonathan Cape.
Burnside, J. (2008), *Glister*, London: Jonathan Cape.
Burnside, J. (2010), *Waking up in Toytown*, London: Jonathan Cape.
Clay, O. (2015), 'Interview with author and review of *Glister*', *Liverpool Echo*, 23 December. Available online: https://www.liverpoolecho.co.uk/news/interview-author-review-glister-novel-10644370 (accessed 9 May 2018).
Dósa, A. (2003), 'Poets and Other Animals: An Interview with John Burnside', *Scottish Studies Review*, 4 (1): 9–24.
Jung, C. G. (1968), *Psychology and Alchemy*, 2nd edn, trans. R. F. C. Hull, London: Routledge.
Martin, S. (2003), *Alchemy and Alchemists*, Harpenden: Pocket Essentials.
Martin, S. (2006), *The Gnostics: The First Christian Heretics*, Harpenden: Oldcastle Books.
Pagels, E. (1990), *The Gnostic Gospels*, Harmondsworth: Penguin.
Rudolph, K. (1983), *Gnosis: The Nature and History of Gnosticism*, trans. Robert McLachlan Wilson, Edinburgh: T&T Clark.
Stevens, W. (2008), *Wallace Stevens: Poems Selected by John Burnside*, London: Faber.

2

John Burnside's Numinous Poetry

Jan Wilm

In the beginning was not the word, and the word was not with God and the word was not God. The word, in the sense referred to by the New Testament here, comes into being through the poet, and the poet's word is secular, uttered by a living, material being; it is the body that writes the poet's words. But the poet is human, the acknowledged legislator of man, chronicler of life and death, recording angel of man's search for transcendence.

If one is schooled in postmodern (or post-religious) thinking, one has likely had to abandon a belief in the transcendental signifier, and one may share Ludwig Wittgenstein's opinion that 'whereof one cannot speak thereof one must be silent' (1922: 23). The category of the unspeakable, the ineffable, is a category that cannot even be spoken of in the negative, as any utterance about the unspeakable returns it to the realm of the speakable. If there is nothing outside of language, outside of language is not nothing disguised as something, the category of outside-of-language simply does not exist. Or does it? If one inverts the idea that there is nothing outside of language, everything that is is only in so far as it is inside of language, only in so far as it can be spoken of. If everything is language, then everything is. Wittgenstein was aware of this and argued, in a letter to Paul Engelmann, that the inexpressible (also, if not only, God) is only lost if one tries to express it, like the slippery fish one clasps too tightly.[1] Wittgenstein saw no need to express the inexpressible, since 'the inexpressible is – inexpressibly – *contained* in what is expressed' (qtd. in Schulte 1992: 75). Language expresses everything, whether expressibly or inexpressibly. But poetry, if one remembers what Roman Jakobson called language's 'poetic function',[2] is heightened language, and so poetic language perhaps expresses just a little more than 'ordinary' language.

If there is a category of the ineffable, of which one must be silent, what does this mean for poems like John Burnside's, which engage with the religious and divine and holy, with poetry which stirs emotions opening onto sensations or experiences of the numinous? Does this poetry sing in a realm of illusion, or worse in a realm of delusion, and will the literary scholar trying to sound or echo it have to forego analysing such poetry, as it speaks what cannot be spoken and can therefore only be treated with silence, or worse, with scorn?

An analysis of how the numinous is actualized, aestheticized and perhaps secularized in poetry – as will be attempted in the following – must be prefaced by a question inquiring further into *how* literature may contain dimensions of the numinous in the first place, especially if the numinous is defined as something language cannot define, as Rudolf Otto, the German theologian who coined the term, does. He describes the numinous as a deep, total and submissive experience of the holy in his work *The Idea of the Holy* (1917), as being at the mercy of this experience, subjugated by it, while unable to describe it fully or to interpret it rationally:

> I shall speak ... of a unique numinous category of value and of a definitely numinous state of mind, which is always found wherever the category is applied. This mental state is perfectly *sui generis* and irreducible to any other; and therefore, like every absolutely primary and elementary datum, while it admits of being discussed, it cannot be strictly defined. (1923: 7)

In order to speak of the numinous not as something that cannot be spoken of but of something that can and is spoken of in poetry, one may begin by suggesting a distinction between (1) literature dealing with religious themes or topics, (2) literature whose contexts of production were shaped by religion and literature which serves religious functions and (3) literature whose aesthetics were formed by religious experience and may provoke feelings and sensations that could be termed religious also. The first of these three thematically and topically religious works of literature might be those that retell religious myths and depict or narrate spiritual images and stories: Gerard Manley Hopkins's poetry, for example. The second of the three, works whose contexts of production were shaped by religion might be those works created for a religious purpose, such as liturgical verse or the poetry of George Herbert and John Donne. This second category often blends with the third, and the third is arguably the most difficult even to describe, comprising those works which were influenced by religious experience and feeling and which aim to provoke similar feelings by the recipient. The credible description of such works of art is doubtless shaped by the describer's religious disposition, since a religious person may find religious flavours in literary works regardless whether they 'are' religious or not, but they may do so more easily if the authors were expressly influenced by religious experience.

To argue that a work of art is religious in impact, that it has a sacred quality, that it stirs feelings of a spiritual nature, is dependent on the one making this claim. It is probable that believers feel a very different set of emotions when listening to Giuseppe Verdi's *Requiem* (1874) than non-believers do, that the non-believer will say the impact of the work is unrelated to numinous sensations and merely related to the work's aesthetic force, to compositional and performative craft and artistry, to the recipient's learning and training in the appreciation of art. Many are the works of art which engage the numinous without encasing themselves in impenetrable spirituality or exclusionary specific religious content, works which are numinous to the believer and secular to the non-believer. But rare are those works of art whose numinous quality may, in fact, also be appreciated by the secular reader not as the secular alone but also as the numinous, as a secularized numinous.

The poetry of John Burnside is a such a rare example. His 2007 collection *Gift Songs*, for instance, features an epigraph from *Genesis*; long poems written as responses to Augustine; and 'Four Quartets', which reference T. S. Eliot's poems of the same name and via the intertext also Eliot's religious preoccupations. *Gift Songs* is perhaps Burnside's most overtly religious collection, referencing religious texts, ideas and images in nearly every poem. Merely one example is part three of the poem 'For a Free Church', titled 'Prayer':

Give me a little less
With every dawn:
colour, a breath of wind,
the perfection of shadows,
till what I find, I find
because it's there,
gold in the seams of my hands
and the night light, burning. (Burnside 2007a: 44)

The titles of the poem and this section prepare the reader for the religious connotations, and thus the implied 'you' might be seen as a devotional address to God, a waiting for God's grace in an ascetic form of worship, whose objective ultimately arrives at the pure perception of natural beauty, the 'perfection' mentioned in the fourth line. The apostrophe to God is a frequent technique in Burnside's poetry, for example in the 2011 collection *Black Cat Bone*, where the poem '"A Garden Inclosed Is My Sister, My Spouse"' (the title is a line from *The Song of Solomon*) features the epigraph '*Matthew 22:14*' (Burnside 2011a: 20). So, the poem refers implicitly to the Bible verse ('For many are called, but few are chosen'), even if it refers explicitly to the Bible citation. Like 'Prayer', this poem also celebrates a sense of waiting with God for the slow unfolding of the world's beauty in a prayer or a devotional contemplation of what is. By supplying only the Bible citation rather than the verse as epigraph, the reader has in a sense to wait for the verse, assuming he or she chooses to look it up in the Bible subsequently or remembers it by heart. Slyly, the poem conveys what it speaks of through a subtle literary technique of delaying or withholding information, and thereby implicitly secularizing its religious content, bringing it into the realm of reading for information or the pleasure of gaining knowledge rather than for religious enlightenment or edification.

Burnside, a chronic user of epigraphs, liberally borrows from the Bible and other religious scripture in his paratexts to steer the reception in an explicitly religious direction. Stripping away the titles I have mentioned, or eliminating the epigraphs, would make his poems more ambiguous religiously for sure. But a poem cannot and should not simply be pruned to one's interpretive needs; it is more prudent and more productive to attend to what is there on the page, which in the case of '*Matthew 22:14*' may confront one with the dilemma of having to interpret merely the word 'Matthew' and the numbers '22:14' before allowing one's interpretive wings to take flight. In such a reading, '*Matthew 22:14*' is, then, paradoxically a non-religious sign, referencing only itself. The effect of quoting the Bible citation rather than the verse it refers to complicates the immediately religious reading, even if it clearly flags religious scripture. This ambiguous effect would not have been achieved had the author chosen merely to quote the verse of Matthew 22:14, 'For many are called, but few are chosen.' This is constitutive of Burnside's dealing with religion in his poetry, and his use of titles and epigraphs referencing religion creates ambiguity, rather than eliminating it through explicit religiosity. Ambiguity inspires interpretation, and so Burnside's vexing use of religious titles and epigraphs might, in fact, supply the serious reader – whether religious or not – with a set of spiritual coordinates to map his or her way around a spiritually overgrown literary landscape.

To analyse more deeply what the status of this poetry's engagement with religion is and in what way the numinous enters Burnside's work, one might try to use the aforementioned three categories to classify Burnside's poetry regarding religion, even if the three categories might be either far too reductive or far too inclusive. His poems are not specifically written for religious purposes; they are not psalms or liturgical hymns. Many of Burnside's poems fall either into the first or the third category: they cite or remodel religious imagery as they narrate or incite feelings that might be called religious, or spiritual. These dimensions of Burnside's poetry are often equivocal, oscillating between the secular and the numinous, such as when biblical images or scenes are located in ordinary, mundane, even trivially secular contexts, as in his early prose poem 'Suburbs', from his second collection *Common Knowledge* (1991). 'Suburbs' begins quite religiously, if 'religious' is understood as referencing religion explicitly rather than evoking religious feelings:

> Wet Sunday afternoon; after the rain a bible wind ripples the sheet puddles on Station Road; along the hedges by the girls' school an elaborate birdsong streams through the wet scent of roses, like a new form of music evolving out of water. (Burnside 2007b: 2)

Time ('Sunday afternoon') and mood ('bible wind') are set by the first line, the place by the title, and here it emerges as a suburban road, possibly traversed on the way home from church. Subsequently, the poem lists 'the spiritual history of the suburb' (ibid.), consisting of precious objects, such as Chinese porcelain, fruits and spices, and a lot of emptiness which surrounds the material inventory of suburbia: 'Nevertheless, something is missing: an absence that is only temporarily filled by the red post van in the lane, or the sound of footsteps crunching ice' (3). Here, suburban space has 'an abstracted quality' (2), its life is described as being 'intended to make it appear real' (3), it mimics the real, something which the poem's clusters of similes mirror stylistically. The suburb can never 'emulate' the 'colour and solidity' of reality (ibid.). The suburb is a spatialized ritual concealing its omnipresent vacuity: 'the last true rituals only happen here: the inhabitants of the suburb are compelled by an attention to detail that was once religious and is now quite meaningless' (ibid.).

By contrasting the categories of the religious and the meaningless, the poem's speaker implicitly laments the absence of religious significance, of the sacred dimension, which might have been present in a pre-modern (and so pre-suburban) existence. This, then, would mean that a spiritual existence has come to an end and was replaced by secular living, with its 'ice-cream and lemons' and 'bottles of gherkins and maple syrup on kitchen tables' (2) – spirituality is lost or concealed beneath the farrago of a materialist present. But like most of Burnside's poetry, 'Suburbs' is not so unambiguous, since the suburb is equally celebrated as a space that may become, through caring decoration of the mundane, through ritualistic repetition, 'finally magical' (2). The care for the ordinary may, over time passed in ritual, assume spiritual proportions, warranting praise.

While the religious life in the suburb has lost its meaning, there is a sense of what might be termed a 'secular spirituality', an appropriately paradoxical term to grasp the two contrastive forces in the poem. 'Suburbs' implies an all-embracing sense of what suburbia is potentially capable of, that the suburb might transcend itself through its symbolical or allegorical reach, in that it might stand for everything else, a miniature of modern social life, not fully urban yet no longer wholly subject to the entirely rural. For this reading, it is, however, necessary that the suburb be merely a copy of the real, so that one's thoughts of that which is symbolically represented by the suburb gains force as it makes its way from the copy to the real. The suburb here is an effigy of the real, and it is its artificiality which makes the real seem purer and almost transcendently beautiful.

Burnside's poem is ambivalent whether the suburb is the object of an infinitely allegorical fragmentation and therefore the stage of a crisis of spirituality or whether the potentially transcendental dimension of the suburb is actually its efficacy, since paradoxically the spiritual emptiness of the suburb becomes a space into which a variety of spiritual experience may be funnelled. The suburb is 'where everything is implied' (5); its spiritual emptiness prepares the ground for a new kind of spirituality, a resurrection of numinous experience, the way in *The Book of Revelation* what is initially called for, as the story goes, is a form of apocalyptic emptying of the world before the Second Coming.

Burnside's poetry is a good example to show how complex a range of feelings and experiences are included in religious, spiritual or numinous phenomena, and how there may not be an unequivocal way to say with finality that a poem is either spiritual or secular. His poems are spaces where the contrastive forces of spirituality and secularity meet in an aesthetic conversation, and where the fine line between the sacred and the profane is teased out of language. To use two very different examples: like the poetry of Wallace Stevens or Philip Larkin, Burnside's work is often philosophical about spiritual presences, feelings and images. Like Larkin's 'Church Going' from his 1955 collection *The Less Deceived*, much of Burnside's poetry tacitly asks the question 'What remains when disbelief has gone?' (Larkin 2004: 59). Even if poetry abandons religion in its organized manifestations, the need for spirituality might remain, often in the self's hunger for wonder and contemplation. Burnside's poems are filled with implicit moments of reaching for such spirituality, with ghostly presences watching the speakers, with moments of near-religious contemplation, with resurrections and life after death, with intimations of immortality and intonations of the music of the soul. The central struggle between spirituality and secularism, posed as a question in Larkin's 'Church Going', is staged in nearly every poem by Burnside – without naïve idealizations of religion and without producing poems of religious edification.

Frequently, this dialogue is crystallized around the problem and attraction of death, and Burnside engages with spirituality most openly and his work becomes, via its constant contemplation of mortality, a celebration of ordinary living that might warrant the term 'numinous'. In his work, death is nearly a state of grace, which inspires not dread but awe in the living and can thus prepare the reader for a feeling of numinosity. Awe of death is inspired in Burnside's work since death is the state that subsumes and subdues all other states. The dead populate Burnside's poetry and prose alike; the dead exude a force over living existence, as when Burnside's narrator in his novel *Living Nowhere* (2003) writes:

> the dead are real, are they not, real and fixed and true? It's the dead who give us, the living, our place in the world: the dead are our roots, the one sure anchor in an otherwise provisional existence. (Burnside 2003: 325)

The ideas of the dead's presence and of 'life' after death seem ostensibly a directly religious topos, if one thinks, for example, of the resurrection of Jesus or the rather grandiloquent resurrection of Lazarus of Bethany by Jesus. But the dead of Burnside's works seem borrowed less from Christianity and closer to myth, fairy tale and folklore. Burnside's dead are ghostly existences, 'scavenger angels' (Burnside 2007b: 6), as 'Suburbs' puts it, roaming the night streets, haunting the breathing state of life with a ghostly silence, a vacuum present beneath being.

Christianity is sceptical of spectres; there are only a handful of ghosts in the Bible, since resurrection in Christianity is resurrection in the physical state, so that a mere ghost is near-blasphemy, a failure by God physically to revive a dead person, a half-hearted or abandoned attempt at full corporeal resurrection – *resurrectio interruptus*, if you like.[3] Burnside's poetic landscape, however, is peopled by all kinds of apparitions and angels; like the paintings of Pieter Brueghel, his works are fond of alerting us to the fact that his poetry borrows liberally from images and ideas across various religions and traditions, not only from the Judaeo-Christian tradition (although this is his major reservoir) but also, the way Jorge Luis Borges's work does, from Buddhism, Hinduism and especially pagan myths, where ghosts as spirits of the dead are quotidian, perhaps even pedestrian or suburban.

Like the suburb, ghosts are simultaneously commonplace and wondrous in Burnside, as ghosts are an expression of in-betweenness. Considering this through the Bible, one sees more clearly the Christian scepticism of ghosts, and one is able to view ghosts in a light that is an important departure from Christianity in Burnside's poetry. The Bible is quite unambiguous on what happens to people when they die: they face judgement (see Heb. 9:27). The sheep are separated from the goats: The believers go to heaven, the unbelievers to hell (see 2 Cor. 5:6–8, Phil. 1:23 and Mt. 25:46; Lk. 16:22–4). The harsh polarity of the Bible permits no third way here, the spirit-state being reserved only for Jesus Christ, and only temporarily. In Burnside's poetry, the ghost *is* the third state, the spirit-state. The poem 'An Essay Concerning Time' from *The Hunt in the Forest* (2009) begins with the lines: 'Only the dead are communal:/intimate under the grass, conversing through snow,/forever gifted with the middle ground' (Burnside 2009: 36). The dead in Burnside's poetry are liberated, 'happy to be free/of hope and fear' (2011a: 36), as the poem 'Day of the Dead' phrases it. The dead remain outside the enclosures of Christian dogma; they 'are', somehow, in a *middle ground* that cracks open the polarity of either dead or alive, of either heaven or hell, of either sacred or profane.

A passage in Burnside's second memoir, *Waking up in Toytown* (2010), reads:

> Much of the time the dead are with us, more present on so many occasions than we give them credit for. At night, I get up and wander about the house, listening to their voices, seeing them as they once were, and the old religious idea that being is a gift seems more acceptable to me than it usually does in the plain light of day. I spend as much of my time as I can being alone, but I never feel completely alone unless the dead are there, in their uniforms and aprons and Sunday best. I know most of them well. (Burnside 2010: 126–7)

As in the poem 'Suburbs', the spaces of Burnside's memoirs are also spaces of ghostly encounters, be they imagined or felt, and as in many of his poems, the realm of the ghostly is nocturnal. At night, it seems, to Burnside's speakers, the ghostly is perceived or argued as being fused with the religious. And the sites of these hauntings and religious or quasi-religious experiences are best found in solitude. In the poem 'A Game of Marbles', the speaker goes to a forest to bury 'the things [he] love[s]' (Burnside 2011a: 39), and as he touches the soil of the ground, he exclaims 'my fingers brush the dead' (ibid.). The dead in Burnside are communal, they root existence and they are in every thing and every place, the way believers, whether in a Judaeo-Christian or a pantheist tradition, may feel that God is in everything. The dead suffuse living existence and lived experience. This way they assume a spiritual quality in Burnside's work. The cycle of poems titled 'Faith' in *Black Cat Bone* links death and faith quite unequivocally through another epigraph, taken from 'The Chapel' chapter in Herman Melville's *Moby Dick* (1851): 'But faith, like a jackal, feeds among the tombs, and even from these dead doubts she gathers her most vital hope' (Melville 2002: 45).

Is death linked to faith because it is outside of language, because it is, ultimately, ineffable? The dead in Burnside possess a spiritual quality precisely because they are elusive, and they are elusive, it seems, even to mortality, as death in Burnside never erases a person. On the contrary, after death, everything that the bereft perceives is suddenly laced with death. Because death disperses a person into the mind of the one left behind, the dead saturate every thing and every place, because the departed is necessarily internalized in the one mourning. Everything the mourner perceives is seen as through a ghostly filter. A line in *Black Cat Bone* reads: 'Everyone becomes/ the thing he kills' (Burnside 2011a: 9).

Yet, the dead cannot be perceived in a concrete way, but merely as a notion, an idea or a hunch, *something almost* glimpsed in a landscape or a half-lit room. Dag T. Andersson has argued that 'the word "almost" [is] perhaps the key word to [Burnside's] poetry' because there is a 'feeling of strangeness' pervading his work, a feeling of strangeness that escapes expression (Andersson 2000: 38). In the opening poem to *Black Cat Bone*, 'The Fair Chase', a group of people are engaged in the hunt for a beast, perhaps a demon, a spirit or a ghost; the speaker mentions the sense of an uncertain presence, which is almost but never fully there.

> What we were after there, in the horn and vellum
> shadows of the wood behind our house,
> I never knew.
> At times, it felt like bliss, at times
> a run of musk and terror, gone to ground
> in broken wisps of ceresin and chrism,
> but now and then, the beast was almost there,
> glimpsed through the trees,
> or lifting its head from a stream. (Burnside 2011a: 3)

What is of interest here is not so much the explicit reference to chrism, to the consecrated mixture of oil and balsam used for anointing at baptism, as it is the reference to the beast being 'almost there', the sense in which the exact nature of what is being hunted the speaker 'never knew', but that it still felt 'like bliss' to him. The significance, it seems, lies precisely in the mystery. Had the nature of the hunted beast been obvious, the beast's nature might have been natural, mundane, but since it remained shaded in a secret, it thrills with the mystique and the suspense of the unknown, the way in which in novels such as *A Summer of Drowning* (2011), Burnside uses the unknown as a technique to create readerly interest and, potentially, readerly thrill from not knowing the precise nature of the *huldra* or the origin of the 'high-pitched shriek' (Burnside 2011b: 310) towards the end of the narrative, something that thrills, perhaps like dread, perhaps like bliss.

Burnside's speakers suffuse the poems with a mysterious and uncertain quality linked to experiences of bliss, states of spiritual blessedness. Andersson argues that it is precisely the uncertainties in Burnside's work, the 'sense of almost', which yields this bliss, since to Andersson, who argues via Walter Benjamin, '[n]aming is losing' (Andersson 2000: 39). Especially in Burnside's collections of recent years, the 'sense of almost' is further accentuated, and one might calibrate Andersson's argument that 'the word "almost" [is] perhaps the key word to [Burnside's] poetry' (38) by saying that equally important are the words 'something' and 'someone'. Speakers are looking 'for something chill and slender in this world' (Burnside 2011a: 17), 'someone is walking home/to the everafter' (18), 'there's something here that chooses to remain' (22), 'the taste of [the self]' is likened to 'the taste of something other' (22), a speaker notices 'the taste/of something in the distance' (Burnside 1995: 'A Folk Story', 12), 'there is something/scratches in the wall' (ibid., 'In the Psychiatric Hospital', 29), 'someone is there – a version of herself' (ibid., 'Cathy', 31) and one speaker remembers 'something he saw through the rain, a face, a wing' (Burnside 1997: 'Epithalamium', 54). There are many more examples; what is important is that 'something' or 'someone' are words of the same order as 'almost', in that they, of course, leave enigmatic and mysterious what to the speakers is utterly profound.

The dead and the various spectres and ghosts populating Burnside's cosmos douse it with mystery, with sensations of the 'enigmatic and mystical' (Andersson 2000: 38); the *somethings* and *someones* in his work produce in his characters and speakers what William Franke terms an 'uncanny awareness', which he sees as 'a channel of divine vision reaching beyond the ordinary sight of mortals and issuing in inspired speech' (Franke 2016: 2). This inspired speech, to Franke, is poetry. Productively, for a consideration of Burnside's work, Franke views this 'uncanny awareness' as 'connect[ing] by heavenly inspiration or even madness with a higher, transcendent source of consciousness, which is to say, with a type of knowing' (2). The epistemological dimension Franke touches upon is evident in many of Burnside's people, and most of them might be termed both poets and prophets for their 'uncanny awareness', their specifically transcendent sources of consciousness, their ecstatic 'type of knowing', which, even if they are unable to put into words what that knowledge is, has such an absolute hold over them that they are forced to submit to it, sometimes for the rest of their lives, sometimes to the point of madness.

The ecstatic, near maddening quality of this form of awareness, consciousness or knowing, which is perhaps ultimately beyond the reach of specific expression, beyond the reach of language, connects to Otto's sense of the numinous. Perhaps Otto's admission that the 'unique numinous category of ... a numinous state of mind' can be 'discussed' while 'it cannot be strictly defined' (Otto 1923: 7) seems like a convenient – perhaps tautological – cop-out to leave the ineffable unmarked by the signs of language and thereby leaving it immune to de(con)struction. Yet, to Otto, the numinous is a *real* experience, whose mystery and ineffability are paradoxically directly responsible for its reality. It is felt, either as sensation or as haunting, and it is so powerful because it cannot be fixed with language and therefore it cannot be argued away. He cites the Book of Job as an example text, from where his idea of the numinous comes forth:

> The *Book of Job* ... is not so much concerned with the awefulness of the majesty of the numen as with its mysteriousness; it is concerned with the non-rational in the sense of the irrational, with sheer paradox baffling comprehension, with that which challenges the reasonable and what might be reasonably expected, which goes directly against the grain of reason. (Otto 1923: 104)

The numinous is a *something* that is there, which can be all but grasped, which can only be grasped almost. This is why the numinous can be productively connected with the 'sense of almost', the mystifying 'experience of something or someone' in Burnside's poetry, an experience which is not only exclusive to religion but is also to do with the experience of mourning, of feeling the mysterious nearness of the dead in everything that is.

The nearness of the dead may be called a numinous presence since they instil a sense of implicit wonder, which has two characteristics: (1) it is so foreign that it is rationally inexplicable and indefinable, and (2) it is so powerful that the speakers are haunted to try again and again to capture and describe it. Because Burnside's dead do not impart terror but awe, they may be called numinous presences in secular surroundings, as the numinous, according to Otto, is stripped of 'human and natural' characteristics of 'terror, majesty, and sublimity' and filled instead with 'a feeling of the *unapproachable essence* of the Divine' (191). Otto wishes numinous experience to be free from ethical dimensions and that it be more terrific than terrifying, more good than ghastly, even if the human being might still feel utterly insignificant in its presence. Because divine essence is unapproachable to Otto, it is paradoxically desired wholly and therefore communicates what is to him the greatest sense of achievement in Christianity, namely a state of grace to aspire to in the future paradise following death. Bringing these ideas in dialogue with Burnside's poetry and the functions of the dead therein, one appreciates that the dead never have that dimension of terror or even sublimity and that the speakers communicate with their dead in a way that is usually hopeful. When a speaker in Burnside comes upon a remote forest cottage, his tone is one of relief when he experiences a feeling of wonder and says: 'My dead were there/ among the tilted stones' (Burnside 2011a: 11). Or a speaker states: 'though it's a long shot, you still believe someone will call/from far out in the hills' (64). The dead are personal, benevolent presences that are with the individuals like second selves, watching, observing and communicating with the often lonely speakers of the poetry, who seem to spend, like Burnside's alter egos in his poetry and memoirs, as much of their time as possible 'being alone', though perhaps they, too, 'never feel completely alone unless the dead are there' (Burnside 2010: 126–7).

It is important to see that the feeling of being in the presence of something wondrous when communicating with the dead like this never creates a desire for death in the speakers themselves. Unlike Burnside's alter-selves from the memoirs, his poetry's speakers never seem suicidal, and none of them actually dies. The dead's presence seems dialectically to make life much more precious and more beautiful. Andersson notes, 'Burnside seeks ... what he calls a "surrender to all life, to the continuum of energy, to all the possibilities of integration"' (Andersson 2000: 38). The enigmatic contemplation of the dead keeps Burnside's speakers in a meditative and wondrous balance in the middle of things. It keeps them in the world. *The dead are our roots, the one sure anchor in an otherwise provisional existence.*

To end on an ending: the poem 'Notes towards an Ending' from *Black Cat Bone* narrates the ambiguous end of a relationship between a man and a woman and correlates this end of two with the end of one, the end of life of a 'feathered thing [they] brought in from the yard' (Burnside 2011a: 25). Death comes to the couple's house personalized in this winged creature that 'came to grief on [their] picture window' (25). Death has brought indeterminacy, to this poem and to this creature's contours, as it's unclear what 'that feathered thing' actually is. It might not be a bird at all, but rather a symbol of their relationship – one may recall that Emily Dickinson wrote '"Hope" is the thing with feathers' (1970: 116). The poem's aesthetics of indeterminacy, its 'sense of almost', might give the ending to 'Notes towards an Ending' a spiritual quality, a non-rational sensation. If one perceives a spiritual dimension there, it's actualized by two things: (1) the enigmatic character of that *something* that died on the *picture window*, and (2) the concrete and secular terms and descriptions that surround it, such as '*dolce vita*', 'Hundertwasser' and 'Reich' (Burnside 2011a: 25).

As in 'Suburbs', the magical, the awe-inspiringly beautiful or spiritual need not be numinous to be felt as such but need merely be filled with a sense of mystery in a materialistically definitive world. The indeterminate and enigmatic ways of almost are strung through Burnside's poetry, and they secularize a numinous dimension by clashing the desire for expression with the inability to express. The words are not with God, but with the things, creatures and feelings of the secular world. By attending to this world carefully, by allowing the enigmatic to remain enigmatic through the choice of an indeterminate aesthetics, Burnside's poetry instils a sense of wonder. His speakers escape the radical need to fasten every sense datum and kill it with names. His speakers' words create the feeling that there may exist something other than the expressible phenomena of the world, and they are able to tolerate that they are inexpressibly contained in the world. Expressing them might, in fact, snatch the words from the speakers and force them to relinquish them to God.

Chapter Two: **John Burnside's Numinous Poetry,** Jan Wilm

Andersson, D. T. (2000), '"... Only the Other Versions of Myself": Images of the Other in the Poetry of John Burnside', *Chapman*, 96: 35–9.
Burnside, J. (1995), *Swimming in the Flood*, London: Jonathan Cape.
Burnside, J. (1997), *A Normal Skin*, London: Jonathan Cape.
Burnside, J. (2003), *Living Nowhere*, London: Jonathan Cape.
Burnside, J. (2007a), *Gift Songs*, London: Jonathan Cape.
Burnside, J. (2007b), *Selected Poems*, London: Jonathan Cape.
Burnside, J. (2009), *The Hunt in the Forest*, London: Jonathan Cape.
Burnside, J. (2010), *Waking up in Toytown*, London, Jonathan Cape.
Burnside, J. (2011a), *Black Cat Bone*, London: Jonathan Cape.
Burnside, J. (2011b), *A Summer of Drowning*, London: Jonathan Cape.
Dickinson, E. (1970), *The Complete Poems*, ed. T. H. Johnson, London: Faber and Faber.
Franke, W. (2016), 'Poetry, Prophecy, and Theological Revelation', *Oxford Research Encyclopedia of Religion*: 1–24. Available online: http://religion.oxfordre.com/view/10.1093/acrefore/9780199340378.001.0001/acrefore-9780199340378-e-205 (accessed 15 August 2017).
Jakobson, R. (1960), 'Linguistics and Poetics', in T. A. Sebeok (ed.), *Style in Language*, 350–77, Cambridge, MA: MIT Press.
Larkin, P. (2004), *Collected Poems*, ed. A. Thwaite, New York: Farrar, Straus & Giroux.
Melville, H. (2002), *Moby-Dick*, ed. H. Parker and H. Hayford, Norton, New York and London: W. W. Norton.
Otto, R. (1923), *The Idea of the Holy: An Inquiry into the Non-Rational Factor in the Idea of the Divine and Its Relation to the Rational*, trans. J. W. Harvey, Oxford: Oxford University Press.
Perloff, M. (1996), *Wittgenstein's Ladder: Poetic Language and the Strangeness of the Ordinary*, Chicago: The University of Chicago Press.
Schmitt, J-C. (1998), *Ghosts in the Middle Ages: The Living and the Dead in Medieval Society*, Chicago: The University of Chicago Press.
Schulte, J. (1992), *Wittgenstein: An Introduction*, trans. W. H. Brenner and J. F. Holley, Albany: State University of New York Press.
Wittgenstein, L. (1922), *Tractatus Logico-Philosophicus*, trans. C. K. Ogden, London: Kegan Paul, Trench, Trubner & Co., and New York: Harcourt, Brace & Company.

3

'A Temporary, Sometimes Fleeting Thing': Home in John Burnside's Poetry

Monika Szuba

Looking into a 'grimoire we cannot read' in an attempt to decipher its grammar, John Burnside questions our being-in-the-world: 'Do I belong here? Do any of us belong on this earth any more?' (Burnside 2014a: 264–5). Consistently returning to the question of home, he emphasizes the necessity of negotiating our dwelling-in-the-world, stressing both the need to belong and the impermanence haunting this endeavour: 'we write, in that same book, random and possibly unintelligible graffiti across the pages' (2014a: 265). Burnside does not idealize or romanticize the natural world, nor is he sentimental about its processes; he notices its unintelligibility. There are, for example, poems in which he addresses the unhomely nature of the earth; the speaker yearns for the reconnection with the natural world, constantly posing the question 'of belonging, a reckoning, and an accommodation, with the world around us, where no home is offered, but everything – including the ultimate mystery of life itself – is shared' (Burnside and Riordan 2004: 21). Burnside addresses 'the real plight of dwelling' (Heidegger 2013: 159), highlighting the constant transformation of place. He frequently returns to a familiar setting, a milieu in which he feels at home, especially when he recognizes his ability to name and thus domesticate the unknown. The act of naming foregrounds the capacity of language to order the world and, consequently, enables the possibility to dwell. Struggling with the ineffable, poetic language invests signs appearing in the natural world with meaning. Yet language also invents, ushering in imprecision and vagueness. Its slipperiness constitutes an important theme in Burnside's work; similar to dwelling, of which it is an inextricable part, language is uncertain, yet indispensable, as Burnside demonstrates.

Dwelling

In 'Building Dwelling Thinking' (1951), Heidegger considers 'our dwelling plight', emphasizing the importance of learning how to dwell properly because how we dwell is who we are. To dwell is to be situated, to maintain a relationship with the world; 'dwelling itself is always a staying with things. Dwelling, as preserving, keeps the fourfold in that with which mortals stay: in things' (Heidegger 2013: 150–1). Yet things remain impermanent; even homelands are illusory, many of Burnside's poems highlighting the plural and provisional nature of home. This is particularly marked in *The Asylum Dance* (2000), where titles indicating sites have a plural form ('Settlements', 'Fields', 'Roads', 'Ports'). Such titles emphasize the dissipation of dwelling, suggesting in turn something intermittent, transient, as opposed to figuring or representing a permanent home. Such impermanence is captured by, and expressed in, the poem that opens *The Asylum Dance*, 'Ports' (Burnside 2000a: 1–8). Its first line – 'our dwelling place' – flows with liquid consonants, figuring a place consisting of light, the weather forecast and snippets of language. Dwelling depends on 'the choice of a single word to describe/the gun-metal grey of the sky' (ll. 6–7), yet the combination of the compound proves the impossibility of such a task. The 'flicker' of the gulls mentioned in the next lines emphasizes the changeable nature of the world, the nouns suggestive of quick motion. The sentence ends with a proper name, Tolbooth Wynd, a close in Edinburgh built in the sixteenth century. The original function of the tolbooth changed over time, from housing council chambers, to a police court and then a prison. Its appearance – turret and clock – makes this construction stand out from the urban landscape; Burnside not only perceives mutability as a condition of what is seen (colour, motion) but reads it in the materiality and historicity of place. The name of the close is a kind of shibboleth for the changeability of purpose, and in turn the changeable world in which we live.

In Burnside's poetry, our dwelling place is defined both as something elusive and fleeting, such as changing light and flitting birds, and as something apparently solid and concrete like a building construction, which changes in its own way. Dwelling is usually tied to memory of place, something no longer there, mere remnants. The necessity to negotiate one's place in the world, a major preoccupation in Burnside, is an ecological concern. Several other poems in *The Asylum Dance*, including 'Settlements', 'Fields' and 'Roads', have a similar structure to 'Ports', the plurality of their titles further highlighting impermanence and hinting at the impossibility of settling in one place. As these poems suggest, the fleeting, frail nature of home is foregrounded in its finitude, in being tied by time in the realm of the earthly household (Snyder 1969). The plurality of the natural world, with its innumerable beings, is emphasized by the worlds accumulated in the first lines of 'Settlements': 'shorelines', 'rocks', 'shallow/sandbanks' and 'reefs'. The coastline with its natural variability is punctuated by manmade light and sound. The first part, 'A Place by the Sea' (Burnside 2000a: 24), is replete with the remains of the fleeting presence of others where the speaker happens to stay – 'powders', 'sacks of grain', 'crumbs' – the objects denoting fragments of existence, found in passing. In search of a firm ground, the self is unmoored, unfixed. What we are left with is 'the ghost of ourselves' (l. 39) and familiar scents and flavours.

We pass constantly, in both a spatial and temporal sense, and Burnside frequently emphasizes this dual aspect of our Being. The final poem from the collection, 'Roads' (Burnside 2000a: 73–85), is preceded by a citation from Octavio Paz's 'A Tale of Two Gardens' (Paz 1991: 291): 'Transcurrir es suficiente,/Transcurrir es quedarse' ('to pass through is enough,/to pass through is to remain'). It echoes the epigraph of the opening poem, 'Ports', a line from Henri Michaux's poem 'Sur étrave': 'Pas de port. Ports inconnus'. Not one but many unknown ports, their unfamiliarity heightened by their transitional nature. Often, the only thing we have is

a glimpse of something, not quite what we thought,
    but just enough, that we can think of home
in this, the most provisional of worlds.
(Burnside 2002: 62; ll. 71–3)

Despite its provisionality (or perhaps because of it), the world should be shared with other beings: 'how we view nature is only part of a wider question … one of belonging, a reckoning, and an accommodation, with the world around us, where no home is offered, but everything … is shared' (Burnside and Riordan 2004: 21). The necessity to share one's home with other creatures and to experience the world together involves the transcendence of borders – identities, the assumption of essences, selfhood – in the hope for reconnection. Our houses hide other beings; there are always guests such as field mice or other animals tucked away in a place consigned 'for woodlice and gnats,/for craneflies and death-watch beetle' (Burnside 2009: 44; ll. 2–4). Even though their ability to metamorphose is often difficult to grasp, and their multiple natures may appear alien (Brown 2006), insects are nevertheless there, present. Short-lived, they emphasize once more the transient fragility of dwelling, reminding us of our own finitude. As Maurice Merleau-Ponty argues, 'it is from the point of view of finality that we perceive analogies in living beings' (2003: 26). Other living beings and their demise remind us of our own. Mortality becomes even more acute when it is perceived in the context of immutability of the natural world: 'Finality is man' (Merleau-Ponty 2003: 24), while Nature and its laws are unchangeable, 'intact'. Burnside's speakers are acutely aware of Nature's unchangeability. Frequently observed from a distance, the non-human world inspires admiration for its unmistakable rhythms. In 'Geese' (*The Asylum Dance*) the ability to return to one's territory after travelling away from it, 'the pull and sway of home' (l. 44), makes scientific explanation unsatisfactory.

At the same time, Burnside also reminds us that the 'natural' world is not always homely.[1] This is stated explicitly in 'Steinar undir Steinahlíthum' (2005), preceded by a citation from James P. Carse. These words – 'Nature offers no home' (Carse 1986: 134) – foreground the inherent homelessness of human beings and the uncompromising fleetingness from which nothing can provide protection. In the poem, the earth is represented as an unknown, unknowable place; its inhabitants cannot guess 'how earnestly the land conducts itself' (l. 10), as it contains a mystery, 'something hidden, rot-cold' (l. 36). What remains is only a possibility of people's prosperity, their deepest emotions buried, 'abandoned to the depths' (l. 38). The unfulfilment of hopes is emphasized by three modal verb forms: 'they should have guessed' (l. 9); 'all they might have been, could they have stayed' (l. 39). The nouns – 'thumbprint' (l.13), 'scribbles' (l. 40), 'snowflake' (l. 16), 'figments of glass and tinder' (l.3) – stress the fleetingness of their existence, as well as the provisionality of 'goods/and movables they prized' (l. 5–6). Provisionality is also captured in the poet's invention of new coinages, such as 'rot-cold' (l. 36). Such formations problematize straightforward mimesis, forcing the reader to consider provisional, unfamiliar relationships as part of a dialectic between the 'natural' and language, between what is and what seeks to represent. Frequently employed by Burnside, the phrase 'a science of belonging' (Burnside and Riordan 2004: 19)[2] – where science means what is known – contains a contradiction, as it is unknown why dwelling proves impossible at times:

> But this was something else: a slighter thing
> and less precise: surrender to new mire,
>   a failure in the science of belonging,
> an aberration, fading on the air.
> (ll. 30–3)

In these lines, there is a shift from 'surrender' to 'failure' to 'aberration', a descent that intensifies the impression of gradually lost agency. The final word, 'aberration', signifies an astronomic cause but may also mean something unexpected, an imperfection, a deviation. The expression 'fading on the air' further emphasizes the poem's themes, with 'air' being frequently deployed by Burnside to foreground impermanence and fleetingness.

As already argued, temporality and finitude are the principal features of Heidegger's conceptualization of dwelling – features aggravated by human activity. In his work, Burnside often demonstrates that people are responsible for the destruction of habitats, emphasized in the opening lines of 'Settlements': 'Because what we think of as home/is a hazard to others' (2000a: 23). Driven by greed and a misplaced desire to belong, we sometimes make our dwelling in an inconsiderate manner, without remembering that this may threaten other beings. In 'Travelling South, Scotland, August 2012' (Burnside 2014b: 51–3), the poet expresses his antipathy to corporations changing landscapes and lives, disturbing habitats, criticizing 'the rule of Mammon'. The poem contains lists of artificial, man-made objects littering the landscape, having replaced animals. Throughout, Burnside plays with dialectics, strengthening an effect of oppositional forces: north/south, land/sea, present/past, light/darkness, inside/outside. There is the almost paralyzing barrenness of wasteland: 'a steady delete/of anything that tells us what we are,/a long/distaste for the blood warmth and bloom/of the creaturely' (ll. 57–60). Structurally, there are frequent enjambments, including the intrastanzaic ones, which may highlight divisions, and yet there is a distinct nostalgia imbuing the poem with sadness at our failure to transcend oppositions:

> a light we could have known
> but failed to see
> by choosing not to find
> the kingdom-at-hand:
> this order;
> this dialectic;
> this mother of invention,
> ceaseless play.
> (ll. 80–7)

The end of the poem refers to the epigraph, 'Necessity is not the mother of invention; play is' (Suttie 1999:18), which stresses the importance of playfulness in creation, a feature frequently undermined in modern society. Thus, by ending the poem with the words 'ceaseless play', Burnside foregrounds the potential sublimity of the animal and plant kingdom, the never-ending reinvention, the play of the world, its delightful unpredictability. These two words introduce a glimmer of hope into the arid wasteland, demolished as a result of our blindness to its abundance.

Sprawling industrialization distances us from the natural world, continuing our disconnection from the wild, which arises from the increasing isolation caused by technological advances. Foregrounding the vision of loss and destruction, and exhorting us to mend what can still be mended, Burnside urges us to share habitats in a non-destructive way. He underlines the necessity to mend the broken relationship, stressing in essays and interviews that the purpose of 'ecological art' is to reconnect us. We have lost the connection with the natural world, he argues, but poetry has the potential to perform an important role in finding unity: 'poetry itself can be seen as a means – a discipline, a spiritual path, a political-ecological commitment – to wholeness and reconnection with the earth itself' (Crawford 2006: 99–100). The reconnection in the poetry of 'we' means 'preserving the environment and studying how we, human beings, should dwell on the Earth without destroying [it]' (Dósa 2009: 117). Our relationship with the natural world may be fraught, but there is still the possibility to mend the broken connection, and this can be achieved by dwelling, often through poetic speech.

Language

In 'Language' (1959), Heidegger postulates speech's inevitability: 'man speaks. We speak when we are awake and we speak when in our dreams' (Heidegger 2013: 187). Such ideas have greatly influenced Burnside's thinking on the subject; as Burnside argues, Heidegger 'reminds us of the importance of language to the new way of thinking that we must discover in order to dwell meaningfully in the world' (Burnside 2000b: 260). For Burnside, the intricate relationship between language and dwelling has remained a focus of exploration throughout his work, as for instance, in the final lines of 'Ports':

> a name for something wanted
> and believed
>   no more or less correct than anything
> we use to make a dwelling in the world.
> (III.II. 101–4)

Interconnected with naming, dwelling depends on the ability to recognize and identify the elements of the natural world in our surrounding. These closing lines evoke an uncertainty by the use of indeterminate words such as 'something' and 'anything', as well as indefinite articles in the two nouns – 'name' and 'dwelling' – which foreground a sense of conditionality and ephemerality. Yet, the title of the poem, 'Kith' (Burnside 2002: 52), emphasizes the significance of familiarity and kinship, as well as Being, which is bound with language. Familiarity may perhaps be felt on a small scale on a parcel of well-known land but proves impossible to achieve in a worldly sense, as the final lines indicate: 'the world we paraphrase/as crease and furrow; grass-blade; robin's nest;//the *terra incognita* of the whole' (ll. 24–6). The lines stress elements of the inanimate and animate world, mostly things seen at close range such as contours of a field, fragments of flora and fauna, the list of nouns devoid of any evaluating words, a mere statement of the natural world's abundance and plenitude. Without representing things directly, language maps the landscape and its objects as phenomena connected to the self, as they are given to the self in the *there is*.[3] Language traces an otherwise non-orderable taxonomy, standing in as a series of elements that could continue perpetually, thereby pointing to an infinite seriality without totality. The expression 'the world we paraphrase' suggests again the vital necessity to name elements of the world using a language that we understand, where the verb 'paraphrase' highlights the limitation of speech to express meaning, as our being in the world is inevitably determined by speech.

Language's uses are emphasized recurrently in Burnside, in the contrast between science and experience, which foregrounds the inadequacy of the scientific method in the face of what is there. In 'Sense Data' (Burnside 2000a: 12), the speaker mentions 'things I couldn't name' (l. 8). This lack of specific knowledge is contrasted with the scientific approach, foregrounded in such quantitative verbs as 'we measured' (l. 1) and 'we counted' (l. 3), as well as in the name of a method: 'chromatography' (l. 5). As science strives to invent a precise language that would contain the world, poetry points to the impossibility of such a task. There is 'some seventh sense' (l. 14), which allows one to listen to its 'deeper pulse' (l. 15). Our inevitable urge to look for labels to mark the world is already foregrounded in the title of 'Taxonomy' (Burnside 2002: 6), which suggests scientific classification, a system grouping plants and animals based on their presumed relationships. This scientific orderliness has its limits – the limits of language – as the following lines propose: 'leaving the rest untold;/the world/unspoken' (ll. 7–9). Things are 'untold', kept secret and the world is 'unspoken': expressed or understood without being directly stated, speech unnecessary. Even if the language of the living world remains beyond our comprehension, it is sensed nevertheless, as the world responds to something in ourselves – 'a meadow answers' (l. 13) – allowing us a moment of self-recognition. We look for things we know and can name. Details such as form, texture, colour help us recognize the familiar. The plants' familiarity creates 'commonplace affection' (l. 4), leading in turn to self-reflection. Yet, exact description is impossible: the colour is 'nothing like' (l. 20) the difference between two plants, 'no more or less/specific than a kale field after rain' (ll. 23–4). The lack of specificity and a certain vagueness or haziness of terms is a recurrent feature of Burnside's writing. The expression 'something like' echoes throughout his writing, underlining the imprecision of language, the impossibility to name emotions and phenomena – a certain impotence. Even though speech proves hazy, imprecise, it remains indispensable to dwelling (see, for instance, Heidegger 2013).

We continue to use words even if they 'slip, slide, perish/decay with imprecision', 'crack and sometimes break under the burden' (Eliot [1936] 2002: 182). As the next stanza from 'Taxonomy' suggests, language inevitably comes when we experience the world, our perception turning into words. The urge to respond to everything we see using language is always there, competing with the tension between *there is* and expression. Echoing Heidegger, Burnside suggests that language is the locus of Being. In the final three stanzas of 'Taxonomy', language participates, as if magically, in uncovering the world. In these lines, magic blends with hints of a religious world, the latter embodied in the single word 'revelation': to reveal, or to lay bare the familiar offers epiphany, truth, or *aletheia* (*Erschlossenheit*), 'the uncovering of beings' (Heidegger 2013: 57). As elements of the vegetal world are revealed, a clearing opens, in which Being takes place, as an instance of the Merleau-Pontyan dehiscence (1968: 117). A term employed in botany, 'dehiscence' refers to the opening of flower buds or fungi when they are ready to release their content, sending the seeds or spores out and into the world. Poetic language likewise performs an act of opening up, uncovering and releasing meaning.

In the second section of 'Taxonomy', entitled 'Fauna', the opening stanza suggests a link between naming and possessing: 'we speak as if they understood the words' (l. 7), 'their fondness' (l. 8) gesturing towards an affinity, a form of belonging. The pronouns 'they', 'their', 'them' used throughout the poem refer to 'these animals' (l. 3), juxtaposed with 'us' in order to foreground the distance between human and non-human animals, as 'they are far from us' (l. 4). A sign of helplessness in the face of the abundance of the natural world, taxonomy offers limited possibilities, as sometimes we are left with filing and naming in no particular order as if to acknowledge their bare existence. Thus, elaborations are a frequent device: a list of plants in 'Taxonomy' ('toadflax', 'fern', 'coltsfoot', 'mint', 'kale') (2002: 6–7) or 'The Unprovable Fact: A Tayside Inventory' ('lobelia/nasturtium/wintersweet/rhubarb and garlic/privet and night-scented stock') (2000a: 65); a list of animals in 'Shapeshifters' ('marten, dog-fox, wolf') (2005: 17); a catalogue of plants in 'A Duck Island Flora' ('cornflowers; bluebells; dogwood; purple vetch;/*kornblomst; blåklokker; skrubbaer; fuglevikke*') (2002: 59). The natural world appears as a site of meanings, which language represents; in its repetitions, language suggests the iterability of the meaningful, repeated listing an attempt to epitomize their significance.

At times, language in Burnside is endowed with a magical function. As we read in 'Koi' (Burnside 2002: 3–5),

> The trick is to create a world
> from nothing
>   – not the sound a blackbird makes
> in drifted leaves.
> (ll.1–4)

Reverberating throughout the poem, the word 'nothing' becomes immediately performative in the second line, as it stands on the verge of the gap above the second line and the dash, suggesting a pause, gesturing towards emptiness: something comes from nothing; the creation of the world is reimagined in 'the gap between each named form and the next' (l. 38). Language is thus the 'nothing' from which something comes: it makes things appear, as in the oft-cited passage from Stéphane Mallarmé's 'Crisis of Verse' (1897), in which the flower is immaterial and thus absent. Only language can make the flower present, its essence evoked through the word denoting it.[4] The poet saying 'flower' assumes the non-presence of its material counterpart. Fundamentally absent, the flower can never be grasped physically, but it can be bodied forth, verbally summoned and evoked. In Burnside's poem, the world is, likewise, conjured up from nothing through speech. Nothing becomes something when it is poetically summoned.

'What was the world like before language?' asks Burnside in poems laden with religious connotations. Biblical allusions abound. The latter is particularly pronounced in 'History' (Burnside 2002: 20), which opens *in medias res* where the first word 'then' suggests a succession of events, reaching the next stage, rhetorically offering a reference to Genesis: 'And out of the ground the Lord God formed every beast of the field, and every fowl of the air; and brought them unto Adam to see what he would call them: and whatsoever Adam called every living creature, that was the name thereof' (Gen. 20:19). 'A breed apart' (l. 3), Adam 'gave names to all cattle, and to the fowl of the air, and to every beast of the field' (Gen. 20:20). After Adam forgets the names of animals, they disappear. Connection is lost, what remains in the absence of animals is myth-making. It is not absence exactly but 'the unvoiced presence' (l. 12), a presence sensed but not named. Reimagined, animals are 'made flesh again' (l. 13), an expression recalling the biblical phrase 'the Word ... made flesh' (Jn. 1:14). The phrase 'made whole' foregrounds the yearning to mend the disconnection, man and animal reunited, the world as one, a world without god's intervention, 'untouched by god' (l. 13).

The figure of Adam returns in 'Septuagesima' from the collection *Feast Days* (Burnside 1992: 1), which evokes a yearning to go beyond language: beyond the constraints of arbitrary signs in search of a different form of signification, when the speaker imagines a moment before Adam names the animals. It is preceded by a citation from Jorge Guillén's 'Los nombres'. There is no welding of language and things: words fail to touch things, remaining on top of a layer covering things, irreducibly unpresentable. It is only through a shared language that we can even come close to the thing *as it is*. In Guillén's poem, wild being takes merely a moment before the thing is fixed, before the rose is rose. The speaker of 'Septuagesima' dreams of the time before names were given by Adam when there was silence, and 'the gold skins newly dropped' (l. 4), surrounded by 'a winter whiteness' (l. 8). Gold and white suggest impeccable purity, perfection before things are tainted. There exists a hint of religious iconography in this image of absolute cleanness, the colours redolent of divine glory, and religious undertones appear also in the use of pronouns: the first-person singular speaking 'I' in the first stanza shifts into a collective 'we', a community of loss in a postlapsarian world. The final two stanzas return to the idea of perfection, offering a Platonic image of forms in which there appears a pre-verbal spectral presence, as lines 10–14 indicate. In the final line of the poem, the preposition 'beyond' offers a transcendental vision, pointing to something lying behind the meaning of words and outside the materiality of things.

In the eponymous poem from *The Light Trap* found in the second section titled '$Φύσις$' ('Physis', after Heraclitus), animals are given names. The poem starts with the words, 'Homesick for the other animals' (Burnside 2002: 23), creating a link between animals and home, gesturing towards our origins. The line expresses a yearning for kinship, inextricably connected with proper dwelling, a concern which reverberates throughout Burnside. The end of the poem is once more a catalogue of names, emphasizing the dizzying plurality of animals and revelling in language. Here, 'the act of naming insects … creates a problematic disjunction between language and materiality' (Brown 2006: xii). All the butterfly names mentioned in the poem are common rather than scientific, their sound poetic. Counting moths in the first stanza, naming familiar forms in the last, naming as poetic gesture. As Brown argues:

> because of a nearly unfathomable number of species, the plethora of insects 'in need of names' … beggars description … the scientific names of insects, which demonstrate both an abundance and an abundant lack in the world

of taxonomy, are often dazzling to the eye (witness *Parastratiosphecomyia sphecomyioides*) but the expressive euphony is also evident: Ephemerella subvaria or Libellula pulchella, Euborellia annulipes or Nannothemia bella. Such expressiveness underscores the ways in which poetry and the natural world collapse into each other, a pattern evident as well in species that take the poetry of their names from some of those most proficient at the art. (2006: xiii)

Language is there to ground us from our first words, as the opening lines of 'De Anima' (Burnside 2005: 36–8) demonstrate. The first line is repeated later in the poem, the list of names different: millipede, beetle, Painted Lady, 'may- or dragon-fly' (l. 49), followed by another list: 'spider and fly/lizard and drowsing cattle/dolphin/skua' (ll. 54–7). The spacing of words foregrounds the accidental nature of knowledge. As Burnside's speaker says, this is 'how mind evolves/one meeting at a time' (ll. 52–3). The shapes and sounds of one's *Umwelt* 'go down like script/unmemorised/and not to be forgotten' (ll. 64–6).[5] Scientific precision proved useless in placing the soul, as the 'old anatomists' (l. 31) tried to locate it 'in all the likely places' (l. 32). Language in its labelling function fails in capturing something so diffuse, 'a total sum of movement and exchange' (l. 17). As Burnside writes in 'Appleseed' (2005: 32), 'the wider rootedness' is what 'we sometimes call the soul/and sometimes spirit' (ll. 3–4), where 'the soul is wild and single' (l. 8). The last words of the poem – 'rooted in the stars' (l. 24) – combine the earth and the sky, resonating with Heidegger's fourfold of earth and sky, mortals and divinities, with fullness being a part of dwelling. The legend of Johnny Appleseed spreading seeds braided into the poem suggests that the earth grounds human beings as part of the fourfold, belonging to, dwelling in it.

Names of insects are spread between commonality and singularity. Both the commonplace and the unique combine in the making of home. Proper names in Burnside occur most frequently in titles, as if mooring the texts: 'Going to Crosshill' (1992: 20), '8 a.m. near Chilworth' (1992: 41), 'In Kansas' (2005: 60–6), 'In Argentina' (2005: 68–72), 'On Kvaloya' (2002: 53–8), 'Insomnia in Southern Illinois' (2011a: 63), 'Saint-Naizaire', 'By Pittenweem', 'Le Croisic', 'Ny-Hellesund' (2007), 'Crane-watching in *Ostprignitz-Ruppin, November 2014*' and '*Midwinter, 2013, Arncroach*' (2017: 66–8). They are most often being referred to as places of transit and the proper names make the references concrete. Singular and general, the ordinary is made special in poetry in the process of isolation, as 'out of several vocables, [poetry] makes a total word, entirely new, foreign to the language, and almost incantatory' (Mallarmé 2007: 211). Suspended between sound and sense, poetic language defamiliarizes words and focuses attention on itself.

Coda: Grammar and Kinship

Poetry is a continuous attempt to translate the 'grimoire we cannot read' – the 'natural' world – in which we are immersed yet cannot decipher, or fully understand. Not knowing how to translate it, we try nonetheless to paraphrase it. As Derrida argues, 'a text lives only if it lives on, and it lives *on* only if it is *at once* translatable *and* untranslatable ... Totally translatable, it disappears as a text, as writing, as a body of language. Totally untranslatable, even within ... one language, it dies immediately' (1979: 102–3). Both translatable and untranslatable, the text of the natural world is approached by Burnside through the iterability of common and proper names as well as the recollection and recurrence of familiar words. The result is a glimpse of an intimate space opened within language which, through defamiliarization, attempts to evoke the numinous and the immanent. Endowing signs found in the natural world with meaning, poetic language helps us dwell. As Bachelard observes, 'we experience an extension of our intimate space' through the poetic (1994: 199). Thus, the poetic functions both as an emanation of inner lives and as a translation of the complex grammar of dwelling.

A fleeting, temporary thing, our dwelling place is shared with other beings, beings that can be named as home, through language. Naming, which demonstrates the need to domesticate, is constantly foregrounded in Burnside. Let us turn once more to 'Ports':

> Whenever we think of home
> we come to this:
> the handful of birds and plants we know by name.
> (ll. 11–13)

These lines evoke a familiar setting, a milieu in which we might feel at home, equipped with the capacity to name. Thus, home is 'grammar and kinship/ wedlock/collective nouns' (2005: 13; ll. 83–5) or else 'the world we paraphrase' (2002: 52; l. 24). The ability to name, to make familiar, to domesticate the unfamiliar, is one role of poetry. Finding a place for words, setting them in a particular order and devising a structure, Burnside has made his home in poetry: mobile dwelling, shared with the reader. In an attempt to read from the 'organic-textual' grimoire, the poet explores the grammar of being as belonging. As he writes, we dwell

> in a world we do not know
> and name the things

one object at a time:
fishing boat, lighthouse, herring gull, clear blue sky.
(2005: 27; ll. 67–70)

Burnside's poetry opens the world for us and opens within us our forgotten Being-in-the-world.

Chapter Three: 'A Temporary, Sometimes Fleeting Thing': Home in John Burnside's Poetry, Monika Szuba

Bachelard, G. (1994), *The Poetics of Space*, trans. M. Jolas, Boston: Beacon Press.
Brown, E. C. (2006), 'Introduction', in E. C. Brown (ed.), *Insect Poetics*, ix–xxiii, Minneapolis, London: University of Minnesota Press.
Burnside, J. (1992), *Feast Days*, London: Secker & Warburg.
Burnside, J. (2000a), *The Asylum Dance*, London: Jonathan Cape.
Burnside, J. (2000b), 'Strong Words', in W. N. Herbert and M. Hollis (eds), *Strong Words: Modern Poets on Modern Poetry*, 259–61, Tarset: Bloodaxe.
Burnside, J. (2002), *The Light Trap*, London: Jonathan Cape.
Burnside, J. (2005), *The Good Neighbour*, London: Jonathan Cape.
Burnside, J. (2006), 'A Science of Belonging: Poetry as Ecology', in R. Crawford (ed.), *Contemporary Poetry and Contemporary Science*, 91–106, Oxford: Oxford University Press.
Burnside, J. (2007), *Gift Songs*, London: Jonathan Cape.
Burnside, J. (2009), *The Hunt in the Forest*, London: Jonathan Cape.
Burnside, J. (2011), *Black Cat Bone*, London: Jonathan Cape.
Burnside, J. (2014a), *I Put a Spell on You*, London: Cape.
Burnside, J. (2014b), *All One Breath*, London: Jonathan Cape.
Burnside, J. (2017), *Still Life with Feeding Snake*, London: Cape.
Burnside, J. and M. Riordan (2004), 'Introduction', in J. Burnside and M. Rioardan (eds), *Wild Reckoning: An Anthology Provoked by Rachel Carson's Silent Spring*, 13-21, London: Calouste Gulbenkian Foundation.
Carse, J. P. (1986), *Finite and Infinite Games: A Vision of Life as Play and Possibility*, New York: The Free Press.
Crawford, R., ed. (2006), *Contemporary Poetry and Contemporary Science*, Oxford: Oxford University Press.
Derrida, J. (1979), 'Living On/Borderlines', in H. Bloom *et al.* (eds), *Deconstruction and Criticism*, 102–10, New York: Seabury Press.
Dósa, A. (2009), *Beyond Identity: New Horizons in Modern Scottish Poetry*, Amsterdam & New York: Rodopi.
Eliot, T. S. (2002), *Collected Poems 1909–1962*, London: Faber and Faber.
Heidegger, M. (2013), 'Building Dwelling Thinking', in *Poetry, Language, Thought*, trans. A. Hofstadter, 143–59, New York: Harper Perennial Modern Thought.

Mallarmé, S. (2006), *Collected Poems and Other Verse*, trans. E. H. and A. M. Blackmore, Oxford: Oxford University Press.
Mallarmé, S. (2007), 'Crisis of Verse', in *Divagations*, trans. B. Johnson, Cambridge, MA, and London: Belknap Press.
Merleau-Ponty, M. (1968), *The Visible and the Invisible. Followed by Working Notes*, trans. A. Lingis. Evanston: Northwestern University Press.
Merleau-Ponty, M. (2003), *Nature: Course Notes from the Collège de France*, trans. R. Vallier, Evanston: Northwestern University Press.
Paz, O. (1991), *The Collected Poems of Octavio Paz. 1957–1987*, trans. E. Weinberger, New York: New Directions.
Philipse, H. (1998), *Heidegger's Philosophy of Being: A Critical Interpretation*, Princeton: Princeton University Press.
Snyder, G. (1969), *Earth House Hold*, New York: New Directions.
Suttie, I. D. (1999), *The Origins of Love and Hate*, London: Psychology Press.

4

Violent Dwellings and Vulnerable Creatures in *Burning Elvis* and *Something Like Happy*

Alexandra Campbell

For Burnside, violence is an ugly and banal reality, a troublingly commonplace experience that occurs through the 'inappropriate or unnatural application of force' upon the 'powerless' figures of women, children, animals and 'terrain' (2006: 127). As critics such as David Borthwick (2009), Scott Brewster (2006) and Astrid Bracke (2014) have noted, this interrogation of force often arises in conjunction with male characters who 'utilize violence as an illusory route to power and self-determination' (Borthwick 2009: 70). Driven by an impulse towards both self-determination and 'self-annihilation', his anxious narratives are 'peopled by bereft sons and husbands, strange counterparts and inadequate father-figures who play sadistic games and whose stories cannot be believed' (Brewster 2006: 188). The violence that permeates through Burnside's prose worlds is symptomatic of a wider 'spiritual failure, a failure to recognise the fundamental imperative to respect and honour "the other"' (Burnside 2009: 128), an 'other' that importantly includes the more-than-human. Across his novels and short stories, anthropogenic, often male-centred, violence emerges as a central rupture that fuels a wider narrative of restoration and recovery. Suggesting that the experience of violence engenders a necessary healing, his works are concerned with 'the possibility of growth, which is a painful thing, but nevertheless an exciting, meaningful and authentic thing ... What I'm writing is always about healing: about healing the world or about trying to heal one's vision of the world' (2009: 131). Poised between obliteration and restoration, the stories contained within Burnside's short story collections *Burning Elvis* (2000) and *Something Like Happy* (2013) explore unsettling ecologies of violence that emanate from a central crisis of masculinity. This chapter offers a new reading of Burnside's masculine figures, suggesting that rather than exhibiting a morbid preoccupation with violence, his stories interrogate the condition of vulnerability as a central component of ecological relation.

Vulnerable Selves in *Burning Elvis*

One cannot deny the pervasive force of what David Borthwick has described as a 'malignant masculinity' within Burnside's fiction (2009: 73). Often writing about 'alienated male characters who have become denatured', his short stories centre on moments where 'something happens which reveals to them that they have been wrapped in a lie, or self-deceit, or social conditioning – that they have been blinded to their true natures' (2009: 73). This dynamic of exposure is central to Burnside's shorter works, where moments of violent revelation offer characters a route towards a necessary healing in which isolation and malignancy give way to a 'meaningful and non-destructive play between self and other' (Burnside 2015: 122). Burnside's first short story collection, *Burning Elvis*, presents a series of twelve stories 'about young men who are suddenly faced with the fact that they had been standing still and that they haven't been paying attention to the world around them and it is time to change' (Burnside 2009: 128). The collection as a whole is haunted by the possibility of 'grace', where moments of brutality give way to the prospect of 'a different life, a state of grace, a cleaner way of being' (Burnside 2000: 68). For many of the disturbed male characters, this 'cleaner way of being' manifests in line with a more open and multispecies sense of kinship, whereby the experience of violence inflicted by, or upon, the male body accentuates the corporeal vulnerability of a self that is newly open to both the risks and the possibilities inherent in relation.

In the collection's titular story, the life of a young man is forever altered as he witnesses the murder of a female friend at the jealous hands of another woman. The story follows the unnamed protagonist as he attempts to come to terms with his inability to rescue Lindy from her sudden and senseless end. Through an exploration of the resulting sense of powerlessness that extends from the protagonist's failure to act, the story highlights the marginalized condition of the male character, whose social paralysis extends from his perception of himself as nothing more than 'an isolated body in a closed space' (Burnside 2000: 3). Across the tale, the protagonist does not lament the death of Lindy but rather mourns his own inability to cultivate a meaningful sense of relation with the world around him. Her murder becomes the 'one defining event' in his life, where the severing of her carotid artery accentuates the protagonist's own severed sense of relation between self and society (Burnside 2000: 26).

Prefaced by a quotation from John Donne, 'No man is an island', the story works to decentre the primacy of the male-driven narrative, forcing the protagonist to recognize his minor role in the broader spectrum of society and to come to terms with the fact that he 'never had anything more than a marginal place there' (Burnside 2000: 22). The story thus problematically positions the death of Lindy as a platform from which the protagonist is able to engender new forms of relation, as he comes to realize 'that the world doesn't revolve around [him]' (Burnside 2009: 130). The shock of the murder is used as a catalyst for the protagonist to come into an awareness that he has heretofore existed trapped 'behind an invisible line' (Burnside 2000: 13), existing in a state of self-imposed disconnection from which he may now be able to recover. The death of Lindy prompts the protagonist to begin looking beyond the bounds of the self and to extend outwards towards the 'more than human "other"' and to begin cultivating a new, better self (Burnside 2009: 121). The final reflections of the protagonist in 'Burning Elvis' thus do not linger over the fate of Lindy but turn instead to the difficult possibility of the protagonist's own renewal. For Lindy, of course, this renewal will never occur, but for our unnamed protagonist, the slow passage of time becomes a source of solace: 'history had passed and nobody knew or cared who she was. Life had moved on. It was a banal and surprisingly comforting thought, and all of a sudden it made me unaccountably glad, like the stillness of a city graveyard, or the first thick fall of snow, that obliterates and renews everything it touches' (Burnside 2000: 27). The sense of obliteration that accompanies the protagonist's radical decentring gives way to a heightened sense of awareness of the external world that fosters the emergence of a more communal and relational mode of being and tentatively moves towards developing 'a meaningful way of dwelling' with the world (Burnside 2015: 120).

In placing the death of a woman as a facilitator for male growth and recovery, 'Burning Elvis' draws attention to a key problem in Burnside's early prose works, namely his tendency to employ female characters as either victims or tools of masculine renewal. Across his fictional worlds, Burnside's women often appear as 'insignificant, two-dimensional characters, existing only in relation to men' (Bracke 2014: 424); their constant objectification becomes a clumsy tool through which to highlight the dangers evident in communities shaped by a 'socially legitimised psychosis, a psychosis intimately connected, unfortunately, with our ideas of manhood, and social worth' (Burnside 2009: 120). While the stories contained within Burning Elvis seek to address the underlying 'social psychosis' of toxic masculinity that legitimizes and normalizes conditions of exploitation, violence and abuse, these narratives also fall victim to such impulses. We see this in the story 'Decency', in which the serialized murders of women in a Spanish seaside town serve to fuel a narrative centred on the (im)possibility of masculine healing and relation. From the opening of the story, the focal character, Robert, is revealed to be yet another marginalized male figure, whose strained marriage and 'detached' state of being forces him out into the streets in search of connection (Burnside 2000: 86). Across the story, Robert's position as a 'neutral observer' of the world around him rather than active participant (Burnside 2000: 85) sees him move further away from his wife Sandra and the society she inhabits, and towards the unsettling character of Gold, whose mesmeric qualities lead Robert on a path to self-empowerment, which manifests in the form of sexual violence. Where Sandra is described as 'the secret enemy of all [Robert's] desires, and even of his deepest sense of self' (Burnside 2000: 87), Gold encourages Robert to pursue a disturbing form of 'freedom' described as 'the freedom to be. Which [is the] polar opposite of everything other people want from you, other people's – expectations. Freedom is the domain of monsters' (Burnside 2000: 96). As a facilitator of Robert's suppressed violent fantasies, Gold becomes emblematic of a particular form of masculine violence, in which violence 'is presented as natural, or even attractive [creating] a social climate in which violence is sanctioned, especially violence towards the powerless' (Burnside 2009: 128). Torn between monstrosity and decency, Robert comes to represent the central anxieties of Burnside's prose works, namely the ways in which masculinity is aligned with 'violence and the need for domination' (Borthwick 2009: 76).

Throughout 'Decency', Burnside examines the ways in which male self-fulfilment is achieved through dynamics of detachment, domination and destruction. Across the story, the isolation of the male central character(s) serves to prohibit forms of meaningful interconnection and intimacy from emerging. The story explores a disturbing form of masculine rage and desire and ambiguously positions Robert as both victim and perpetrator of violence. Importantly, while the sexual violence is initially presented as a viable means through which Robert is able to achieve self-empowerment, the story also presents glimpses of an alternative pathway to self-determination, one derived through an openness towards the other. This sense of openness occurs at several key moments in the text, namely when Robert is positioned at the extreme edge of society. At one moment in the story, as Robert is precariously positioned on a cliff face, his body and mind become open to a range of new sensations: 'he felt himself altered, receiving signals and stimuli he normally missed – a gust of scent on the air, a flicker of movement among the hibiscus shrubs at the square's edge, a new resonance ... that sent tremors through some fine cord in his spine that he had never been aware of until that moment' (2000: 86). For Robert, the 'sanctuary' of the cliff face brings both comfort and a sense of risk, where the threat of self-annihilation brings a sudden awareness of his own embodied mortality that allows him to feel 'more alive, more rooted in the world' (2000: 86). This strange awakening of the flesh presents Robert with a renewed possibility of connection and relation to not only other people but the wider more-than-human realm. Here, Burnside attempts to provide an alternative construction of masculine selfhood as something previously performed through the violent subjugation and objectification of women, to something cultivated in relation to a primal sense of corporeal vulnerability. No longer presented as a ghostly figure that haunts the fringes of society, Robert's embodied position within the world induces a state of acute perception, developing a form of sensorial attentiveness that might allow for the possibility of future connection.

As with 'Burning Elvis', however, throughout 'Decency' female victimhood is problematically presented as a facilitator of masculine growth and recovery. As Julika Griem has suggested, the closing dream-like image of Robert gradually being eaten away by 'a school of tiny fishes ... biting softly into his flesh, eating him away slowly, quietly, without pain' (Burnside 2000: 117) subjects him 'to a violent self-annihilation that leaves open the possibility of a cathartic and healing transformation' (Griem 2015: 95). However, this final cathartic transformation is punctuated by images of the murder and rape of a local woman. It is left unclear whether these moments are real or imagined, but they remain central to Robert's navigation of a distinctly fraught sense of self. At the end of the story, Robert's desire for a 'place where he could rest, and think of himself as happy and free, and intrinsically, incontrovertibly decent' highlights the possibility of renewal for the central masculine figure, but one that is first made possible through committing acts of indecent and inexcusable brutality (Burnside 2000: 117). Throughout *Burning Elvis*, Burnside is attuned to the hazards evident in patriarchal modes of relation, whereby the moral ambiguity of his stories highlights the difficulties evident in cultivating forms of interconnection that remain reliant upon modes of subjugation and dominance. While the continued use of female characters as a device for male recovery remains problematic throughout the work, the collection is invested in exploring alternative systems of relation that might emerge from instances of bodily vulnerability in which the male body is opened towards the wider world.

As Burnside has suggested, phenomenological modes of being-in-the-world are central to his understanding of ecological relation, where a 'walking human – or for that matter, any human being standing in the open, exposed, aware, at risk, untrammelled – is able to attune him or herself to the rhythm of the earth, the feel of a place, the presence of other animals, the elements, sidereal time, the divine' (2006: 101). This seamless relation between earth, animals, the sky and the divine draws from Martin Heidegger's essays on dwelling, in which he argues that in order to dwell – understood as the act of inhabiting and recognizing one's place in the world – man must not only exhibit an acceptance of nature but must exhibit 'a profound openness to the other, an acceptance of the essential nature of the earth's elements, including humanity' (Borthwick 2009: 77). Consequently, for Burnside the act of dwelling necessitates 'both a recognition of the spiritual importance of connection with the earth and the political importance of *being* open', where the act of being open and 'exposed' is both dangerous 'but it is also essential to being human' (Burnside 2006 italics in original: 101–2).

In *Burning Elvis* this sense of being open, exposed and at risk gives rise to the possibility of altruistic relation as engendered through conditions of somatic vulnerability. As Erinn Gilson describes:

> Vulnerability is regarded as definitive of life, a condition that links humans to nonhuman animals, and an experience that roots us in the corporeality of our existence. It is also a state that is intimately tied to violence, acts of which render us more vulnerable while also laying bare a preexisting vulnerability of which we have been ignorant. (2013: 4)

In suggesting that vulnerability holds an ethical potential, Gilson places vulnerability as the basis of social life, arguing that 'only by being vulnerable can one extend oneself beyond oneself' (2013: 2). In relation to the male characters within *Burning Elvis*, their proclivity towards violence reveals an innate vulnerability of the self, where acts of violence do not result in securing the male body against an external other but lay it open to reciprocity and relation. Understood in these terms, vulnerability is not simply a subjective disposition but, rather,

> characterizes a relation to a field of objects, forces, and passions that impinge upon or affect us in some way. As a way of being related to what is not me and not fully masterable, vulnerability is a kind of relationship that belongs to the ambiguous region in which receptivity and responsiveness are not clearly separable from one another. (Butler 2016: 25)

While the reciprocity between self and other is integral to the cultivation of empathy and community, there are also dangers evident in this openness, where being open risks being 'affected by forces outside our control, the effects of which we can neither fully know nor fully control' (Gilson 2013: 3–4). Across *Burning Elvis*, Burnside draws together the self and other, the known and the unknown, in to a dialectical system of relation through which his male characters may begin to cultivate a 'meaningful way of dwelling with the land, with water, and with the sky' (2015: 120).

Throughout *Burning Elvis*, Burnside's ambiguous men acknowledge that vulnerability 'may surely inspire care, love, and generosity, but it may equally inspire abuse, intimidation, and violence ... as vulnerable bodies, we are always available to both care and injury, and are similarly capable of offering care to, or inflicting injury on, others' (Murphy 2011: 579). This complex dialectical relationship between injury and care manifests through a disturbing story that centres on themes of death, trauma and the vulnerability of the body. In 'Dada', Burnside presents a macabre tale of another unnamed male narrator who has decided to 'keep' his grandfather's body after death. Throughout the narrative, Burnside once again hones in on a definitively violent form of masculinity as the narrator relates the details of a childhood shaped by fear: 'I was frightened of him ... He never spoke, he would just stare at me, as if I was some stray animal the women had taken in. I sometimes thought ... he would have killed me with his spade, the way I once saw him kill a rat he caught, in the corner of the yard' (Burnside 2000: 173). Across the story, women, animals and children perish at the hands of alienated and denatured men. However, as the story unfolds, the tender actions of the unnamed grandson serve to collapse and undermine the dominating rationality of masculine violence that fuels the narrative.

In 'Dada', the death of the patriarch allows for a new mode of relation to emerge, where the violence of the grandfather is juxtaposed against the grandson's tender actions after his death. Deciding that 'Dada's better off in the bath than he would be in the graveyard', the protagonist does not disown his abusive grandfather after death but instead chooses to alter their previously violent relationship into one of preservation and care:

> I look after him. If I've been out for the day, I go in to see him as soon as I get back. I brush off the craneflies and dust, and start from where I left off, talking to him, washing his skin, replacing the ice around his body. It's a long process, but I'm determined to make someone new ... I'm making him the gift of a new life: I'm teaching him to be something he never even dreamed of becoming. (183)

The protagonist's macabre safeguarding of Dada's body reformulates the previous violence of their relationship, presenting a narrative framed around the possibility of healing and restoration as opposed to power and control. Given the opportunity to reform his relationship with his grandfather, the protagonist constructs a new narrative of their lives:

> I'm determined to make someone new, and now that he is in my mind, I can see him differently. I can trace him back to an origin I must have forgotten was there: a bright afternoon, a beach, Dada in his dark-red swimming trunks, taking me into the water and telling me I needn't be frightened because he's with me, he'll hold me up … I am weightless and free. (2000: 183)

The sense of trust and freedom that emerges in these swimming scenes highlights a form of vulnerability that does not incite suffering but instead instils vulnerability with a transformative function that allows for new narratives of care, grace and possibility to arise. The 'unexpected abandonment' (Burnside 2000: 183) the protagonist feels as he surrenders his body to the memory of Dada prompts a simultaneous 'surrender of [the male] need for power and control over the other' (Borthwick 2009: 76). By embracing this new relational self, the protagonist formulates an alternative history for both himself and his grandfather, one that offers the potential for both characters to 'move onto something new' and to pursue a form of dwelling that is centred on an ethics of care and relation as opposed to one governed by fear and isolation (Burnside 2000: 183). As the second half of this chapter argues, for Burnside, vulnerability not only offers the potential for human relation and masculine renewal but further exposes humanity's obligations towards the wider more-than-human world.

Creaturely Connections in *Something Like Happy*

Burnside's works are attentive to the 'the vulnerability and otherness of the natural world', where the continued mystery of the natural world is acknowledged and respected, giving 'way to a more chastening ethos of personal, bodily finitude and respect' (Clark 2011: 140). In his second short story collection, *Something Like Happy*, the ecological potential of vulnerability is explored through stories that attend to the 'creaturely' relations of human and nonhuman kinship. Understood as the 'wild, the soulful animality of live being', for Burnside, a sense of the creaturely is something that contemporary society is fundamentally lacking (Burnside 2012). Due to forms of history that have been set forth by 'big corporations and their employees in our state governments', Burnside laments the forces of 'conflict and consumption, of production and power that den[y] us elements of our very nature, as human animals' (Burnside 2006: 92). Across *Something Like Happy*, the experience of vulnerability again plays a vital role in fostering an ecological ethics of relation between the self and other, where instances of violence and exposure are employed as a means of renewing 'our kinship with the creaturely world' (Burnside 2012).

The ethics of a creaturely way of life have been most recently explored in the work of Anat Pick, who defines 'the creaturely' as the shared vulnerability of human and non-human animals. Suggesting that 'fragility and finitude' are the key coordinates of vulnerability, for Pick the creaturely is not only fundamentally ecological – fostering relation between and across human and non-human lives – but 'inherently ethical' (2011: 3). As Pick notes, within the Western world, animals are often viewed as nothing more than 'material bodies pitted against human mindfulness and soulfulness' (2011: 4). In order to overcome this damaging mind/body dualism, a new understanding of the human must emerge in relation to conditions of vulnerability, finitude and exposure. For Burnside, recognizing that 'my creaturely self is kin to the creaturely everywhere' allows for an expanded sense of self that is felt in relation 'not with some [external] other, like "Nature", or "the biosphere", but with the inclusive and continuous realm of animate being' (2012). His adoption of the term 'creature' itself provides a 'powerful antidote to anthropocentrism', avoiding the duality of human/non-human (Pick 2011: 6). While the physical body may be exposed to conditions of harm, injury and suffering, as Pick suggests, the vulnerability of the body may also constitute a proscriptive 'corporeal plea against violence' (2011: 14). Across the stories 'Godwit', 'Roccolo' and 'Slut's Hair', Burnside plays with the dynamics of protection and exploitation that stem from the bodily dimensions of creaturely vulnerability; in doing so, his stories cultivate an ethics of responsibility and care that stem from a sense of expanded multispecies kinship.

In 'Godwit', the story of two young boys hunting for a rare black-tailed godwit continues in the same vein as Burnside's earlier fiction. From the opening line, the story instils a sense of unease regarding the fate of its central protagonists: 'Back in the old days, before Fat Stan went to prison, we used to go out on the Sands every afternoon, to watch the seabirds and hunt for godwit' (2014: 101). The story centres around the beguiling mystery of the 'Sands', a liminal space that blurs the boundaries between the human and non-human. While the Sands are presented as a space that threatens the coherency of the human subject, it is also described as a site that only the two boys are capable of navigating: 'Everybody knows that the Sands are dangerous, a couple of people have even died out there, but that day, we were invulnerable, we were hypersensitive to everything and we knew exactly where to place our feet' (2014: 106). Across the story, the bodies of the boys find synergy with the birdlife on the shore, their movement through the precarious landscape as 'light-footed' as birds 'and ever so tender' (106). From the story's opening, Burnside draws a division between Stan and Jamie's relationship to the Sands: where for Jamie, it is a space of wonder and restoration, 'a place to escape to, to get away from the rest of the world', for Stan it is a space to be mastered and brought under control as signified through his obsessive drive to hunt the godwit (105).

The two boys represent two different pathways for masculine relation. As the story unfolds, Jamie's decision to invest in the lives of others is contrasted with Stan's banal decline into drug-fuelled chaos and violence. In failing to capture the rare bird, Stan's desire for domination is transposed from the more-than-human realm to the local pub, where in an act fuelled by 'pride, fear and shame', he stabs a young man, 'callously robbing [him] of his life and his future' (114–15). Describing Stan as 'absent from the world that other people lived in', Burnside highlights the dangers evident in the containment and closure of the self, suggesting that Stan's self-imposed absence engenders his capacity to inflict violence against others (117). The character of Jamie emerges in contrast to this containment of self, where in an attempt to alleviate his sense of 'emptiness' and isolation he walks out into the treacherous Sands:

> It was cold and the fog got thicker the further I went, and I kept thinking something would happen – I didn't know what, but I know I was waiting for something as a I walked out across the Sands towards the place where the godwit lived. A ghostly figure at the tide line, a patch of nothingness where a person could fritter away in a matter of seconds, or maybe the hint of a body moving towards me through the fog like a hunter. (118)

Here, Jamie's precarious position mimics that of the hunted godwit from earlier in the story. His perilous foray into the fog is driven by a sense of hope, self-annihilation and the vague possibility of change that ultimately ends with a conflicted sense of 'relief and disappointment' as he finds himself back on dry land (119). Where Stan embodies a form of masculinity centred on greediness, domination and self-destruction, Jamie's positioning as the hunted instead of the hunter opens the possibility of an alternative form of kinship to arise between human and non-human, where the animal encounter does not serve to solidify an anthropocentric hierarchy but rather opens the possibility for reciprocity and relation.

Bird hunting is also a central factor in the story 'Roccolo'. The story traces the disturbing ritual of the character Eloise, who every year ensnares a young boy on his summer holidays and forces him to witness the sadistic ritual of the Roccolo. Luring a bird into the hide, she 'quickly and without hesitation, but with great care and accuracy, pierc[es] the bright small button of the eyeball with a silver needle' so that the bird's cries might entice others to enter the tower (208). The ritual of the Roccolo is centred around a perverse intimacy, where Eloise's courtship of young boys into the bird-hide presents one of the first narratives in which Burnside explores a feminine capacity for violence. As with his disturbing male characters, Eloise's disregard for non-human life engenders a wider capacity for violence and domination. Much like 'Godwit', the vulnerability of birdlife is transposed into the violence enacted between human beings, where those who abuse or kill animals are revealed to be utterly denatured themselves and thus incapable of true connection or joy. The story's closing image of Eloise's father rescuing the trapped bird, and by association the boy, disrupts the cycle of her cruel ceremony; his careful touch guiding the bird 'straight up into the light' halts the ritual of violence and prohibits any further harm from being inflicted (234).

This impulse towards salvation as directed through the liberation of animals is explored most fully in the story 'Slut's Hair'. Centring on an extreme act of domestic violence in which the protagonist's husband forcibly extracts her rotting tooth in an act of drunken dentistry, the story explores the connections between systems of patriarchal domination that legitimize the domination of vulnerable creatures and the ways in which humanity has become exiled 'from the land, from other animals ... from a lived sense of justice' (Burnside 2015: 113). In the wake of her abuse, Janet begins to hallucinate the existence of another vulnerable body in the house in the form of a

> long-haired, powder-blue mouse with tiny feet and a sharp, clever face ... She was surprised to realise that she wasn't afraid, but the animal was. It was terrified, in fact, and desperate to get out, scared and lost and far from its own kind, its wet, black eyes gazing up at her, so shiny and wet and hopeless that she felt a sudden, desperate need to gather it up and spirit it away before Rob got home to save it, in other words – because Rob would kill it. (Burnside 2014: 43)

The presence of the fantastical blue mouse – real or imagined – inspires a renewed sense of self-confidence and purpose in Janice, where the fragility and vulnerability of the mouse immediately awakens a need to protect and to shelter. Newly 'decisive and confident, and most of all, calm', her strong desire to save this creature that is nothing more than a 'little sack of hair and bones' correlates with a new sense of self-worth, courage and potential for a different life (43). Throughout the story, Burnside plays with the 'cross-species vulnerability of bodies' (Pick 2011: 10) in order to draw out a new ethics of relation between the self and other that further demonstrates how 'we do not, and cannot, "live" apart from the rest of the [nonhuman] world' (Burnside 2015: 121). Through their multispecies alliance, Janice's decision to keep the mouse secret and safe even when it unravels into nothing more than a 'fistful of dust' reveals the dynamics of responsibility evident in ecological modes of relation (Burnside 2014: 46). At the end of the tale, her decision to place her own body between that of the mouse and her husband ensures that this creature who had 'come to her and nobody else' remains treasured, safe and a source of personal strength (46). Her kinship with the fantastical mouse emerges in opposition to the 'feelings of separateness that make [humans] capable of damaging the world in which [they] live' (Burnside 2015: 122). Their multispecies alliance signals a need to rethink the divisions between human and non-human, nature and culture, that engender conditions of exile and separation, and in doing so suggests a potential path forward for a more inclusive and relational mode of dwelling to emerge.

As these stories exhibit, openness towards the other offers the potential for both harmony, and serious harm. Through his insistence on cultivating a creaturely mode of being in the world, Burnside in his work serves to limit the conditions of harm by highlighting the need for a heightened respect for, and responsibility towards, the other:

> Our responsibility is to respect and protect all living things. To honour this vast 'Other', however, we must also respect all habitat: for we cannot honour other living things if we damage or destroy their sources of shelter, nourishment and play. Thus we must honour all things, from the air, to rocks and soil, to trees, to all waterways, to the ocean, to the wind, to pond life, to Arctic mosses, to temperate forest, to silt, to reedbeds, to glaciers. (2015: 121)

Across his short stories, Burnside's ecological vision expands anthropocentric notions of community and kinship to include all creaturely beings. His stories thus provide an understanding of human nature that is not solely defined by 'the mystery of ... cruelty' but also highlights an innate capacity for care and connection that is able to heal the damage of previous systems of thought and relation (Burnside 2011). For Burnside, to exist in this world without recognizing an inherent interconnected and creaturely nature is to live a diminished life. Where his poetic works broadly seek to express the ways in which this creaturely life might be pursued, across these short story collections the traumatized, bruised and bleeding bodies of his characters warn us of the dangers of what living a diminished life means: to be coarsened, cruel and desperate for connection.

Chapter Four: **Violent Dwellings and Vulnerable Creatures in *Burning Elvis* and *Something Like Happy*, Alexandra Campbell**

Borthwick, D. (2009), 'The Sustainable Male: Masculine Ecology in the Poetry of John Burnside', in H. Ellis and J. Meyer (eds), *Masculinity and the Other: Historical Perspectives*, 63–85, Newcastle upon Tyne: Cambridge Scholars Publishing.

Bracke, A. (2014), 'Solitaries, Outcasts and Doubles: The Fictional Oeuvre of John Burnside', *English Studies*, 95 (4): 421–40.

Brewster, S. (2006), 'Beating, Retreating: Violence and Withdrawal in Iain Banks and John Burnside', in J. McGonigal and K. Stirling (eds), *Ethically Speaking: Voice and Values in Modern Scottish Writing*, 179–99, Amsterdam and New York: Rodopi.

Burnside, J. (2000), *Burning Elvis*, London: Vintage.

Burnside, J. (2006), 'A Science of Belonging: Poetry as Ecology', in R. Crawford (ed.), *Contemporary Poetry and Contemporary Science*, 91–107, Oxford: Oxford University Press.

Burnside, J. (2009), 'John Burnside: Poets and Other Animals', in A. Dòsa (ed.), *Beyond Identity: New Horizons in Modern Scottish Poetry*, 113–35, New York: Rodopi.

Burnside, J. (2011), 'John Burnside: Interview', *Granta Magazine,* 16 August. Available online: https://granta.com/interview-john-burnside/ (accessed 5 July 2017).

Burnside, J. (2012), 'The Hyena Is My Favourite – My Totem – Animal', *The Guardian*, 20 January. Available online: https://www.theguardian.com/books/2012/jan/20/author-author-john-burnside (accessed 5 July 2017).

Burnside, J. (2014), *Something Like Happy*, London: Vintage.

Burnside, J. (2015), 'John Burnside', in M. Fazzini (ed.), *Conversations with Scottish Poets*, 111–23, Aberdeen: Aberdeen University Press.

Butler, J. (2016), 'Rethinking Vulnerability and Resistance', in J. Butler, Z. Gambetti, and L. Sabsay (eds), *Vulnerability in Resistance*, 12–28, Durham: Duke University Press.

Clark, T. (2011), *The Cambridge Introduction to Literature and the Environment*, Cambridge: Cambridge University Press.

Gilson, E. (2013), *The Ethics of Vulnerability: A Feminist Analysis of Social Life and Practice*, London: Routledge.

Griem, J. (2015), 'John Burnside's Seascapes', in U. Kluwick and V. Richter (eds), *The Beach in Anglophone* Literatures *and* Cultures: Reading Littoral Space, 87–107, Farnham: Ashgate.

Murphy, A. (2011), 'Corporeal Vulnerability and the New Humanism', *Hypatia*, 26 (3): 575–90.

Pick, A. (2011), *Creaturely Poetics: Animality and Vulnerability in Literature and Film*, New York: Columbia University Press.

5

'This Learned Set of Limits and Blames': Masculinity, Law and Authority in the Work of John Burnside

Ruth Cain

John Burnside, a poet and writer of the magical and gothic as well as the brutally down-to-earth, is less well known as a commentator on matters of politics and law.[1] Yet his work, and his own commentaries upon it, constitute a profound set of observations on the current global moment, its injustices and dangers, and the political, economic and psychosocial structures which have formed and maintain it. Burnside commented in 2011, for instance, that 'on an almost disastrous scale, we see what we expect to see, what we have been told to see – which preserves certain power structures (political, yes, but also "moral" and "intellectual") rather nicely ... I just don't fancy giving in' (McCarthy 2011: 26). He has been a fierce critic of the rigidity and inhumanity of all institutions that embed class and gender distinctions, particularly the traps of a power-fixated masculinity. His anarchic and even revolutionary statements, recently made in the dispiriting context of a marked swing to the right in Western politics and the hollow triumph of a demonstrably bankrupt financial system, mark Burnside out as a writer unafraid to politicize the personal and aesthetic.[2] Indeed, he sees art as 'a model of order, a world view [that] proposes an alternative to the disinformation and lies that permeate the atmosphere we grow up in' (McCarthy 2011: 33).

Burnside's novels and autobiographical works consistently question and problematize the interactions of gender (particularly masculinity), class and labour. He explores these issues from the point of view of a son of the displaced British/Scottish working class, who both lived out and abandoned his mother's desire for him to 'better himself'. In his work, Burnside foregrounds deeper attempts to understand, create or embody laws of life and death: mastery, violence, technical knowledge, the fundamental need to feel 'at home' and to exist in the moment, on this earth. 'The rare, intense, unsettling beauty' of his work is usually counterpointed by a vivid sense of threat and danger (Brewster 2006: 180). His work displays a particular 'ambivalence towards masculine power and the paternal' (Brewster 2006: 180) alongside a piercing set of insights into the vulnerabilities, disappointments and hollows at the heart of disaffected, angry working-class masculinity. This is informed by a highly political awareness that, under the mass of social and individual pressures, including class and gender norms, individuals can become 'agents of limitation' in each other's lives (McCarthy 2011: 26).

In this chapter, I analyse how Burnside's writing works against what he identifies as the 'Authorised Version': a Bible of disappointment and lowered expectations, composed of restrictive class and gender mythologies, social and ecological violences, and convenient (often religious, but also cultural and political) lies. He comments in an interview:

> there is more to empiricism than trusting the five (why so few?) senses that we have been trained from birth to use, by people with very strong vested interests in having us behave well. That some of those people loved us, or at least had our best interests at heart, is neither here nor there. They were agents of limitation, tasked with ensuring that the doors of perception should remain acceptably muddied. (McCarthy 2011: 26)

The apparatus and operation of his 'Authorised Version' is rather more complex than that of direct legal, or even social, oppression, making his oppositional stance somewhat more nuanced than mere anarchic rebellion against the powers that be. Like the market-neoliberal capitalism of which it is both a part and an effect, it is a highly adaptable system for the internalization of conformity and restriction, a personal as well as a political creed; 'this learned set of limits and blames' (Burnside 2014: 41). As cultural theorist Mark Fisher (2009) describes, the *ennui* and hopelessness of the individualized, consumption-obsessed societies in which we must live penetrate deep into subjectivities and relationships. As such, our broadly 'Western' social and political system (whether we name it capitalism or neoliberalism) can come to resemble a religion. The deadening hold of religious doctrine and its long legacies of internalized repression also form part of an Authorised Version, as the old-established punitive authoritarianism of, for instance, Christianity and conservative morality may work alongside capitalist realism. As such, Burnside's Authorised Version is a complex set of internalized prohibitions, a psychic and social constitution, sharing with law its powers to command and restrict.

For Jacques Lacan and his followers, the 'Law of the Father' represents that foundational, internalized Law, which provides the subject with language and meaning. To access language, the Lacanian subject must make a choice to accept the Law of the Father and reject the prelinguistic realm of the Real. The Real is associated with the lack of personal and bodily boundaries of the foetus and infant, and thus with the maternal, animality, the supernatural or surreal and madness (including ecstatic or spiritual states) (Lacan 1985). In psychosocial terms, the Law of the Father represents patriarchy (male control of property, bodies and resources) as well as linguistic structures and constraints. I discuss below how the troubled masculinity of his characters echoes the prohibitions (laws) which create language (see Cain 2011). Thus, as well as representing psychic prohibitions, in its current incarnation, the Authorised Version is the rapacious socio-economic inequality and authoritarianism of (post-)austerity: 'All around us, officials of the Authorised Version take it upon themselves to parcel out the real as a marketable commodity and, out of sheer gall and not much else, would have us believe that the whole world belongs to them. Yet nothing could be further from the truth' (Burnside 2014: 44–5). Burnside valorizes a political and personal refusal of both convention and violence, a meditative aesthetic of surrender to time, to 'disorderly order' (44) and to the natural world, which for him represents an escape from the crushing laws of working-class masculinity in which he grew up. The refusal to accept the Authorised Version demands a difficult, painful act of opening up the self; perhaps particularly hard for men, who may ally themselves more rigidly with the Law of the patriarch (on masculinity and the Lacanian Law of the Father, see Frosh 1994). Burnside has commented that 'the men I've thought were worthwhile were always people who had exercised some kind of surrender – the surrender of the security of their own power to a kind of openness' (McDowell 2003).

Burnside made a timely and rather apocalyptic statement in a 2011 interview, saying that he is

> preparing ... for what is to come, which in my view is the inevitable collapse of a stale civilisation dedicated to the financial enrichment of a few, at the imaginative, moral and spiritual expense of the many. At this stage, *refusal* is significant: to say, yes, you have managed to damage us in countless ways with your fifth-rate socialisation (I won't say education) system and your forced work programmes, but I still refuse to accept that this way of

> living is inevitable – and I have one useful tool, *Imagination*, with which to continue the mental fight. (McCarthy 2011: 26)

Poetry for Burnside is a privileged mode of imaginative refusal of the conformity, consumerism and individualization implicit in the 'capitalist realism' (Fisher 2009) and repression that reproduce a learned set of limits; 'poetry is a heightened way of saying, *Look how thoroughly we are all in this together* ... It's a space carved out away from the Authorised Version' (McCarthy 2011: 27). Yet, just as the Lacanian Real beyond the Law and language of the patriarch threatens chaos and psychosis, aesthetic and ethical escape from the laws of Authorized civilization is shadowed by the eerie glamour and deadly wisdom of the 'cruel beauty' Burnside detects in nature – a beauty which has undeniable connections with the cast of sociopathic and violent (usually male) characters which populate his fiction. He has said:

> I do take solace in the natural world – though I hope that's not an easy solace. I do hope that I come up against the harsh, the bloody, the seemingly cruel in what we think of as nature – including human nature. And I hope I preserve a sense of the mystery of that cruelty. Sometimes it's a very beautiful cruelty – it's not cruel per se, of course, it only seems so to us, because we are attached to our own interests – and, on occasion, a sense of that beauty lifts one above one's attachment. (Allen 2011: np)

Since Burnside refuses to sentimentalize nature, the ethical aspects of his Unauthorised Version (the political refusal, the constructive anarchy) are haunted somewhat by the dark double, both animal and spectral, which stalks his poetry and prose. This double is masculine, despite the recent appearance of a shadowy kind of feminine doubling in the figure of the glamorous/murderous *huldra* in his novel *A Summer of Drowning* (2011). The double in Burnside's writing walks half-unseen alongside the supposedly rational (male?) individual: 'someone else is close beside him, other to his other' (2011: 60). In the concepts of the '*thrawn*', or the 'dark side of the fair', to which he frequently refers in his most recent autobiographical work *I Put a Spell on You* (2014), Burnside explicitly valorizes the wild, sinister and uncivilized, in political as well as aesthetic terms: 'wildness is a path of rigorous unlearning and lifelong recovery from one's "education" ("socialisation")' (McCarthy 2011: 27). The practice of being *thrawn*, meaning 'crooked' or 'perverse' or 'contrary', is for him 'an essential and virtuous wildness' which is explicitly and anarchically *political*:

> to be *thrawn* is already to take a first step towards shrugging off the State in all its manifestations and so to commence working for the spontaneous

expression of individual and local life – not an easy matter, as there is so much socialisation and Authorised Version garbage to *unlearn* ... So much to root out that was seeded in us as defenceless children – all that guilt and obedience and weakness we were taught over our father's knee and in primary school. (2014: 40–1)

Still, in his work, the wild/dark side retains a thoroughly amoral power to extinguish innocence, to subjugate human life to a natural order in which our place is uncertain, to say the least. This is what must be so rigorously learnt from the *thrawn*. In what follows, I examine how the gendered and ethical contradictions at the heart of Burnside's concept of the *thrawn*, reflected in the extra-legal, anti-cultural Unauthorised Version, which he posits as an alternative to political and gender/class conformity, make his work both elusive and compellingly insightful.

Femininity as Alternative/Real: The Lost Girl and the Marzipan Doll

As I have noted, Burnside's work most frequently features male protagonists and is notable for its intense portrayals of male violence, anger and coldness. Burnside's work demonstrates an intriguing set of contradictions with regard to women and femininity: despite the masculine focus of his own oeuvre, he has remarked that he considers 'the experience of women' to be 'more poignant and more interesting' than men's,

> in working class life especially. In the past I was quite concerned with writing about the problems of male working class life: the violence, and the sense of powerlessness. But growing up and watching the women around me, their lives seemed more nuanced. They weren't blinded by an illusion that you could prove yourself by being violent or whatever. (O'Malley 2013: np)

And yet, as Astrid Bracke notes, the women in Burnside's earlier fictions at least (the exception being 2012's *Something Like Happy*) are somewhat two-dimensional, usually viewed in relation to men (Bracke 2014: 424). In *I Put a Spell on You*, Burnside associates the commonplace closure of sensitivity and empathy in young adult males with the figure of a 'lost girl' (a form of anima, perhaps – like the dead workmate, Helen, in *Waking up in Toytown*, 2010), which he locates in the male psyche as symbolic of the loss of something associated with openness and emotion, the traditionally feminine Real. In

A Summer of Drowning, a young female narrator recounts the disturbing story of a local 'lost girl' who comes to embody the Icelandic myth of the *huldra*, a beautiful and deadly female spirit luring men to their deaths. The alluring enchantress is, again, a somewhat traditional feminine image – as, in a different sense, is the 'anima', which the 'lost girl' seems to personify; but if one examines his work as a whole, Burnside rarely subscribes to a traditional, wholesale feminization of nature, wildness and the abject. Nonetheless, the femininity of *Summer*'s narrator appears somewhat incidental, since in many ways, she replicates the solitary, emotionally closed male narrators of, for example, *Living Nowhere* (2004) and *The Locust Room* (2001); and as noted, it is in his depictions of masculinity and male violence that Burnside's writing is often at its most troubling and resonant.[3]

In his depictions of his mother and of other working-class or downtrodden women (in, e.g., *Waking up in Toytown*), Burnside demonstrates rare insight into the traps posed for women by the mythology of romantic love and the crushing institutionality of marriage. In a poem in the collection *Black Cat Bone* (2011: 36), 'Day of the Dead', he writes chillingly of the 'corpse-groom ... pledging his troth, by default/to a marzipan doll/with eyes that no longer/remind him of someone else; ... and happy to be free/of hope and fear,/he listens for the wind ... silence trailing after, like the sleep/he thought would end/in sugarcraft and satin'. He remarks: 'The wedding in *Black Cat Bone* ... is ... the shadow of marriage *as institution*, that grotesque condition in which love becomes a legal contract and husbands and wives are set upon one another as instruments of the overall machinery of conformism and social control' (McCarthy 2011: 35). Burnside's insights into gender and the traps it lays for both women and men are central to his delineation of the *thrawn* as a place of encounter with the Real and with what lies beyond the Laws of language and signification and the crushing rules of human institutions and authorities. If, as the character Rob says in *The Mercy Boys*, 'the whole world is about men being fucked up' (Burnside 2000: 243), Burnside demonstrates how the 'fuckups' of men represent a shadow-side of the *thrawn*, one which cannot simply be derided as 'unnatural'. The confrontation with the Real comes up against the predatory and psychopathic nature of the 'stoat in the soul' (Burnside 1992: 4).

Sociopathic Masculinity and the Real

As noted, Burnside's work regularly features acts of extreme cruelty and narrators who speak coldly of brutal acts: for example, the chilling poem 'Wrong' (from *Swimming in the Flood*, 1995), where an adolescent killer murders 'a luckless child' (Borthwick 2009: 9). The narrator of Burnside's horrific novel *The Dumb House*, another murderer of luckless innocents, tries to understand the twin babies in his 'care' as 'wet machinery' (1997b: 82). His shift to interrogating the truth of human language by denying the twins access to words from their birth onwards is equally cruel and doomed. In a final irony, it has the side-effect of forcing the twins into communication through eerily beautiful songs which remain incomprehensible to him. This icy, abusive man's pose of 'scientific' detachment covers a deeply emotional fascination with the abject, a desperate desire to triumph over the Real of both language and the body – that Real which, in the form of the twins' wordless song and the bloody failure of his 'experiment,' eventually engulfs the narrator in insanity and chaos. Yet he still maintains a classically patriarchal/capitalist concept of free choice, which the narrative clearly shows to be illusory. When a mute teenager, Lillian, future mother of the twins, comes to his bed – although he is well aware of her absolute vulnerability, and that her already-abused body is all she has to offer him – he still sees her 'choice' to approach him as rendering her his to possess and control, sexually and in every other sense (1997b: 107). Later, he allows her to die shortly after childbirth, interpreting this also as her 'choice'.

Given Burnside's engagement with political issues and crises, there is a clear political aspect to his depictions of male sociopaths. Market-liberal economies, with their increasingly authoritarian and inequitable social hierarchies, are frequently described as 'sociopathic' (Bakan 2012). The narrator of *The Dumb House*, like other sociopathic anti-heroes of contemporary fiction (e.g. Crake in Margaret Atwood's *Oryx and Crake*, 2003, and Frank in Iain Banks's *The Wasp Factory*, 1984), presents the monstrous shadow-side of conventional masculinity and 'success'. He is the creator of his own emotionless and oddly bureaucratic world, caught in fantasies of a final conquest of language and the flesh. What is striking are the ways in which this sociopath (and others in Burnside's fiction, such as the rapist in *The Locust Room*) still embodies aspects of *wildness*, amounting to a shadow of Burnside's own Unauthorised Version of art, masculinity and language. For instance, Burnside says this of his own work:

> any work of art ... is a model of order ... it's the map that has all the lines of ownership and privileged pillage that is a fiction – and a bad one at that. And the way I would define 'lie' is exactly that: a bad fiction. (McCarthy 2011: 33)

The narrator of *The Dumb House* seeks to create order through knowledge. He confuses 'ownership and privileged pillage' – the privilege/pillage of sexual and physical control over women and children, for instance – with the attainment of truth. Read in the light of Burnside's memoir *A Lie about My*

Father (2006), written several years before the 2011 interview in *Agenda*, which I quote above, his work demonstrates a certain complicity with men like this narrator who have become sealed off from emotion and empathy. Such men are inevitably associated with his abusive and dishonest father: Burnside convicts himself of telling lies, in his memoir of his father: the son is '*just as much a lie* as [his father] ever was' (2006: 232, italics in original). The abuser, liar and psychopath are the double or dark Other of his work. His own attempt to create art from his paternal relationship is by his own admission tainted with failure: 'bad fiction'. He writes, 'these are my words, and *this* is the real lie about my father. I cannot talk about him without talking about myself, just as I can never look at myself in the mirror without seeing his face' (2006: 231). The autobiographical elements of *The Locust Room* and *The Mercy Boys* connect Burnside with '"Gothic" elements of his own paternal inheritance of violence, darkness, guilt and an inchoate internal wildness that finds its authenticity in the giving and receiving of pain, or in unsettling memories of road-kills and carrion, enacted in the verse' (McGonigal 2006: 241). Burnside's poetic narrator longs to escape from the trap of 'containing, like a cyst, my father's soul, his cryptic love, his taste for carrion' (Burnside 1997a: 9).

Burnside's male psychopaths are also articulate, and occasionally even sympathetic, monsters. *The Dumb House*'s narrator tells us that 'the trick and the beauty of language is that it seems to order the whole universe, misleading us into believing that we live in sight of a rational space, a possible harmony' (1997b: 8). The reader may empathize with the aesthetic quest to find the truth and source of this 'harmony' – until he or she has to witness the brutal and bloody methods used to locate it. Any sympathy for Burnside's monsters is thus hedged about with horror at their brutality, entitlement and lack of empathy or remorse.

The figure of a disruptive double or doppelgänger, the one who walks too close behind us, is a trope of masculine crisis and subjectivity in contemporary literature (Cain 2011). In Burnside's work, the double is simultaneously a magical companion in the world of natural enchantment, which his poetry in particular illuminates, and a disturbing reminder that whatever laws hold true in nature (the 'disorderly order' of the *thrawn*) are not those of human morality. It is thus that the sociopathic male may represent a grim truth about nature, the predatory/destructive nature of (masculine?) humanity. In *A Lie about My Father*, Burnside's father/double becomes (partially) accessible when his son comes to a (partial) comprehension of his rage, frustration and ultimate loneliness. Understanding of the lying, false father is only possible when the full *social* context of the man – his bleak childhood as an abandoned 'foundling', his history of failed confrontations with 'the authorised textbook lies of citizenship and masculinity and employment we are all obliged to tell' (Burnside 2006: 309) – is read back into the story of the abusive alcoholic liar, who can be forgiven at last for inventing what felt to him like a better self and for failing to live up to the demanding construct of the authoritative, inspirational Father (Cain 2011: 22).

The double/Other traditionally faces us with what we would rather repress and deny in ourselves and in Burnside's work reminds us that even we are, occasionally at least, part of the 'cruel beauty' of nature. The motif of the double reappears in *The Locust Room*, where Burnside emphasizes the strange kinship of the solitary, nocturnal Cambridge rapist of the 1970s with the solitary, nocturnal main character, Paul. When the novel speaks from the rapist's viewpoint, he says that he 'should have been an animal – a polecat or a wolverine' (Burnside 2001: 148). The rapist knows all too well the terror of the Other within and beside the self:

> that invisible assembly of movement and steps and even breathing that matched him in every way, but was not himself – like that invisible presence the Arctic explorers described when they came home from being lost, walking for hours or days in the snow and the dark with a single, unseen companion. (2001: 148)

In *A Lie about My Father*, the paternal familiar is similarly experienced as a dark pursuer split off from the self: the father returns unwanted at Burnside's Halloween bonfires, but by the end of the text, Burnside reaches a fragile accommodation with him. The 'secret other' whose weightless grace Sconnie discerns in *the Mercy Boys* (Burnside 2000: 52) has its shadowy counterpart in an amorally transcendent world, remote from human attachments and concerns. The realm of the other, another aspect of the inhuman Real, disturbs because its rhythms are alien to us; the dead, and the animal, are part of it, and the 'stoat in the soul' knows this.

The 'pink-eyed wonder' of the 'stoat in the soul' (Burnside 1992: 4) is, Burnside teaches us, that aspect of humanity that is truly an *inseparable otherness* close to the Freudian concept of the uncanny. For Freud, 'the uncanny is that class of the frightening which leads back to what is known of old and long familiar' (1919, quoted in Dolar 1991: 6). Lacan translated Freudian uncanniness as extimacy, a concept combining the closeness of intimacy with a shocking, alien exteriority, as the double terrifies us when we see its exact resemblance to ourselves (Lacan 2006: 224, 249). Burnside unfailingly confronts his readers with the sinister and predatorial in ourselves and those we live among. For him, brutality and evil exercise a mesmeric power, as the narrator of *The Dumb House* assuredly does. McGonigal notes this 'gnostic tension of darkness and light' in Burnside's work (2006: 242; see also, Peter Childs's chapter in this volume). We might relate the shadowy/fraternal/paternal double (in which Brewster [2006] sees echoes of the ethically perfect and eternally demanding Other of the philosopher Emanuel Levinas) as a representative of this creative and empathic duality. In the title poem of *The Myth of the Twin* (1994), the 'someone' who shares a night of silence with the poet is finally defined as 'the common soul' (53). But this common soul is clearly troubled, doomed perhaps to spend a great deal of time in the dim purgatorial realms, from which Burnside crafts his inchoate magic.

Gender, Class and the Violences of the Authorised Version

The challenges posed by Burnside's 'gnostic' sensibility include a piercing demolition of the traps laid for both women and men by the constrictions of gender, as observed in his working-class childhood in industrial communities in Scotland and Northamptonshire (of which more later). Nonetheless, as noted, women often appear as points of alterity, and as embodiments of the failure or limit-point of language and meaning, in Burnside's work. This immediately recalls Jacques Lacan's claim that women are excluded from language, 'other' to human and symbolic law (and thus akin to the Real). Feminist psychoanalytic theory has extensively explored the positioning of women as 'other' to the (rational, normative) male and thus allied with the natural, animalistic and supernatural (Mitchell 1975). Lacan, in characteristically provocative and elusive style, asserted that woman *does not exist* – in that a female subject cannot attain singularity (or subjectivity) through language: '*the* woman can only be written with "*The*" crossed through. There is no such thing as *The* woman, where the definite article stands for the universal' (Seminar XX Lacan 1985: 144). Jacqueline Rose's 'Introduction II' to this seminar clarifies the significance of the 'woman who does not exist' for 'real' women: 'as negative to the man, woman becomes a total object of fantasy (or an object of total fantasy) elevated into the place of the Other and made to stand for its truth ... this is the ultimate form of mystification' (1985: 50).

Note, for instance, the distant, impenetrable mother Angelika and the elusive *huldra* in *A Summer of Drowning*, and in *The Dumb House*, the invented language of the 'foreign' woman glimpsed in the narrator's childhood, the mute or semi-conscious Lillian and Karen, and Luke's mother's last sounds: 'a kind of sob, though it was more than that, more deliberate, almost articulate, like a word in some foreign language that I didn't understand, rooted in some dark, wet place, the beginning of decay perhaps, the beginning of annihilation' (Burnside 1997b: 75). This dark place is the realm of the abject and Real, the place where language runs out, where signs and boundaries fail. As Scott Brewster observes, 'the abusive, aphasic relationships with Karen Olerud and the rescued vagrant Lillian, reproduce this silenced maternal voice ... the nameless twins sing their indecipherable songs, transcending the gap between human and animal ... plugged into a current of instinct and blood-knowledge' (Brewster 2006: 185). In Burnside's fiction, what women might say of life and relationships is often mysterious and elusive, sketchy, like the portrait of the narrator by her distant, goddess-like mother in *A Summer of Drowning*: reflecting, perhaps, the pointless but powerful romantic idealisms in which Burnside describes his mother and other working-class women indulging, mortgaging their lives to the empty promises of popular love songs and romance novels. The mother in *A Summer of Drowning* has a queenly mystique, which clearly escapes the downtrodden women of Burnside's own life-story, women who expect nothing from the world but betrayal. This mother has escaped the laws of the Authorised Version, but her portrayal remains idealized and ambivalent, somewhat inhuman. Her 'aphasia' is that of hauteur and withdrawal, rather than trauma and abuse. For the women of Burnside's autobiographical childhood, the 'Authorised Version' of marriage and childrearing tarnishes the dreams of girlhood and leaves women like his mother with only snatches of song to express past longings. The 'lost girl' trope Burnside uses to represent an elusive or lost masculine romanticism in *I Put a Spell on You* suggests that girlhood in itself represents access to a raw emotional experience and vulnerability, which women are less likely to leave behind; while by contrast, his own memoirs suggest that this vulnerability in the actual lives of women tends to translate all too soon into escapist fantasies of 'happy ever after', which encourage feminine conformity and domestic entrapment.[4]

In a recent interview, Burnside was asked about the theme of 'new beginnings' in his work. He remarked:

> that is a theme that I have looked at many times, by asking: how we are born into a world that is already defined for us by our parents, teachers and authority figures. We are expected to appreciate that world, or approve or disapprove of it, in very subtle ways that are imposed upon us. So for example in the poem 'History' from the collection, *The Light Trap* [2002], I'm asking: can we unlearn that, and come to the world afresh? Can we unlearn all those values that are imposed upon us, to try and figure out if the things that we are taught are actually reasonable and logical? Or are they just based on the ideas of the privileged in society? (O'Malley 2013: np)

The 'new beginning' thus combines the favoured elements of refusal and retreat, demanding ethical engagement with the wild realm of 'unlearning' and desocialization described above. The surrender of gracious men, the 'solitude of the craftsman', has 'traded the social, traded the human, for something else' (Burnside 2001: 231). Brewster calls this 'responsible disengagement' (2006: 193). Note, for instance, Derek's 'appropriate refusal' of violent revenge in *The Locust Room*. Derek longs for 'another system ... based on the ordinary, possible decency of which people were capable' (314). Burnside's outline of an ethical method of refusal of violence and brutality cannot entirely be reconciled with the predatory malevolence of some of his characters and poetic voices. The anger and violence of the phantom father who approaches the Halloween bonfire is not, despite the son's best efforts at rapprochement and re-embodiment, ever entirely neutralized into the 'good fraternal/paternal phantom' (Brewster 2006: 196). The 'dead and damaged' may 'become familiar: moleskin/figures amongst the lupins/nodding and waving': but as McGonigal remarks, they 'combine love and menace in intimate fashion', 'with their blue smiles and mottled bodies/shuffling, pressing closer, making room' (McGonigal 2006: 237, quoting Burnside 1988: 15). Thus, the ethical realm of the Unauthorised is a haunted one, and its ghosts are not necessarily friendly.

To escape from the prisons of the Authorised Version is thus to live in a series of acutely observed, yet fragile, moments: 'a life full of landmarks, a life of endless detail. It was something to believe in, this life of observed moments – an escape, somehow, from time' (Burnside 2000: 22). It is through such 'observed moments' that Burnside retrieves a tolerable image of his own father, recalling a view of him tending his garden alone (Burnside 2006: 323). He had already used a similar image in *The Locust Room*'s closing passage, with Francis in his father's garden. Francis merges into the paternal body as it experiences a rare moment of simple satisfaction (372–3). So, perhaps, Burnside imagines his father temporarily at peace as part of a process of rehabilitation and eventual forgiveness (Cain 2011). However, we should note that in *The Mercy Boys*, Alan, the dreamer of this world of perfected moments, finally enters a permanently perfect 'weightless' instant by drowning himself (Burnside 2000: 265). Burnside recalls (using a poetic first person, which may or may not directly recall his own experience) the deadly allure of near-drowning:

> what I remember best is the water's answer,
> the shadow it left in my blood when it let me go
> and the tug in my bones that remained, like a scar, or an echo
> concealing the death I had lost. ('Learning to Swim' 2009: 1)

Burnside's work is far too complex, its insights far too *thrawn*, to offer safe or generalized solutions for the incommensurable problems of contemporary subjectivity, gendered and political violence, which they address. These problems emerge as endemic to language and to the imposed limitations of patriarchal political and economic order which leave us with the raw horror and fascination of the Real. Burnside thus teaches 'responsible disengagement' from the internal and external horrors his work forces us to face: '... a special skill some men possessed; nothing more than an intuitive understanding, an acceptance of gravity that allowed them to pass through the world with a certain grace' (Burnside 2000: 52). Thus, refusal of authority, limitation and blame can become a 'joyful project', since 'if reality belongs to anyone, it belongs to those who refuse to possess it' (Burnside 2014: 44–5).

Chapter Five: 'This Learned Set of Limits and Blames': Masculinity, Law and Authority in the Work of John Burnside, Ruth Cain

Allen, R. (2011), 'John Burnside: Interview', *Granta*, 64, 16 August. Available online: http://www.granta.com/New-Writing/Interview-John-Burnside (accessed 11 November 2014).
Atwood, M. (2003), *Oryx and Crake*, New York: Anchor.
Bakan, J. (2012), *The Corporation: The Pathological Pursuit of Profit and Power*, London: Hachette UK.
Banks, I. (1984), *The Wasp Factory*, Basingstoke: Macmillan.
Bracke, A. (2014), 'Solitaries, Outcasts and Doubles: The Fictional Oeuvre of John Burnside', *English Studies*, 95 (4): 421–40.
Brewster, S. (2006), 'Beating, Retreating: Violence and Withdrawal in Iain Banks and John Burnside', in J. McGonigal and K. Stirling (eds), *Ethically Speaking: Voice and Values in Modern Scottish Writing*, 179–98, Amsterdam and New York: Rodopi.
Borthwick, D. (2009), 'The Sustainable Male: Masculine Ecology in the Poetry of John Burnside', in H. Ellis and J. Meyer (eds), *Masculinity and the Other: Historical Perspectives*, 63–85, Newcastle upon Tyne: Cambridge Scholars Publishing.
Burnside, J. (1988), *The Hoop*, Manchester: Carcanet.
Burnside, J. (1992), *Feast Days*, London: Secker and Warburg.
Burnside, J. (1997a), *A Normal Skin*, London: Jonathan Cape.
Burnside, J. (1997b), *The Dumb House*, London: Jonathan Cape.
Burnside, J. (2000 [1999]), *The Mercy Boys*, London: Jonathan Cape.
Burnside, J. (2001), *The Locust Room*, London: Jonathan Cape.
Burnside, J. (2002), *The Light Trap*, London: Jonathan Cape.
Burnside, J. (2006), *A Lie about My Father*, London: Jonathan Cape.
Burnside, J. (2009), *The Hunt in the Forest*, London: Jonathan Cape.
Burnside, J. (2010), *Waking up in Toytown*, London: Jonathan Cape.
Burnside, J. (2011), *Black Cat Bone*, London: Jonathan Cape.
Burnside, J. (2013 [2011]), *A Summer of Drowning*, London: Jonathan Cape.
Burnside, J. (2014), *I Put a Spell on You*, London: Jonathan Cape.

Cain, R. (2011), '"Imperfectly Incarnate": Father Absence, Law and Lies in Brett Easton Ellis and John Burnside', *Journal of Law, Culture, and Humanities*, 8 (2): 1–25.
Crown, S. (2011), 'John Burnside: A Life in Writing', *The Guardian*, 26 August. Available online: http://www.theguardian.com/culture/2011/aug/26/john-burnside-life-in-writing (accessed 19 November 2014).
Dolar, M. (1991), '"I Shall Be with You on Your Wedding-Night": Lacan and the Uncanny', *October*, 58: 5–23.
Fisher, M. (2009), *Capitalist Realism: Is There No Alternative?*, London: Zero.
Freud, S. (1955), *The Standard Edition of the Complete Psychological Works*, ed. James Strachey, vol. XVII, London: Hogarth Press.
Frosh, S. (1994), *Sexual Difference: Masculinity and Psychoanalysis*, London: Taylor & Francis.
Lacan, J. (1985), *Feminine Sexuality: Jacques Lacan and the École Freudienne*, eds. Juliet Mitchell and Jacqueline Rose, trans. Jacqueline Rose, London: W. W. Norton.
Lacan, J. (2006 [1968–1969]), *Le Séminaire XVI: D'un Autre à l'Autre*, Paris: Éditions du Seuil.
McCarthy, P. (2011), 'Interview: John Burnside', *Agenda*, 45 (4)–46 (1): 22–38.
McDowell, L. (2003), 'Poet Sees the Plight', 'Seven Days' Supplement, *Sunday Herald*, 19 January: 10.
McGonigal, J. (2006), 'Translating God: Negative Theology and Two Scottish Poets', in J. McGonigal and K. Stirling (eds), *Ethically Speaking: Voice and Values in Modern Scottish Writing*, 223–46, Amsterdam and New York: Rodopi.
Mitchell, J. (1975), *Psychoanalysis and Feminism*, London: Penguin.
O'Malley, J. P. (2013), 'Interview with a Writer: John Burnside', *The Spectator*, 18 January. Available online: http://blogs.spectator.co.uk/books/2013/01/interview-with-a-writer-john-burnside/ (accessed 11 November 2014).
Rose, J. (1985), 'Introduction – II', in *Feminine Sexuality: Jacques Lacan and the École Freudienne*, eds. Juliet Mitchell and Jacqueline Rose, trans. Jacqueline Rose, 27–58, London: W. W. Norton.
Steedman, C. (2002), *Landscape for a Good Woman: A Story of Two Lives*, London: Virago.

6

Consequences of Pastoral: The Dialectic of History and Ecology in *The Light Trap*

Tom Bristow

Consequences of Pastoral

In the history of British ecological poetry, *The Light Trap* (2002) is as significant as Ted Hughes's *Hawk in the Rain* (1957) for bringing a new audience to a theme: ecology. While publication did not allow for inclusion in Jonathan Bate's *Song of the Earth* (2000) – which set the terms and tone of ecocriticism for a generation – in terms of literary merit, the collection reads well against Seamus Heaney's *Electric Light* (2001) and *District and Circle* (2006). Burnside's particular engagement with ecology from this moment onwards suggests that *The Light Trap* can be regarded as important to his oeuvre as *Life Studies* (1959) is to Lowell's pursuit of autobiography. *The Asylum Dance* (2000) put Burnside on the map; *The Light Trap* placed him on a par with Michael Longley, Don McKay and Mary Oliver.

For Empson, literary uses of language may undertake forms of cultural work; literary styles and devices imply or afford 'social ideas' (1935: 23). For Alpers, pastoral is about the role of literary works in cultivating forms of community, communication and 'ethical stability in one's present world' (1982: 6). From the first collection, *The Hoop* (1988), to *The Asylum Dance*, Burnside's pastoral enquires into the conditions of possibility for stability when person, planet and place – and thus society – are subject to change and destruction. *The Light Trap* takes on a new disposition in Burnside's oeuvre. An interpretation of desirable dwelling anxiously marked by concerns for home, heritage and the impossibility of a *locus amoenus* is bathed in golden hues, refracted light, transcendence and joy in this volume. To what effect might this new comportment to world portend scenarios and subjects that do not, or simply cannot, exist anymore?

Pastoral operates in conditions of social and economic life – and alongside emotional practices – to which this literary tradition remains meaningful today. In my view, pastoral's dialogic nature and reflexive consciousness ultimately faces up to its own constructed nature; the awareness of conceits, inherited forms and themes enriches the texture of combined practices that the enjoyment of pastoral rests upon. These practices might be understood in light of the shepherding of affects that pastoral embodies. Are there specific environmental affects that pastoral can claim literacy for over other genres? This question seems neither to interest critics of pastoral through Western literary history nor today's ecocritics; the latter scholars seek out only the elision between the idea of pastoral as an artificial construct in a text and thematic allusions to pastoral ideology as a form of environmentalism. For Iain Twiddy, reading Burnside within the pastoral tradition, the very bridge between these impotent states of dwelling (the artificial and the allusive) rests upon the foundations of 'intimacy' and upon an uncanny 'sense of belonging' (2013: 149). In Burnside's hands, the bridge is conjured up through the spectre of vulnerability haunting celebration and wonder of nature's manifest delights. In *The Light Trap*, the speaking subject is often stirring a dispassionate and disturbed consciousness; however, unlike the earlier poetry, this period begins with a move away from anger and frustration that modulates the solipsism of Burnside's very early work and commences a path towards spiritual uplift. It is curious to me, and I think ecologically sound, that this uplift comes from dispossession thought most keenly, which is the gift of Burnside's spirited materialism.

The pastoral tradition is defined by its simplification of the complex; it is the codified examination of opposing ideas, or outlooks (e.g. country, city). Organized and arranged systematically in three sections, *The Light Trap* deconstructs the opposition between ecology and history by reducing the relation to three constituent parts that are meaningful to both terms, reinterpreting the relations between the two by casting fresh outlooks on the interplay rather than opposition (as witnessed in the use of light and dark). This emphasis on interplay and contradiction adds to an ongoing theme of the unhelpful dichotomy of dwelling and departure for a species that will always be lost or not quite at home in this world. The divisions of the text are 'Habitat,' 'Phusis' (after Heidegger) and 'World', which give rise not to an exchange of logical argument but to ways of accounting for our inhabitation of space: the affective, cultural, psychological and material attributes of our sense of place.

This ecology of mind and matter, world and cognition inheres to the point of non-distinction and communality in *The Light Trap*; it learns from flux, contradiction, reconciliations and the Rilkean dialectical, where 'all things are shown in terms of one another' (Cohn in Rilke 1989: 16). Resident in Burnside's literary ecology, this emotional disposition and practical comportment to the question of otherness does not create an ecological subject; it is the site of feeling that inheres in a *voice*, which describes persons and the scenes in which they are a part as if both are constituted through the lexicon of nature.

Form

The Light Trap is the second collection within Burnside's dwelling trilogy, framed by *The Asylum Dance* and *The Good Neighbour* (2005). It is the poet's most intricately conceptual collection to date, decisively enforcing themes of division and unity through twenty-seven poems divided into three sections of nine. With regular appearances of a blackbird taken from Wallace Stevens's poem 'Thirteen Ways of Looking at a Blackbird' (1954), Burnside's collection can be read as a transatlantic extension to the Pragmatist representation of 'uncontainability and irreducible plurality' symbolized by the conjoined bird and number (Eeckhart 2002: 138). The blackbird motif binds together three sections to the collection, which are further divided into loose groups of triplets. The bird, oscillating between figure and ground in these poems, and across sections, enables each poem to embody both singularity and triangulation.[1] This theme terminates with the secular man, woman and blackbird that appear in the closing poem 'A Theory of Everything', a third term for the two poems titled 'History' that end the first two sections. It is clearly worked out. The divisions entitled 'Habitat', 'Phusis' and 'World' relate to Burnside's ecological appropriation of Heideggerian thought. Furthermore, each cluster of three poems contains a single lyric that stresses one of the following themes: (i) the condition of the human, which Burnside writes out as homesickness; (ii) the relationship of mind and world, which is offered within the tones and registers of a lament; and (iii) the need for attunement – to be aware or responsive – a misanthropic theme and third term that Burnside understands through the philosophical concept, decreation: a form of destruction of the privatized subject where the 'I' dissolves into its surrounding environment, collapsing subject-object dichotomies (the inflection is sometimes ecological, sometimes spiritual, oftentimes both).

These emphases watermark sections one to three of *The Light Trap*, respectively, and I take these for my reading of the dialectic between history and ecology throughout this collection.

Melancholia

As we shall see, *The Light Trap*'s intertextual hinterland comprised of ideas from many disciplines frames themes of loss and animality in curious and enlightening ways. The third section explicitly draws from Walter Benjamin's thesis on language, which is the dialectical result of the conversation between the first and second sections of the volume. The compound of Paul Shepard's human ecology and the figuration of loss in 'History' (1) frame the first section; a phenomenological investigation of the natural world parsed by the senses and an ethics of inclusion and care, as forwarded by 'History' (2), frame the second section. To fully enjoy the dialogue that extends across these domains, we might afford ourselves the luxury of travelling through Burnside's Germanic hinterland, well indicated before this collection yet reaching an apotheosis in the dwelling trilogy (Benjamin, Heidegger, Rilke).

Shepard's Lacanian semiotics argues that language structures the unconscious. His work on animals, the human and nature (1978, 1982, 1996) argues that culture traps humans in early adolescence, which reduces intimacy with the wild and offers normalized life devoid of the natural psychogenetic development that humans need. The Orwellian undertone of a shrinking vocabulary implies that we are growing in our alienation from roots in nature – that ultimate vicissitude which made imagination and intelligence possible for the human – as biodiversity (i.e. elements of our language, our biological creative vocabulary) is reduced (Shepard 1978). Read that again. In these works, it is stressed that we lack a vision where interdependence between language and culture is inclusive of animals and terrain. Shepard's notion of 'minding' clarifies this relationship: 'What is meant here is something more mutually and functionally interdependent between mind and terrain, an organic relationship between the environment and the unconscious, the visible space and the conscious, the ideas and the creatures' (1978: 35). And that outlook is the very emblem for this collection that runs from the Hopi symbol on the front cover to the postmodern ecological appropriation of Stevensian poetics in the final line.

Spirited and idealized negation to the fall into ecological impoverishment can be located in the epigraph to the first section of *The Light Trap* (Shepard, above) and in the central line, 'homesick for the other animals', that is a Romantic spilling of energy running across the division marked between the first section ('History' (1) and 'The Light Trap'). The line is the volume's conceptual core (Burnside 2002a: 10) pregnant both with desire for an impossible equality with a dominated other and with a counterpoint to such desire: the clearing away of hope and its cognate affects to lament the loss of the other. In Burnside's early work this world took us to paganism, husbandry and violence; in this, his second period, we find the tension between domination and lament taking us towards Octavio Paz, Walter Benjamin and contemporary American poets who ordinarily would not be read in this complex intertextual light.

Hanssen reads Benjamin's efforts to differentiate his writing from Heidegger's as one crystallized in the concept of the *kreatur*, the de-limitation of the human subject within a thesis of natural history that incorporates transience and decay. Such emphases denote a non-human history coloured by a critique of the philosophy of the subject (Hanssen 1998: 2); and – with great appeal to Burnside – it offers insight into the possibility of the named entering the nameless. Benjamin's attentiveness to the social world of language injects contingency and alterity into the idea of nature (and transcendental philosophy), thus standing as one of many significant modifications to the Linnaean model of an infinite chain of being that rose during eighteenth-century historiography before the advent of evolutionary theory. Furthermore, Benjamin's humanistic subject is considered in terms of the present being salvaged by the incomplete potential of the past.[2] It is defamiliarizing to read of this in Anthropocene times obsessed with the impossibility of salvation for the complete annihilation of the future. However, the elegiac mode of *The Light Trap*, captured in the phrase 'homesick for the other animals', embodies a line of post-Romantic thought supercharged for our times of ecological collapse and yet critically distant from the cynicism of latent, discordant environmentalism amplified by Anthropocene media.

Animals

For Rilke, animals present back to humans the notion of submerged humanism in the recesses of the heart, which is to be realized via loss of self. Heidegger argues that the human needs the animal's face (*Antlits*) to see the open. In 'What Are Poets For?' (1946), the need for the non-rational is motioned less than the idea of being brought into relation with God via human distinction to creatures. It is thus that 'nature' in Heidegger's Rilke is not divisional, as it 'is not contrasted to history'; it is life, not biological, but *physis*: 'Being in the sense of all beings as a whole' (Heidegger 1971b: 101). From here we have confidence to fathom that minding the animals reflects back upon the human world; Burnside has evoked a German-Jewish tradition of the creaturely to emphasize possibilities of relation resonating not with deep time but with ecological and conservationist thinking. In the fourth of the Duino elegies contemplating playfulness and harmony, Rilke asserts that 'our blood does not forewarn us/like migratory birds' (2–3). The fact that the animals are world-poor suggests that man, as world forming – is not absorbed into the environment but can view it as a site of possibility. This seems unfashionable, but the intention is to underscore the project or mode of being that understands how we are thrown into the world and how we can act in space and time; it is an emphasis on poetic and political comportment rather than the perspective or experience of one person. The distinction between *weltbildend* and *weltos* to Heidegger is that an enormous sadness burdens the latter animal realm (1995: 273). In Rilke's fourth elegy, man is a latecomer to himself; in the eighth elegy, the human is backward looking, his eyes like 'traps' surrounding the world as it 'emerge[s into] freedom' (Rilke 1989: 4). The metaphor of fleeing from the womb is the pain or 'enormous sadness' (42), which, due to memory of the first and now distant home, provides the condition that 'we live here, forever taking leave' (73). This is an unmistakably Burnsidean sentiment (theme) and psychological schema (affect) that can be discerned in early poetry up to its crystallization in terms of dwelling and departure in *The Asylum Dance*. Respite from melancholia comes where there is no 'World', 'that pure/unseparated elements which one breathes/without desire and endlessly *knows*' (16–19). Such breathing is a mode of inspiration, not projecting out but placing self as empty to receive/dissolve into world; casting this subject as a more-than-human person suggests the need to enter into nothingness in Burnside's spiritual lexis. Thus we understand the interest in Benjamin and Simone Weil, who, once placed in Burnside's literary ecology, seem to chime with Romantic dispositions of freedom, which can be felt as 'unuberwachte' (18): free without burden of supervision and healed in 'timeless/stillness' (17–18). This Rilkean mode relinquishes an appropriative vision of a known future that is there for us; conversely, the poetic stance is configured such as to enable an entering into only the 'boundless,/unfathomable' (36–7). We witness value in loss once more. But loss in this collection is held within the mysterious site of creation, pregnant with possibility.

Mourning

'On Kvaloya' is home to the blackbird – Burnside's bird of mourning, and 'portent of death and loss' (Burnside 2006b: 18) – coupled to Adamic and Orphic naming as degrees of ecological attunement and praxis. The poem makes an explicit move from linguistic entrapment to ancient Indian Dharmic religion (to the oldest literate community in India renowned for their fylfot, the holiest symbol or peaceful swastika of 'well-being' now eclipsed by twentieth-century usage). The section titles read, 'Learning to Talk', 'Metamorphosis', 'Tern' and 'Jain'; they are attempts to transform the human into bird and make evitable self-control, spiritual independence and equality. This is the human moved into the nameless as in the final movement's presentation of the body and mind 'attuned,/to gravity' (4: 31–2), offering Burnside's version of immersion into animal life as discerned in Thomson's reading of Mary Oliver's exemplification of contemporary pastoral elegy. This dilution of the ego, the decreation of self, was formerly figured as the realization of the nature of the soul in Burnside's earlier poetry. It should be viewed microscopically, too, as suggested by *The Light Trap*'s abstracted hyperlocalism.

The poem's first section begins with nine sestets toying with 'the rim of sound' (1: 6), 'inattention' (18) and the 'still[ness]' (19) of home. The first phrase relates to Heidegger's notion of nearness given by the property of language 'to sound and ring and vibrate, to hover and tremble' (Heidegger 1971a: 98), the poetic saying of world as projection of energies. The others suggest passivity (or the relinquished 'I') in the attunement to world and the repetition of the provision of endurance in nature viewed as a momentary balance before fulfilment, respectively. I explicate these in respect to the collection as a whole while simultaneously wishing to indicate how form and subject interrelate.

The second section is a sonnet fragmented into two quatrains and sestet but is looser than its predecessor and crafted rhymelessly, suggesting an increase in 'a foreign tongue' (7) and the 'unsure' (12), yet also plugged into the 'certainties' (11) of the meadows. The last sections, 'Tern' and 'Jain', are pinned into triplets and quatrains, respectively, propagating expansive space that would complement the loosening of the first half of the poem. 'Tern' is composed of five triplets but only three semantic units. The first short objective reportage of clipped lines moves into a subjective keyhole, sustaining the remainder of the poem. There is more than trilogic form promoting the 'I' here.

> I've heard it said:
> we are
> what we imagine;
> but just now,
> turning for home,
> I caught the storm
> shaping a bird
> from the swerve
> of the not-yet-seen.
> (3: 7–15)

The final movement represents the illumination of the other world, or epiphanical attunement held in the connection to nature. This glimpse portends Burnside's later prose versions of epiphany as *turning* with the sway of the world, that is the encounter of a flock of the incredibly seasonally camouflaged ptarmigan (2006a: 113), and the heightening of the otherworld, symbolized by isolation and silence, threaded by the call of the red-winged blackbird (2005: 60, 70). This is not traditional fluidity of post-structuralist identity politics. Intertextually, we circle back to Emerson via Stevens, while the poem's concern for animals is haunted by Rilkean homesickness.

> I stopped dead: in a clump of buttercups
> a creature stirred; then far out in the grass
> another wave, until I realised
> that everything was moving, one long tide
> of animals
> in flight from where I stood,
> and for that moment, I was powerless,
> afraid to move, inept, insensible.
> (4: 13–20)

Phenomenology influences Burnside's poetics profoundly, yet its emphasis on deep connection and witnessing seems to invite him to ensure any experiential emphasis is checked as to avoid the pitfalls of the ahistorical. To read, what is an understated and less impactful poem than others published more widely than in the collections alone, 'On Kvaloya' intimates that the death of the self leads to a new brotherhood 'of animals' and a loose anchor in place subject to unpredictable change that the poetico-philosophical stance can transcend and survive. The poetry tells this in its own way: Burnside's use of the 'wave' represents a phase in personal history, the play of wind on the grass and the global interlocked biosphere underlined by the grammatical movement inwards from colon to semi-colon to comma, intimately related to movement beyond the 'I' and the senses. Another trilogy if you will. Likewise, breath, undulation and mind are processes expanding as one in this poem. This ego-free realization and sensitive attainment of powerlessness heals the homesick, while the 'insensible' turns to the idea of home as unplanned and contingent gathering of subjectivity – self as assemblage, perhaps, as suggested by the verb and collective noun 'clump'.

Moreover, the significant line is given over to the seamless order 'of animals' alone, indicative of the progression in form of the poem as a whole from the tight and military arrangements to the shaping of breath in the final section's quatrains: another stress underlining power (in terms of looseness and binding), solidarity and attunement. We have been witness to these themes in Burnside's early poetry, but they have not been distilled into such dense metaphoric compression by the turn to the creaturely in the same manner that *The Light Trap* has as its goal in evoking Shepard and Benjamin.[3] Rilke's reconciling *poiesis* marks 'the divinization of the immanent world' (Bate 2000: 263) and the potential for action or new ecological praxis. However, one must read Burnside's voice as differentiated from the Romantic point of alienation, the position on the edge of experience. It is on the edge of life. Close to extinction. And for Burnside, Rilkean sensitivity enables the ear to attune to how the world enfolds the mental being, which must be taken to contemporary empirical evidence and/or experience. Couple this mobilized sensitivity with the poet's reading of Shepard (above) and Gregory Bateson's literacy for life (as organism plus environment) and you have an understated sense of suicide. So, it is most curious that this new sensitivity of 'divination' emerges amidst so much loss.

Lament

Burnside's Orphic allusions in *The Light Trap* are Rilkean practices of enchantment: to sing into existence, not to name, codify or map:

> Then Adam forgot the names and one by one
> the creatures died. ...
> Sometimes he wondered if they died en masse
> or if a single female had remained
> for months in the forest,
> lamenting the loss of her kind.
> ('History' (1): 1–2, 7–10)

Loss is the point of relationship between world and humans, and it is the anthropocentric vehicle for subjectivity nuanced by worldliness 'homesick for other animals' (14). In a complementary fashion to proleptic mourning in twentieth-century elegy, Burnside's repurposing of our first story of life and its decline is neutral with respect to nostalgia: 'how he loved them more for being lost/became his only myth'. It is not until the poem is found to register, what Rae calls a synecdoche for millennial loss (Rae 2003), that the lines start to take a hold on our less abstract and storied present. 'History' *Piliocolobus badius waldronae*, the critically endangered species of monkey, discovered in 1933 and the first old-world primate declared extinct in the twenty-first century.[4] Such timbre gears the collection towards the Sixth extinction and saves the poem (and this section) from the transcendental abstraction that species thinking can mistakenly generate (see also the final stanza of Burnside 2017).

Burnside's polemic can be heard in the line-endings 'one', 'apart' and 'lost' that betoken the untimely meditation that 'at last' signifies man's destruction and irreversible alienation from the world he laments. The loss of animal ancestry and global biodiversity is Burnside's challenge to linear history. This is indicated by his use of Shepard (in section one), who reads the central theme of linear history as 'the rejection of habitat' (1982: 43), that New Testament 'antiorganic and antisensuous masterpiece in abstract thinking' ('Puritans' 1982: 5). For Burnside, this disconnection from habitat indicates a requirement to rethink the condition of homesickness.

As with the final lines to this collection that suggest referentiality over originary experience, 'On Kvaloya' and 'History' (1) signify the casting of words for the light to catch rather than possessing world through names and projecting enlightenment upon it. Light in *The Light Trap*, therefore, extends the German Idealist shift from interpretation of spiritual truth to the understanding of human action by promoting *the bidirectional way* that meaning is communicated. While Stevens has argued that 'what we said of it became/A part of what it is' ('A Postcard from the Volcano' 1955: 15–16), Burnside is less postmodern; his work leads us to the North American definition that Scigaj has cast upon the theory of ecopoetics: the larger sense of recreation that is the song of the earth. For this idea, we can turn to Scigaj's reading of A. R. Ammons:

> [an] outward movement from alienation and loneliness toward a more comfortable acceptance and celebration of the natural world parallels a deepening understanding of how the creative act of perception and its recreation in language is homologous to the operations of the energy-driven ecosystems of our planet. (1999: 85)

One qualification: homologous and equally threatened. Here, a poet does not necessarily have to write about distinct ecologies backed up by empirical observation, although this would be useful. Such ecopoetic outwardness might rest in the shade of enchantment while mindful of the need to bridge wonder and worry; Burnside's Heideggerian move towards the open (above) can be paraphrased in terms that colour *The Light Trap* as follows: the human as one occurrence of *physis* alongside that of the plants and animals comes as the accomplishment of inaction that enables beings to exist in the 'nameless' ('The Origin of the Work of Art' 1993: 199) where we do no harm.

Burnside expects a lot of his reader and it needs some working out: although alone in his language world (Heidegger 1993: 205–6), by not determining how things appear (1993: 210), a human self can turn to the 'recollection of [the] history that [primordially] unfolds itself' (211). Here, for Burnside, we become ecologically literate Earthlings. While Heidegger states that a dialogue with materialism is required before the holy region avails itself to thinking, Burnside enters an alternative provision of world. Through Wallace Stevens (under the influence of Simone Weil – see Weil 1952 and Stevens 1951), Burnsidean unfolding includes meditation on the themes of proximity and involvement to envision how the self might dissolve into the unfolding conditions of life.[5] Settlement upon the provisional in this manner suggests what Priest, reading Merleau-Ponty, conceives as soul: 'what the unity of my consciousness consists in' (1998: 233), the nature of experienced space thoroughly within things (234–5). The poem, therefore, is a version of the temporal comportment of phenomenological intentionality (*verhalten*): embeddedness in living nature holding humans captive quite differently from indulgent subjective perspectivism.

Erasure

It is my feeling that human and technological frameworks, which locate a conception of livelihood as *begreifen*, trouble the maturing of ecopoetics in *The Light Trap*. At times, the phenomenological emphasis can appear ahistorical; however, Burnsidean temporality is one of arrest, closer to awe than quietude. In its most serene manifestation, it assumes the tone, though not the doctrinal implication, of a prayer.

The post-secular equilibrium of science and philosophy positions Jorie Graham as one of this century's finest poets of phenomenology and metaphysics. 'The Visible World' (*Dream of the Unified Field*, 1996) reads phenomena as 'upthrown' (9, 40) from 'the absolute' (1), 'deranged/and rippling' (10–11). Burnside and Oliver proffer the overlapping of instances carried and cradled by the non-contingent soul, what Thomas has rightly understood as 'an awareness of a universe only briefly troubled by human presence' (2008). In the context of the Anthropocene perspective, this looks decidedly dated. For Graham, the challenge is to bring and make this 'pellucid moment; here on this page now/as on this patch/of soil, my property' (19–21); she attempts to disentangle things yet retain supernatural dynamism in abstractions that are beyond the human frame and at the edge of poetics. For Burnside, the challenge is to hook this problem of property to the question of harm and loss, while also spelling out the modulations of a less egotistical lyrical 'I' yielding a smaller footprint on the world and on the page.

Blackbird

The lighter footprint leads to greater white space, or expansive verse; moreover, at times it leads to an unpoetic space that is an unfinished semantic site where the *work*, not the form of poetry, comes into play. To be frank, this is a site, Simic argues, that is best suited to prose (2005: 29). In *The Light Trap* we witness this unfinishedness as a willed move to emptiness teaming with spiritual nostalgia confused by mental vacancy. Again, Burnside pushes his general reader into unchartered territory. In the Weilean poetic as read in Graham, this willed move urges the reader 'to read the poem back from its fragmentary status' (Baker 2006: 139), rather than reading an accumulation of lines as a journey towards meaning. 'Unfolding from the earth'. In Burnside, the contingent, loose array of poetic elements from intertext, to voice, to natural phenomenon and thematic emphases, all ripe with potential historical, cultural and ecological relations, are not exalted for their potentiality. What would be new there? No, they transfix the reader in their relationality, best exemplified in the work of the closing poem of the collection. By offering up such a fresh fragmentation at such a late stage, one can be forgiven for rereading the collection immediately in the light, not of any ending, but of rebirth. The *Light Trap*'s literary merit may lie on both the lightness of this conceit rather than on its imperial tenacity; further merit might be rewarded for integrity, whereby loss is felt at a critical distance from supercharged Anthropocene nostalgia.

> the sound of water rushing through the pines
> towards us and a scent
> unfolding from the earth, to draw us in
> —a history of light
> and gravity no more–
> for this is how the world
> occurs: not piecemeal
>   but entire
> and instantaneous
> the way we happen:
> woman blackbird man
> ('A Theory of Everything': 7–16)

The final poem to *The Light Trap* elevates the dual action of gravity and light as 'loose[ning] and bind[ing]', setting free and gathering where one can 'settle' in the site of movement in time (the 'reach'). This poem can be read as an invocation of the imagination enfolding the world inspirationally; conjoining these two most consistent metaphors in Burnside's palette instances a brushstroke that is in itself part of the essence of the world, registering the dialectical nature of the collection.

Heidegger speaks of things flashing (*blitzen*), as an entrance 'into its own emitting of light' (1977: 45). In 'A Theory of Everything', Burnside seems to know this as he attempts the extensiveness of Rilke's tenth elegy considering 'place and settlement, foundation and soil and home' (1989: 15). The fourth and seventh lines echoed in 'woman blackbird man' (Burnside 2002b: 17) suggest a form of disclosure where man, as much as his human other and creaturely other, is gazed upon and gathered in nearness. The blackbird – as transmigratory symbol of mourning that evolves into an Orphic messenger of relation and mutual belonging in *The Light Trap* – is one that postulates the unity of the relationally dynamic 'I' rather than positing it as fixed ground. The effect is that the poem echoes the traces of prosperity from primal grief, as viewed in Rilke's principality of lament in the ninth elegy – the 'protocosmic' thinking in daily relationships afforded by the witness to the naming of constellations. In ecopoetic Heideggerian terms, this naming, once including the speaker on equal terms, constitutes the worlding of elements together: a gathering impregnated with potential and disclosure (49). On the other side of the Atlantic, the shallow artwork speaks of the occluded void as 'the attempt to rebuild the shattered community of we' (Graham 2003: 57). Transatlantically, rather than mourning that considers death as terminus, Burnside's bird recalls the 'birdvoice of the deathlike one', the soul not destined to death but 'going under' into the realm of vespers, ghostliness and the land of traces (Heidegger 1971b: 197). Deathlike here is a euphemism for an ecopoetic hauntology that should be read as instigating an unstable experiential world of the third person in its presencing and occasional flight.

This redress to singing and lament has come into being through a curious dialectic between history and ecology in *The Light Trap*. In an attempt to bring these ideas to a conclusion, we can note a vacant modality urged by the poem as primary ontology and means to secure phenomenological experience as reference point, which measures the self in relation to the unnamed fabric of the immanent world. In Burnside's oeuvre it becomes the invisible ecological processes and relations of the planet often mapped but overlooked in our histories of human action. Burnside's involved and dispersed self, extended across media and time, reminds one of what Poirier has noted as 'compensatory emphasis' of the transitive, leading to substance (1992: 136). This ethical move of diluted self-assertion that speaks for the world trumps the griefwork ordinarily understood within elegy theory anchored in a model of the psychoanalytical self (Ramazani, Sacks, Spargo). The fluxional emphasis within Burnside's abstract vitality of qualia – the way and how the world occurs – reinstates the contradictory refraction and blurring of the linguistic and the affective while it is at its most attentive and most empirically grounded, thus refreshing compensation in pastoral terms.

Conclusion

Observations of habitat modulating the emotional ambivalence between valence-carriers of peaceful repose and excursions into night: these are watermarks on John Burnside's poetry and its engagement with the rejection of 'civilized life' and a willingness to locate philosophical truth in nature and in solitary existence. In short: pastoral.[6]

William Empson argued that 'emotions well handled in art are somehow absorbed into the structure; their expression is also made to express where and why they are emotive' (1947: 372). The tripartite structure of *The Light Trap* is a result of the properly dialectical nature of Burnside's thinking; his conceptual framework resists static oppositions or mere dualities often simplified in pastoral, positing instead the triplicate of mental imagining, perceptions of space and social practice. The latter of these – a critique of the social world as a system of objective relations independent of individual consciousness – might be observed under the dilution of selfhood and subtextual spirituality.

Burnside's refusal to set the natural world into relief solely through the experience of a subject of urban landscapes or to distil glimpses of an ecologically unified world as either non-foundational or obscured by the veil of modernity nonetheless brings up the spectre of the pastoral. Pastoral haunts the collection in the metaphors for environmental and political consciousness that I have drawn attention to, as well as in the intertextual allusions to a poetics of relinquishment that speaks to the elegiac mode. To be of the world is to live in the world, and *The Light Trap* remains a pastoral in that its appeal to the common life is never an easy one. For those seeking union with nature yet aware of the limitations to nostalgic longing for that which is lost, active consciousness concerned with recalibrating itself must register 'the prized tension of awareness' as result of attempting an equilibrium with respect to 'proximity to and distance from nature' (Slovic 1996: 353). Intrinsically defined by its *tempo* fleshing out the ethical affordance of deep structures combining with extrinsic poetics of allusion and reference (intertexts), this generative scheme in *The Light Trap* inherits certain ideological contexts and textures that are clearly of the radical far left and philosophical tradition of continental concerns for freedom. The middle point of the dwelling trilogy is an amalgam of information and interpretation deeply indebted to Burnside's engagement not only with German writing but American writing, too. The resultant linguistic moment marks the legible distillation of the theme of writing as a social practice, which in the final analysis resides in the text's style coloured unmistakably by ecological motifs in this collection and onwards in Burnside's publications with Jonathan Cape to date.

Chapter Six: Consequences of Pastoral: The Dialectic of History and Ecology in *The Light Trap*, Tom Bristow

Alpers, P. (1982), 'What Is Pastoral?', *Critical Inquiry*, 8 (3): 437–60.
Baker, T. C. (2006), 'Praying to an Absent God: The Poetic Revealing of Simone Weil', *Culture, Theory and Critique*, 47 (2): 133–47.
Bate, J. (2000), *The Song of the Earth*, London: Picador.
Benjamin, W. (1996), *Selected Writings*, eds. M. Bullock and M. W. Jennings, Cambridge, MA: Harvard University Press.
Blair, R. (2015), 'Introduction: Why Pastoral?', *Australian Literary Studies*, 30 (2): 1–18.
Burnside, J. (2002a), 'An Interview [with Allison Funk]', *Sou'wester*: 8–22.
Burnside, J. (2002b), *The Light Trap*, London: Jonathan Cape.
Burnside, J. (2005), 'Travelling into the Quotidian: Some Notes on Allison Funk's "Heartland" Poems', *Poetry Review* 95 (2): 59–70.
Burnside, J. (2006a), 'Learning to Fly', *Granta* 94: 103–16.
Burnside, J. (2006b), 'Underground Routes', Rev. of *District and Circle*, by Seamus Heaney. *The Scotsman*, 1 April 2006: 18–19.
Burnside, J. (2017), 'Arthur Rimbaud at Scamblesby, 1873', *London Review of Books*, 39 (1), 5 January: 30.
Costello, B. (2010), 'Fresh Woods: Elegy and Ecology among the Ruins', in Karen Weisman (ed.), *The Oxford Handbook of the Elegy*, 251–71, Oxford: Oxford University Press.
Eeckhart, B. (2002), *Wallace Stevens and the Limits of Reading and Writing*, Columbia, MS: University of Missouri Press.
Empson, W. (1935), *Some Versions of Pastoral*, London: Chatto and Windus.
Empson, W. (1947), 'The Structure of Complex Words', *The Sewanee Review*, 56 (2): 230–50.
Graham, J. (1996), *The Dream of the Unified Field: Selected Poems 1974–1994*, Manchester: Carcanet.
Graham, J. (2003), 'The Art of Poetry No. 85', *Paris Review*, 165: 52–97.
Hanssen, B. (1998), *Walter Benjamin's Other History: Of Stones, Animals, Human Beings and Angels*, Berkley: University of California Press.
Heidegger, M. (1971a), *On The Way to Language*, trans. P. D. Hertz, London: Harper Row.
Heidegger, M. (1971b), *Poetry, Language, Thought*, trans. A. Hofstadter, New York: Harper Row.
Heidegger, M. (1977), *The Question Concerning Technology and Other Essays*, trans. W. Lovitt, New York: Harper and Row.
Heidegger, M. (1993), *Basic Writings*, ed. D. F. Krell, London: Routledge.
Heidegger, M. (1995), *The Fundamental Concepts of Metaphysics: World, Finitude, Solitude*, trans. W. McNeill and N. Walker, Bloomington: Indiana University Press.
Poirier, R. (1992), *Poetry and Pragmatism*, London: Faber and Faber.
Priest, S. (1998), *Merleau-Ponty*. London: Routledge.
Rae, P. (2003), 'Double Sorrow: Proleptic Elegy and the End of Arcadianism in 1930s Britain', *Twentieth Century Literature*, 49 (2): 246–75.

Ramazani, J. (1994), *Poetry of Mourning: The Modern Elegy from Hardy to Heaney*, Chicago: University of Chicago Press.
Rilke, R. M. (1989), *Duino Elegies*, trans. S. Cohn, Manchester: Carcanet.
Sacks, P. M. (1987), *The English Elegy: Studies in the Genre from Spenser to Yeats*, Baltimore, MD: Johns Hopkins University Press.
Scigaj, L. (1999), *Sustainable Poetry: Four Ecopoets*, Lexington: University Press of Kentucky.
Shepard, P. (1978), *Thinking Animals: Animals and the Development of Human Intelligence*, Athens: University of Georgia Press.
Shepard, P. (1982), *Nature and Madness*, San Francisco: Sierra Book Club.
Shepard, P. (1996), *The Others: How Animals Made Us Human*, Washington, DC: Island Press.
Simic, C. (2005), 'The Spirit of Play', *New York Review of Books*, 52 (17): 28–30.
Slovic, S. (1996), 'Nature Writing and Environmental Psychology: The Interiority of Outdoor Experience', in C. Glotfelty and H. Fromm (eds), *The Ecocriticism Reader: Landmarks in Literary Ecology*, 351–70, London: University of Georgia Press.
Spargo, R. C. (2004), *The Ethics of Mourning: Grief and Responsibility in Elegiac Literature*, Baltimore, MD: Johns Hopkins University Press.
Stevens, W. (1951), *The Necessary Angel: Essays on Reality and the Imagination*, London: Faber and Faber.
Stevens, W. (1955), *Collected Poems*, London: Faber and Faber.
Thomas, M. W. (2008), 'Full Fathom Five', Rev. of *Sea Change* by Jori Graham, *The Guardian*, 3 May. Available online: https://www.theguardian.com/books/2008/may/03/featuresreviews.guardianreview25 (accessed 16 August 2019).
Thomson, J. (2002), '"Everything Blooming Bows Down in the Rain": Nature and the Work of Mourning in the Contemporary Elegy', in J. S. Bryson (ed.), *Ecopoetry: A Critical Introduction*, 153–61, Salt Lake City: University of Utah Press.
Twiddy, I. (2013), *Pastoral Elegy in Contemporary British and Irish Poetry*, London: Continuum.
Weil, S. (1952), *Gravity and Grace*, trans. E. Craufurd, London: Routledge and Kegan Paul.
Whitman, W. (1954), *Preface to 1855 Edition of Leaves of Grass*, ed. E. Holloway, New York: Doubleday.
Whitman, W. (1992), *Song of Myself*, New York: Petrarch Press.

7

Walking the Tightrope: Félix Guattari's *Three Ecologies* and John Burnside's *Glister*

Phill Pass

In a 2011 essay entitled 'Walk the Tightrope' written for the *New Humanist*, John Burnside outlines an idiosyncratic and anarchic vision of political transformation sufficient to bring about meaningful and sustainable ecological change. Unsurprisingly, for any attentive reader of Burnside's oeuvre, this transformation is at root ecopoetical, arising from the proper nurture of the creative imagination and its ecological sensitivity.[1] As Tom Bristow observes, any meaningful, ecopoetic alternative to 'the problematic legacy of toxic capitalism' must be 'neither socially conservative nor a lyrical song of the earth performed in a political vacuum' (Bristow 2015: 15). Instead, it requires 'a clear lens on how the human is located within the appearance of the world in its many manifestations' (15). For this reason, Burnside's ecopoetical vision begins, of necessity, with a willingness to 'abandon the received image' that has been 'handed down' to us, and, without any 'expectations of success', to undertake the search for a new way of seeing (Burnside 2011).

The object of such a search for Burnside is the fluid and ludic forms of 'order' which these received ideas overlay, and partially obscure – an organic organization that is not 'imposed upon the world' from without but is rather emergent and 'intrinsic to all things' (Burnside 2011). Founded upon a conviction that the universe is a complex and 'self-ordering system', Burnside's political vision is opposed to any hierarchical form of order that is externally imposed by 'kings, or parliaments, or the police state', and which results in the 'institutionalisation of the imagination' (Burnside 2011). Both anti-hierarchical and grounded in an appreciation that order can arise 'spontaneously, from pretty much anywhere in the system', Burnside's politics of emergence places responsibility for any ecopolitical transformation in the creative potential of the individual to realize new ways of thinking and being; for him, 'we are all agents for change, one way or another', through our capacity to learn to see anew, or to deny such insights (Burnside 2011). An embrace of an alternative, playful creativity, is thus seen as a highly political act; just as any meaningful, alternative politics must, at root, be both playful and creative.

In this respect, Burnside's polemic echoes Martin Heidegger's belief that poets are most necessary in an epoch of environmental and cultural destitution characterized by a facile reliance upon technoscientific innovation and the dominance of mass media (see Heidegger 2001b: 87–140). Defining poetry as a disclosure, a 'projective saying', which, in its broadest sense encompasses all forms of artistic creation, it is only the transformative potential of such creative praxis that can reveal the very extent of our pervasive destitution (Heidegger 2001a: 70). As Burnside observes, while we may live in such 'a time of corruption', an era 'when so many have turned from "politics" in disgust', the ecopoetical potential of our creativity means that 'the idea of an emergent politics is, in fact, incorruptible, because it depends upon the shifting tide of imagination' (Burnside 2011). Ecopolitics and ecopoetics are thus two sides of the same coin: just as the fluidity of our ecopoetical imagination allows us to be sensitive to the shifting patterns of the 'beautiful' and 'spontaneous play of the universe', so too it is 'the real *realpolitik*' of an emergent and creative ecopolitics that 'calmly recognizes and imaginatively works with the play of emergent order' – an undertaking which 'imposes nothing at all', and whose outcome 'is, inevitably, the pursuit of justice' precisely through an absence of self-interested, extrinsic imposition (Burnside 2011). Within such political praxis, as long as we find a way to shed the institutionalization of our ecopoetical imagination, alternate forms of social and political organization – more harmonious and ecologically sustainable ways of living – still remain possible.

As personal as such an evocation of the intrinsic interrelation between ecopoetics and ecopolitics may be, for Burnside it is not wholly without precedent. An analogous celebration of the emergence of inherent order is, he observes, 'actually a very old idea: it is, in the true sense of the word, anarchism' – the liberation of both creative expression and political praxis; the celebration of a perpetually emergent state of being 'so beautiful that we needed the massive edifice of church-and-state to blind ourselves to it' (Burnside 2011). Without both expressive and political freedom – a liberation that must first begin with our manifestation of mindful being – we cannot adequately appreciate the transformative role that the individual can play in the age of the Anthropocene. Viewed in such terms, the task of an ecopoetic sensibility is self-evident and lies precisely in the necessity of critiquing and transforming the pernicious societal conventions that, elsewise, we may passively perpetuate and reinstate.

In its repeated emphasis upon radical subjective and social transformation as a prerequisite for meaningful ecological change, Burnside's essay advances a comparable (if more impressionistic) argument to that in Félix Guattari's 1989 text *The Three Ecologies*. Like Burnside, Guattari attempts to address the cause and impact of what he terms our 'ecological disequilibrium' (Guattari 2005: 27). Befitting a thinker whose typical preoccupations are the questioning of the possibilities of social interrelation and subjectification, however, the main concern of Guattari's essay is not the disturbance – or disequilibrium – of the physical commons. Rather, the material degradation of the physical environment is but one abuse of three interrelated ecologies that comprise Guattari's 'ecosophy'. As he states, 'we are talking about a reconstruction of social and individual practices which I shall classify under three complementary headings, all of which come under the ethico-aesthetic aegis of an ecosophy: social ecology, mental ecology and environmental ecology' (41). While this threefold focus results in an oddly immaterial essay, which, paradoxically, has very little to say about specific forms of abuse of the material commons, Guattari's text does provide a useful means of conceiving of the impact of environmental degradation in both social and subjective, as well as purely material, terms. In advancing a theory of three inextricably interrelated ecologies, Guattari provides a means of suggesting that the degradation of one form of ecology *necessarily* leads to an abuse within the realm of the other two: or that the contamination of the material commons necessarily shares an origin in the equivalent pollution of the *socius* and of our possibilities of becoming. It is in this respect that Guattari's theoretical framework provides a useful critical paradigm with which to conceptualize Burnside's ecopolitical polemic: a formal, threefold means of evaluating the extent to which the ecopoetical and the ecopolitical potential of the self is either variously liberated or constrained.

When the polemical call of 'Walk the Tightrope' is viewed in terms of this threefold ecosophy, a broad analogue can be seen between Guattari's conception of a subjective and social ecology, respectively, and Burnside's more impressionistic evocation of the ecopoetic imagination and an ecopolitical emergent order – the primary shaping factors within both of their respective ecosophies. Both the expressive and political freedom for which Burnside advocates comprise sustainable forms of Guattari's 'complimentary headings', through which meaningfully sustainable environmental change can be enacted. The call-to-arms with which Burnside concludes his polemic is thus reflective of this imperative that underlies a threefold ecosophy:

> The corruption of the capitalist world is so blatant now – the machinery is creaking so loudly and the Emperor is so well and truly naked – that it is tempting to turn away, but we have to resist that temptation ... and, like the medieval reformers, who left their cells and their retreats to nail their demands to the doors of the cathedral, our main obligation now is to turn off the TV, set aside the commercially produced fodder of self-help books and cosmetic mysticism and godlessly, playfully but in all seriousness step out on to the tightrope and walk. (Burnside 2011)

The concluding demand of Burnside's essay is thus a call for a transformation in the realm of subjective ecology, an ecopoetical reimagining of the destitution of our age that will allow the emergent potentialities of our social ecology to become apparent, beginning the arduous and delicate process of an ecopolitical transformation which will enable meaningful and sustainable environmental change.

It is precisely towards this polemical call, to an inextricably interwoven ecopoetical and ecopolitical imperative, that Burnside's novels have been increasingly devoted. While ecological concerns were never far from the surface in the author's earlier fiction, with the publication of *Living Nowhere* (2003), ecopoetics and ecopolitics came to prominence – a trend that has continued in his subsequent novels: *The Devil's Footprints* (2007), *Glister* (2008) and *A Summer of Drowning* (2011). Of these later, more overtly ecopolitical works, *Glister* is perhaps the most explicitly systematic in its exploration of the need for ecopolitical transformation – a particularly strident thesis nailed to the cathedral door of late-stage capitalism. Forming a key part of what Graeme Macdonald has termed a 'cluster' of contemporary Scottish novels that work at 'imagining scenarios where individuals and groups of limited political power confront the social and economic causes of ecological disaster and environmental ruin', *Glister* expertly 'registers the damage late capitalism and excessive consumerism has produced in local sectors of Scottish society' (Macdonald 2012: 227).[2] Befitting such ecosophical concerns, and paralleling Guattari's threefold understanding of ecology, the novel's focus is upon the desolate post-industrial wasteland that surrounds and (barely) sustains the economically and ecologically ravaged communities of Inner- and Outertown. Told mostly in a series of third-person narratives, interwoven with the first-person voice of Leonard (one of the unfortunate children of the Innertown slain by the Moth Man, a quasi-supernatural killer), Burnside's novel uses a wide spectrum of viewpoints and perspectives to show the inextricable interweaving of social and environmental injustice and ecology, as well as the pervasive mental ecological destruction that such pollution causes. Equally as crucial, however, is the manner in which Burnside illustrates how such forms of injustice are anchored upon, and interleaved with, an equal impoverishment within the ecopoetical imagination of the residents of the fictional Homeland Peninsula.

Perhaps as a result of this multiplicity of perspectives, combined with the post-apocalyptic tenor with which Burnside evokes the contained, corrupt and desolated world of the Homeland Peninsula, *Glister* can be seen as a paradigmatic work of threefold ecosophy, illustrating how interwoven, and inextricable, the impact of the pollution of the physical commons is upon our social and subjective existence. One such example of this interwoven depiction occurs in Leonard's account of the manner in which even snow-cover cannot erase the lingering trace of the landscape's toxicity, however perversely beautiful it may appear to be. Nor can it obscure the accompanying social and subjective pollution that Leonard both observes and directly experiences:

> And then there's the way it's all transformed, how it all looks so innocent, as if it couldn't hurt you in a million years, all those drums of crusted and curdled effluent, all those pits with their lingering traces of poison or radiation, or whatever it is the authorities want to keep sealed up here, along with the dangerous mass of our polluted bodies. Under the snow, it all looks pure, even when a wet rust mark bleeds through, or some trace of cobalt blue or verdigris rises up through an inch of white, it's beautiful. (Burnside 2009: 64)

As viscerally striking as such images are, the novel does not allow the reader to overlook the tripartite ecosophical pollution that comprises such environmental degradation; an accompanying, and equally pernicious, corruption can always be observed within the spheres of social and subjective ecology. Though, as the narrator states, 'the people believed' that the chemical plant that has shaped life on the peninsula 'was essentially safe', crucially they only 'believed, of course, because they *had* to believe' (10). Since 'the Innertown's economy depended almost entirely upon the chemical industry', it is seeming economic necessity that demands social and subjective complicity – an end best served by a hierarchical social order within which the 'people in the Outertown, up in the big houses', 'the Consortium', 'the safety people' and 'the powers that be' are able to invest all of their time and effort 'in ensuring that things ticked over without too much fuss' (10). As *Glister* shows, only a hierarchical relationship between the Outertown and the 'Innertown folk, the ones who actually worked at the plant', could sustain the patently nonsensical message 'that the danger was minimal' (10). The extrinsic nature of such a social order is thus an edifice purposely built to either obscure or at least justify the pollution of the physical commons, requiring those at the bottom of an imposed social structure to participate in a limiting and self-abnegating blindness 'through sheer force of will' (10). Hierarchy and economic coercion are shown to be necessary in ensuring that the people of the peninsula felt it was required of them 'to believe they were safe because there was nowhere else for them to go', and that 'they wanted to trust the managers and politicians because there was nobody else for them to trust' (10). Despite ample evidence to the contrary, 'naturally, they worked hard on being convinced' (10), harnessing all of their creative efforts to invest themselves within the prevailing social order and its subjective fiction of a necessary and sustaining hierarchy – a monopolization of the inhabitants' creative potential that leaves them unable to adequately undertake any 'interrogation' of 'how [their] home might be spiritually (re) inhabited, how the contemporary human subject might be re-enchanted by nature' (Borthwick 2009: 65) or 'how poetic consciousness can illuminate or imagine conditions such as settlement and alienation' (Bristow 2011: 150).

Yet, as *Glister* so ably demonstrates, the myth of economic dependence that prevents such ecopoetic meditation is only sustained by the seeming reality of economic production; once economic output ceases, the extrinsic order loses the supposed solidity of its foundation. As 'Walk the Tightrope' suggests, a moment of potentiality is created as the previous edifice begins to collapse, leaving a vacuum in which another edifice may emerge, or an intrinsic, anarchic order may instead re-establish itself. Within Burnside's novel, this potentiality is perhaps best illustrated by the generational gap that has emerged upon the Peninsula, following the closure of the chemical plant. The majority of the adults in the Inner- and Outertown continue to cling to the compromised remnants of the corrupt *socius* upon which their lives were structured. For the adolescents of the Homeland Peninsula, however, both the physical landscape and its accompanying social structures are so self-evidently polluted that, absent of continuing economic benefit, the impetus to invest within the remnants of the prevailing social order is no longer sufficient. Instead, the Peninsula's youth are left to try and fashion some form of personal, individual meaning, some spirituality – a subjective transformation that, as Burnside has observed, is easiest to undertake in the kind of liminal space where the self is most 'susceptible to change, where being is raw, as it were, where identity is less fixed, more open to possibility' (Burnside 1996: 203). Within the physical and social wasteland of the Homeland Peninsula, it is the abandoned chemical plant that offers the kind of liminal space required for such a transformative undertaking:

> Maybe it seems daft to talk about reverence, but this complex of ruined buildings and disused railways that runs as far as I can walk in any direction, whether along the coast, or inland through scrubby woodlands and fields of gorse, this apparent wasteland is all the church we have. (Burnside 2009: 66–7)

A liminal space within the Peninsula's youth can fashion 'a secret ceremony, a private ritual' (67). Lacking any social or material support, the alternate subjectivities that the teenagers of the Homeland Peninsula devise through these idiosyncratic ceremonies and rituals are fragile, tenuous things, destabilized by the simplest look or glance. Yet, they still comprise a necessary and needed attempt, however ineffectual, to fashion a new form of self from the detritus that has been left behind.

Thus, through this interwoven, threefold depiction of the impact of pollution – its interrelated physical, social and subjective consequences – *Glister* highlights that the more immediate and visceral physical manifestations of environmental pollution are but one facet of a far more pervasive and complex compound toxicity. As a result, the novel comprises a successful and powerful critique of the inviolability of incrementalist environmental change that strives to address and ameliorate the impact of pollution in terms of physical ecology alone. As Guattari observes, a diverse range of 'political groupings and executive authorities appear to be totally incapable of understanding the full implications' of anthropogenic environmental destruction and have instead been 'generally content to simply tackle industrial pollution and then from a purely technocratic perspective' (Guattari 2005: 27–8). Such half-hearted, cosmetic efforts lack what Guattari terms 'an ethico-political articulation' of the inherent interrelation 'between the three ecological registers' that alone 'would be likely to clarify these questions' (28). This is exemplified, most eloquently and effectively in Burnside's novel, through the depiction of Brian Smith's Homeland Peninsula Company. As the narrator observes, with the closure of the chemical plant, Brian Smith 'was ready to take advantage' (Burnside 2009: 39):

> Nobody wanted to take on the job of cleaning up after the Consortium, but Brian Smith saw that money would have to be thrown at this particular problem. It was politics, pure and simple. Nobody out in the wider world cared about the people in the Innertown, or the environment … but it was in all their interests to have somebody local – somebody like Brian Smith – make a good show of developing and regenerating the area with the subsidies and grants they made available. (39–40)

Burnside's novel thus suggests that the refusal on the part of those in power to acknowledge the inextricable interweaving of all three ecologies, and a refusal to do more than address the solely physical manifestations of industrial pollution in a purely technocratic manner, arises out of self-interest rather than ignorance. In this respect, Burnside's novel diverges from Guattari's work in its willingness to ascribe an intentionality to such behaviour, suggesting that, at a fundamental level, the aim of incrementalist environmental strategies – such as those represented by the Homeland Peninsula Company – is incompatible with meaningful and effective environmental change. Rather, *Glister* proposes that such initiatives merely exist for predominantly cosmetic purposes, precisely because 'the politicians needed to be seen to be doing something', and thus 'nobody checked to see if Homeland Peninsula could deliver a safer, cleaner Innertown; what mattered was that Brian Smith created the illusion of preparedness, the illusion of competence' (40).

Interested predominantly in appearance and the evasion of any (costly) responsibility, business-as-usual capitalism, as *Glister* highlights, cannot ameliorate the degradation of the physical environment to any meaningful extent, precisely because it represents the attempt to promote ostensible change in one ecology alone, whilst simultaneously striving to prevent any social or subjective ecological change that would threaten corporate profits and relative privilege. As both *Glister* and 'Walk the Tightrope' emphasize, it is only an extrinsic hierarchy that would allow vast capital accumulation and income inequality to be sustained, at the expense of threefold ecological devastation. It is thus in the interests of those who benefit from such social and subjective pollution to perpetuate that damaging hierarchy at any cost – maintaining the very creative and cultural asymmetry that brought the chemical plant into being, bringing about the environmental devastation of the Homeland Peninsula. As *Glister* highlights, without a revolution in prevailing forms of social and subjective ecology, any policy of incrementalist environmental change will only perpetuate the ongoing destruction and desolation of the physical environment and will not even begin to adequately redress the environmental damage that has already been done.[3]

While Guattari's and Burnside's texts thus differ in their respective willingness to ascribe a motive to the favouring of technocratic *fixes* over radical, ethico-political solutions, in regard to the manner in which they believe true and sustainable environmental change to be possible, there is a substantial degree of overlap between the two writers. As with the call that concludes 'Walk the Tightrope', Guattari's proposed solution to a lack of official motivation for truly addressing the crisis of social and subjective ecology (or at least his path to the finding of such a solution) begins with the enacting of meaningful change in our Social and Subjective Ecology. As he repeatedly states, what is needed most is the shattering of the dominance of mass-media and its imposition of derivative, given-forms of subjectivity that have pernicious environmental impacts – a conscious movement towards a post-mass-media age and an accompanying diversity in forms of subjectification. For Guattari, it is such a transition in our subjective ecology – what I would term as the raising of an ecological form of consciousness that accompanies the de-institutionalization of the ecopoetic imagination – that will bring about a meaningful change in our social praxis and the manner in which we make use of the material commons: a proposed solution which, to borrow from Leonard's lexicon, 'isn't that complicated, it's just difficult' (Burnside 2009: 59).

While *Glister* broadly echoes this paradigm, Burnside's novel does offer a further important caveat to the assumption that underpins Guattari's ecosophy, highlighting the difficulty of the path which *The Three Ecologies* suggests as the means of achieving meaningful environmental change. Unlike most of the other characters within Burnside's novel, Leonard does not seem to possess a derivative, mass-media-inspired form of subjectivity – one solely the product of school, television, mass-marketing and the crushing banality of Innertown's heteronormative, bourgeois values. Rather, as Elspeth, Leonard's erstwhile lover, observes, Leonard gives the appearance of possessing a subjectivity largely of his own fashioning, embodying what David Borthwick terms a characteristic 'resistance' within Burnside's work 'to the kind of homogenising influence he perceives in capitalist methods of disseminating meaning' (Borthwick 2011: 134). Seemingly possessing the antithesis of such a mass-media-derived sense of self, Leonard has instead attempted to form his alternate, divergent subjectivity through an engagement with radical works of art, the polluted material reality of his physical environment and an acute awareness of how vacuous and endemically corrupt the *socius* has become on the Homeland Peninsula. However, as *Glister* shows, in spite of the acuity of this awareness, and the alternative material from which Leonard fashions his own subjective plane of consistency, his divergent, rhizomatic subjectivity is insufficient to overcome the toxifying effect of the social and environmental pollution with which he is surrounded.[4] As his involvement in the stalking and subsequent killing of local recluse and wrongly suspected child-murderer, Andrew Rivers, demonstrates, the pervasive toxicity of the Peninsula's social ecology, its crushing pressure to enact some form of conformity, is such that its pollution is not so easily escaped or transformed (*deterritorialized* in Guattari's lexicon), even if the dominance of a mass-media form of subjectivity is successfully rejected. The inextricability of a tripartite ecology results in an inertia that accompanies the threefold nature of pollution – and thus degradation within each ecology makes meaningful change in either of the other two spheres alone that much harder to initially achieve, without a co-extensive, tripartite praxis of global alteration. In essence, the chain reaction Guattari seems to envisage in *The Three Ecologies* is not so easily begun in one ecology alone, precisely because, as *Glister* shows, the dominance of capitalism has arisen as a result of an interwoven, threefold ecological pollution – a form of toxification that is ongoing, and sustained, through the co-interaction of each field upon the other and that of the other two ecologies.

Yet, while Leonard's divergent form of subjectivity alone is insufficient to withstand the pollution of the *socius* that Burnside depicts, *Glister* is not a wholly dystopian novel. Instead, it offers a glimpse – admittedly a rather dim glimpse – of something approaching hope and of the possibility that the transformation envisaged in *The Three Ecologies* may in fact be achievable. This is represented in *Glister* by the nomad figure (in both Burnside's and

Guattari's lexicon) of the Moth Man, a deterritorializing character, who, through an act of ecopoiesis – a making in its original, equiprimordial sense – fashions a work of art that highlights the problematic manner in which the crisis facing the Homeland Peninsula exists in all three ecosophical spheres. And as would befit a society and an environment that has become so polluted and toxic, such a work of art takes the form, on a material level at least, of something brutal and cruel – the killing and torture of a succession of young boys, culminating with the slaying of Leonard. As Morrison, the local, corrupt policeman observes, even when the Moth Man's working is viewed purely according to its brutality and legal transgression, some form of *poiesis* still remains evident, a symbolic act of transformation:

> as he stared into Mark Wilkinson's pale, muddied face, he understood that his death had meant something to his killer, something religious, even mystical … it was nothing rational and it was certainly nothing he could have put into words … it was something about the arrangement of the boy that struck him, an arrangement in which he sensed the reverence of a last moment. (Burnside 2009: 29)

As much as Morrison may wish otherwise, he cannot deny 'that there had been reverence here, a terrible, impossible tenderness – in both the killer and his victim – for whatever it is that disappears at the moment of death, an almost religious regard for what the body gives up, something sublime and precise' (29). It is precisely this ritualistic and spiritual quality – the literal sacrifice underlying the *poiesis* – that forces the viewer to acknowledge that the world the novel depicts must be near-irredeemably polluted, not only for such an act to occur and go unexplained, covered up and unpunished but also for it to be such an effective symbol. Sunk in his own inequity, Morrison's reaction to the Moth Man's working is to try and 'deny this sacrifice', to attempt to erase the truth of this observation, its acknowledgement of the endemic and pervasive pollution of the *socius* and the subjective ecologies that characterize life on the peninsula – to somehow 'invalidate it' (29). As the narrator observes, 'Morrison had to fight the temptation, then, to cut the body down, to undo the ceremony of what had been done to him, to cover him up and not let him be seen like this by anyone else' (29).

Experiencing what the Moth Man enacts from the perspective of the sacrificial victim, rather than the viewer, Leonard confirms such a reading, acknowledging that, on one level at least, it is a working made to shock the Innertown into ecological consciousness, highlighting the iniquity and threefold pollution that lies at its core. As he observes, 'I see, at that moment, that I'm not doing this for my own sake, I'm doing it for [the Moth Man]', for those who populate 'the Innertown, everyone on the peninsula, maybe everyone everywhere' (253). While the work they fashion ultimately frees Leonard from the interwoven prison of the Homeland Peninsula's tripartite, polluted ecology, the Moth Man does not himself obtain release, for, as Leonard notes,

> he has to stay, he has to go on with his work. He *is* the necessary angel. I have an image of him going from house to house all along the peninsula, picking off the Morrisons and the Jenners and the Smiths, one by one. That's what I see in him, at the last. An angel going from door to door. The Angel of death. The angel of absolution, gathering the souls of the wicked – not as a punishment, but because God has forgiven them at last, and is releasing them from the hell they have fallen into. (254)

But precisely in ending with such an observation – with the seeming necessity of an angelic figure and with Leonard's transition to another plane of existence – the very structure of Burnside's novel highlights the depth of the environmental challenge we face in order to enact meaningful and sustainable ecological change. Without the artistic, ecopoetical praxis of a quasi-supernatural figure, a kind of techno-shaman described as a 'Necessary Angel', *Glister* offers no indication of how a radical alteration in social ecology, and a reterritorializing of the ecological consciousness underpinning individual subjectivity, is truly possible – a concern Guattari likewise never adequately answers in *The Three Ecologies*. As a nomad, who appears and disappears within Burnside's text, we do not learn how the Moth Man has fashioned such a divergent subjectivity; nor do we learn how he has been able to sustain such a radical conception of self in the face of an endemically corrupt society. If an angelic being is truly needed to bring about a meaningful change, then how can those within a hopelessly polluted *socius* adopt such a role? Or do such individuals have to wait for an angel to miraculously appear and free them from the toxically polluted threefold ecology in which they are complicit? Thus, rather than ending with a reconstruction of the Homeland Peninsula, *Glister* concludes with Leonard's transcendence and a statement of the necessity of an ongoing revolution in social ecology, which perhaps only the Moth Man's continuing efforts can enact – a refusal of closure that highlights the extreme nature of the environmental challenges the society faces if it is to fashion a truly environmentally sustainable form of social ecology. Viewed in such a light, *Glister* may not suggest that any radical change will necessarily be achieved, but it is nevertheless apparent from reading this novel that change remains the only means to ameliorate our current ecological crisis. Only by our walking the tightrope of an ecopoetically and ecopolitically emergent order, in hope more than expectation, will we begin to fashion new forms of individual being and social interrelation that do not sink back once more into the business-as-usual capitalism of our pervading neoliberalism, and the environmental devastation that it enables.

Chapter Seven: Walking the Tightrope: Félix Guattari's *Three Ecologies* and John Burnside's *Glister*, Phill Pass

Borthwick, D. (2009), 'The Sustainable Male: Masculine Ecology in the Poetry of John Burnside', in H. Ellis and J. Meyer (eds), *Masculinity and the Other: Historical Perspectives*, 63–84, Newcastle: Cambridge Scholars Publishing.

Borthwick, D. (2011), '"The Tilt from One Parish/into Another": Estrangement, Continuity and Connection in the Poetry of John Burnside, Kathleen Jamie, and Robin Robertson', *Scottish Literary Review*, 3 (2): 133–48.

Bristow, T. (2011), 'Environment, History, Literature: Materialism as Cultural Ecology in John Burnside's "Four Quartets"', *Scottish Literary Review*, 3 (2): 149–70.

Bristow, T. (2015), *The Anthropocene Lyric: An Affective Geography of Poetry, Person, Place*, Basingstoke: Palgrave.

Burnside, J. (1996), 'Poetry and a Sense of Place', *Nordlit*, 1: 201–22.

Burnside, J. (2000), 'Strong Words' in W. N. Herbert and M. Hollis (eds), *Strong Words: Modern Poets on Modern Poetry*, 259–61, Tarset: Bloodaxe.

Burnside, J. (2006), 'A Science of Belonging: Poetry as Ecology', in R. Crawford (ed.), *Contemporary Poetry and Contemporary Science*, 91–106, Oxford: Oxford University Press.

Burnside, J. (2009), *Glister*, London: Vintage.

Burnside, J. (2011), 'Walk the Tightrope', *New Humanist*, 7 December. Available online: http://newhumanist.org.uk/2701/walk-the-tightrope (accessed 30 April 2012).

Deleuze, G. and Guattari, F. (2004), *A Thousand Plateaus: Capitalism and Schizophrenia*, trans. B. Masumi, London: Continuum.

Guattari, F. (2005), *The Three Ecologies*, trans. I. Pindar and P. Sutton, London: Bloomsbury.

Hardt, M. and Negri, A. (2009), *Commonwealth*, Cambridge, MA: Harvard University Press.

Heidegger, M. (2001a), 'The Origin of the Work of Art', in *Poetry, Language, Thought*, trans. A. Hofstaedter, 15–86, London: HarperCollins.

Heidegger, M. (2001b), 'What Are Poets For?', in *Poetry, Language, Thought*, trans. A. Hofstaedter, 87–140, London: HarperCollins.

Macdonald, G. (2012), 'Green Links: Ecosocialism and Contemporary Scottish Writing', in J. Rignall, G. H. Klaus, and V. Cunningham (eds), *Ecology and the Literature of the British Left*, 221–40, Farnham: Ashgate.

Žižek, S. (2010), *Living in the End Times*, London: Verso.

8

'A Kindred Shape': Hauntings, Spectres and the Poetics of Return in John Burnside's Verse

David Borthwick

Robert Louis Stevenson declared that the 'mark of the Scot' is their remarkable sense of kinship with the dead, in which the individual 'cherishes the memory of his forebears, good or bad; and there burns in him a sense of identity with the dead' (1998: 131). During a 2008 radio interview, John Burnside alluded to Stevenson's remark, agreeing that: 'I feel that the dead are with me ... [I have] a very strong sense of people I've lost, people who have died before I was even born, just a sense of that community, the living and the dead' (*Private Passions* 2008). This sense of the living and the dead as occupying a single continuum, existing as a 'community', an ecology of belonging, is something which Burnside has described in his first volume of memoir, *A Lie about My Father* (2006), where he talks of 'ghosts who are so like ourselves that we are all interchangeable: living and dead; guest and host; house-holder and spectre; my father, myself' (2006a: 4).

Ghosts appear with remarkable consistency across Burnside's poetic output to date. In 'The Dead', from *The Myth of the Twin* (1994), the speaker talks of the deceased 'still passing though:/weavers and children, and women with songs in their/heads' (1994: 8). In 'Haar', from *The Good Neighbour* (2005), we are told:

> Now, as the haar comes in,
> I look for ghosts,
> children with dip-nets, women with salt in their faces,
> men going out before dawn in the coats that will drown them. (2005a: 18–20, 19)

In 'An Old Photograph of West Fife' from *A Normal Skin* (1997), the speaker summons visions of 'towns that no longer/figure on the maps//Of thin men printed in coal' (1997: 34–5, 34). But the line of thought moves to entertain:

> ... darkness and the echo in the woods
> Come out to touch my face and make me strange
> an arm's length away from the dead
> or a mile from home. (35)

Even this brief range of examples shows the problematic diversity of Burnside's dealings with ghosts. The ghosts we find in his poetry defy some of the traditional functions of the revenant or returning spirit. Burnside's ghosts are not those of Thomas Hardy's 'Spectres that Grieve' (1914), who describe themselves as

> The hurt, misrepresented names, who come
> At each year's brink, and cry to History
> To do them justice, or go past them dumb. (1930: 310–11)

Burnside's ghosts lack voices; they do not provide any specific moral injunction to which his cast of poetic speakers must respond. For example, these are not the 'lurid manifestations of the purgatorial period' in the later middle ages; these are not ghosts of the nineteenth century who, says R. C. Finucane in his *Cultural History of Ghosts* (1984), 'were as likely to appear and disappear in a translucent mist, or walk through walls, as they were to knock on doors before entering' (223). These are, in short, not the ghosts of the popular imagination. Yet Burnside's ghosts do share, in some crucial respects, some of the key qualities we expect of a haunting, and these are what make ghosts so problematic, and so compelling. Colin Davis (2005) has spoken of 'the figure of the ghost as that which is neither present nor absent, neither dead nor alive ... it occupies the place of a Levinasian Other: a wholly irrecuperable intrusion into our world, which is not comprehensible within our available intellectual frameworks, but whose otherness we are responsible for preserving' (373).

Indeed, the ghost provides an injunction to the extent that there is no established convention for how to live with a ghost once it has made itself known. The ghost is an aporetic figure which, for John Wylie, represents 'the very conjuration and unsettling of presence, place, the present, and the past. In this sense, it may be understood as a riposte to phenomenologies of being-in-the-world' (2007: 172). A ghost may be seen as a threat in that it challenges sensory perception, confounds rational thought and disrupts the experience of linear time. The appearance of a ghost begins a process of uncertainty for, as Wylie contends, '[t]he spectral ushers in an endless process of returning, without ever arriving. In neither coming from somewhere nor going anywhere, the spectral constitutes an incessance [sic] that belies origins or ends: a haunting' (2007: 171). And yet, the speakers Burnside employs in his poems are not haunted in the sense of exhibiting fear or terror at the appearance of ghosts; rather, these are figures which are looked for, welcomed even, and whose presence is accepted as a necessary given, despite the intrusion they perhaps ought to represent. In 'Responses to Augustine of Hippo' (2007), the opening lines herald the appearance of the dead in late winter:

The snowdrops are here;
and sometimes the dead we have washed
and buried:
the sweet-mouthed, arthritic mothers we rarely noticed
polishing spoons in the small hours
polishing mirrors;
the men in our kitchens blurring with silicosis;
the gradual dead
drifting between the trees like gusts of wind
and finding a visible form. (3–19, 3)

If the snowdrops themselves are revenants, returnees who emerge apparently from nothing and whose presence is not under our control, then they are, in some respects, also haunting the present, emergent as part of the concentrated observance of the visible world to which Burnside's poetic speakers so frequently respond.

In Burnside's verse, perceiving ghosts is part of the same continuum of studied observance that permits his speakers' sensual submersion, often in an outdoor or 'natural' setting. But in addition to this, Burnside's ghosts are not just seen; they look right back. In 'Animals', from *The Light Trap* (2002), a ghost is seen in an empty house: 'a presence: we could see it from the yard//shifting from room to room in the autumn rain/and we thought it was watching us: a kindred shape' (18–19, 18). In *Specters of Marx* (1993/1994), Jacques Derrida describes the gaze of the ghost as producing a 'vertiginous asymmetry: the technique for having visions, for *seeing* ghosts', he says, 'is in truth a technique to *make oneself seen* by ghosts. *The ghost, always, is looking at me*' (1994: 168). A problematic relationship is established through this looking, then, where the present haunts the past as much as the past haunts the present – yet there can be no way to securely verify the perceptions of either gaze. In addition, sequential time is disrupted and made permeable. In *The Hunt in the Forest* (2009), a more descriptive account is given of the watchful emergence of spectral presences, and of their qualities, in the poem 'An Essay Concerning Time':

> Only the dead are communal:
> intimate under the grass, conversing through snow,
> forever gifted with the middle ground,
> only the dead are immune
> to clockwork,
> in its sleeve of zinc and lime.
> Lying awake, they slide beneath the blades
> and, though they see us, when we light our fires
> at daybreak,
> though they know us through our songs
> And customs,
> they are leaving us behind,
> released from the local need
> to manage time,
> passing through aeons as if they were long afternoons. (2009a: 36–41, 36)

This section of the poem presents something of a reversal. Instead of the dead being left behind in their historical periods, it is we, as mortals, who are being left behind, lost to time, victims of 'clockwork' linearity. It is the dead, too, who are 'communal', forming a community below the earth (as opposed to visibly on it, in this case), and instead of the watchful reception *of* the dead accomplished by many of Burnside's speakers, it is here the dead who act as observers of our 'songs/and customs'. In short, it is we, the living, who are historical and trapped in our mortal realm. It is the spectral figures who possess freedom for, as Derrida notes, 'a specter is always a *revenant*. One cannot control its comings and goings because it *begins by coming back*' (Derrida 1994: 11).

This section I have quoted from 'An Essay Concerning Time' is entitled '*kairos*': that is, the right or opportune moment (sometimes translated as 'the supreme moment'), as opposed to *chronos*, chronological or sequential time. This is pertinent since Burnside's haunted speakers are forever trying to pin down the single moment and document it scrupulously; one might say that many of Burnside's speakers strive to document a moment of *kairos* such as:

> that point, to the nearest second,
> mid-afternoon,
> when someone indoors looks up, and the window darkens,
>
> not one thing after the other, but both at once:
> this knowledge we have that no one is truly absent,
> and nothing is ever the same as the shape it resembles. (Burnside 2009a: 38)

In 'Fields', from *The Asylum Dance* (2000), the speaker implores: 'Be quick when you switch on the light/and you'll see the dark … the otherlife of things/ before a look/immerses them' (35–44, 42). What these moments share with Burnside's cast of ghosts is that they disrupt epistemological certainty, reveal the provisionality or even the falsity of what we might regard as objective reality, as casually seen, the complacently inhabited. In his musings on spectres, Derrida talks of a ghost as a force which 'secretly unhinges' linear time and so works, in Wylie's words, to 'displace the present from itself' (Wylie 2007: 172). What emerges, Derrida says, is a '*non-contemporaneity with itself of the living present*' (Derrida 1994: xix). Derrida's spectre, claims Colin Davis, opens its percipient up to 'an essential unknowing which underlies and may undermine what we think we know' (Davis 2005: 377). It is a 'deconstructive figure hovering between life and death, presence and absence, and making established certainties vacillate. It does not belong to the order to knowledge' (Davis 2005: 376).

Yet the 'order of knowledge', the settled (if wavering) consensus on the limits of the objectively known, the epistemology of the 'real', is something which John Burnside seeks to question across the breadth of his output. He has argued in several essays that the politics of the 'real' are open to challenge, indeed interrogation. Citing Paul Elulard's remark that 'there is another world, but it is in this one', Burnside says: 'to speak of another world has, historically, been to commit an essentially mystical or religious agenda, and so to a province of wishful thinking normally inhabited by children and the simple-minded, as opposed to the real, factual, less deceived world of grown-ups and rationalists' (Burnside 2005b: 60). Yet, he argues, to seek 'another world' within this one is actually to recalibrate one's attention to the world; it is, in Burnside's words, to seek out

> the missed world and, by extension, the missed self who sees and imagines and is fully alive outside the bounds of socially-engineered expectation

– not by some rational process ... but by a kind of radical illumination, a re-attunement to the continuum of objects and weather and other lives we inhabit'. (Burnside 2005b: 60)

It is, he says, a 'spiritual and political discipline' which opposes the 'self-imposed limitations and inherited fears' of wider society, evading what he calls 'the hydra-headed monsters of entertainment and consumption' (Burnside 2005b: 60).

Burnside's poetics, then, has a deeply political agenda in opposing the very nature of accepted reality as an artifice. 'Our minds are unable to process more than a mere fraction of the data that surrounds us,' claims Burnside, and 'what we see as "reality" is the result of a constant and necessary filtering process.' But, he argues, 'too much of that filter has been constructed for societal reasons ... to constrain our secret selves' (Burnside 2008: 58). What we really fear, Burnside avers, what we really are haunted by, is not the spectral figures of ghosts. What we are terrified of is what lies beneath, and behind, the thin veneer of the filtered experience we grandly term 'reality'. Burnside is fond of evoking an otherworldly void to make his point, often selecting the vision presented by Jean-Paul Sartre in his infamous statement 'nothingness *haunts being*' (my emphasis), which Burnside interprets to signify a moment of insight in which 'we look into nothingness and we see either a personal abyss or a generative source' (2006c: 64). What we call reality can, at certain times, or in certain places, seem like 'an image projected on to a cinema screen', argues Burnside, and the invisible field at our backs is, he says, 'recognised as a void – a nothingness – that is, nevertheless, the actual, or essential reality of the world' (Burnside 2008: 55). What his poetry amounts to is, in his own words, 'a technique for reclaiming the authentic, a method for reinstating the real, a politics of the actual' (Burnside 2006b: 95) which permits acknowledgement of the paucity of human understanding, the ultimate mystery of being in the world, which manifests itself, as Maitreyabandhu has said, in a form of animism, in the sense of 'a kind of imaginative empathy: an unmediated, intuitive resonance' (Maitreyabandhu 2011). The intuitive response to the world is something Burnside advocates as an ethics of what he calls the 'wild mind' (Burnside 2009b). Burnside invites us to entertain that we can experience direct and imminent continuity with the world using our bodily senses, that we can achieve brief moments when the actual and the imagined are blurred into a wider sense of the possibilities of the world: a moment approaching what the Surrealists called '*le hasard objectif*', the 'objective chance', in which one is confronted, often unexpectedly, with an alternative order within, or alongside, the present one, an interruption which creates experiences usually unnoticed in ordinary perception – experiences of liminal states, boundary crossings, which are essentially a confrontation with the self.[1]

So where does this leave us in terms of Burnside's ghosts? The ghosts we find in Burnside's poetry are, I would argue, multivalent entities. They are indeed very much about respecting and acknowledging continuity and fellowship with the past, but they are not ghosts in the sense of figures who have literally returned from the dead. Rather, these ghosts are emblematic of possibility. These are Derridean ghosts for, as Derrida argues, 'the specter is also ... what one imagines, what one thinks one sees and which one projects – on an imaginary screen where there is *nothing* to see' (Derrida 1994: 125, my emphasis). They are means of engaging with the possibilities of the heightened moment, *un autre monde*, the 'nothingness' at our backs, of musing on where we have come from, and where we are going, of arresting linear time in the moment to permit detailed reflection and to enable the potential for creative rupture. For Colin Davis, the Derridean spectre highlights 'an essential unknowing which underlies and may undermine what we think we know' (Davis 2005: 377); more than this, Davis avers, the spectre 'gestures towards a still unformulated future' (Davis 2005: 379). Indeed, if the figure of a ghost represents a confrontation of the self, a spur to look beyond the immediate and complacently given, then they must also represent the possibilities for other selves to come.

It must be acknowledged, however, that even while these spectres may be seen to represent an invitation to a future to come, they have much in common with Derridean spectres in that none of Burnside's poems iterate what kind of a future this might be. While they rise in moments rich in the potential for luminous insight, it is never clear that any such insight is rewarded. Mark Fisher treats spectres as nonexistent actors, understanding them psychoanalytically as persisting 'virtualities': 'reverberant events in the psyche become revenants', he says (Fisher 2014: 19). Fisher follows a distinction made by Martin Hägglund in respect of Derrida's hauntology. Hägglund describes the spectre as an actor which 'has no being in itself but marks a relation to what is *no longer* or *not yet*' (Hägglund, cited in Fisher 2014: 18). This distinction between 'the *no longer* and the *not yet*' (Fisher 2014: 19) complicates a hauntological understanding of Burnside's spectres: they are caught between being visions of a past which has come to an end or stimuli for a confrontation with the possibilities of selfhood in the present: are these moments those of transcendent insight, or does their repetition represent a problematic sense of stasis? Despite Burnside's descriptions of the possibilities of evading contemporary ontological norms, the spectral presences in his verse may not represent any actionable evasion of it. Fisher describes the 'no longer' as that 'which is (in actuality is) *no longer*, but which *remains* effective as a virtuality (the traumatic "compulsion to repeat", a fatal pattern)', while the 'second sense of hauntology', he says, 'refers to that which (in actuality) has *not yet* happened, but which is *already* effective in the virtual (an attractor, an anticipation shaping current behaviour)' (Fisher 2014: 19). Spectres, then, may be repetitions of the past or anticipations of the future. They retain possibility as their central character – but the 'compulsion to repeat' (without forward movement) might also be read in the frequency with which ghosts appear in Burnside's work and in the similarity of various encounters. These spectres are multivalent, then, but they are also ambivalent – vacillating between emblems of continuity and possibility, and that of repetition and infinite delay: they can be read in more than one way to be figures 'on an imaginary screen where there is *nothing* to see' (Derrida 1994: 125).

Future possibilities and confrontation with the self are also surely represented in the figure of the double, or *doppelgänger*, which appears in Burnside's verse almost as often as often as ghosts do. In *The Myth of the Twin* (1994), the opening poem, 'Halloween', has the speaker locate himself in liminal space. He says:

The village is over there, in a pool of bells,
and beyond that nothing,
or only other versions of myself,
familiar and strange, and swaddled in their time
as I am. (1)

In *The Good Neighbour* (2005), the title poem talks of a man who 'watches what I watch, tastes what I taste:/on winter nights, the snow; in summer, sky' (Burnside 2005a: 3). For Dag T. Andersson, such figures exist as 'a reminder of something we should have seen but could not, something which we lost before it could awaken the slightest premonition in us' (Andersson 2000: 35). For sure, these are partial figures, perhaps even more ambiguous than their ghostly counterparts, but they may be read differently to the way in which Andersson sees them: not only representing loss but rather also as the speakers' embodying an intense moment of self-projection: the self othered and observed, as the ghosts earlier observed the living, immersed in their own quotidian and yet with the knowledge of a wider, more inclusive reality enveloping them, a greater range of possibilities. Again, the quotidian is opened up to intuitive scrutiny, and the speaker led to take account of a more rich and less boundaried reality, even if this is confined within a series of potent moments.

In his most recent collection, *Still Life with Feeding Snake* (2017), Burnside brings together the figures of the spectre and the doppelgänger, which coalesce in the figure of a 'lost cosmonaut', which is also an altered embodiment of a sibling who died in infancy. In 1964, cosmic background radiation (residual activity from the earliest point in the creation of the universe) was discovered. This ancient signal is used as a means of considering how conventional scales of time might be confounded – how the past persists in the present – and the ways in which this discovery lends 'the universe/more mystery than anyone imagined?/No limit to the possibilities/or none we could detect?' (Burnside 2017: 27). In 'With the Discovery of Cosmic Background Radiation, My Brother Returns from the Hereafter as a Russian Cosmonaut', the deceased sibling becomes a part of this wondering, beyond the earth and among ancient particles 'floating in space,/in your orange suit' (25). 'Octaves below the frequencies we hear', the speaker muses, 'inferred from microwaves and static' – 'that could be you, or me, or someone else,// the man I might have been, the child he was' (Burnside 2017: 27). There is an elegiac tone, here, an acknowledgement of loss, but also the recognition, fifty years after the discovery, of the ways in which these spectral echoes from the past continue to reverberate in the present. The poem maintains Burnside's long-lived concerns with retaining and negotiating with past events and his insistence on wider senses of what constitutes lived reality.

Despite his emphasis on arresting time into potent moments of singularity, Burnside himself concedes that 'we cannot, in our actual experience, stop time in its tracks. The only way in which this linear flow, through a series of indefinable points, can be evaded … is by artifice: the lyric seems to break time's flow, not by freezing it, as a snapshot does … but by celebrating transience' ('Poetry and a Sense of Place' 1996). In a more recent interview, he has declared that 'poetry's concern is with the present. That is, with eternity – which we experience as the "present moment" … Poetry, for me, is one of the means by which we dispute the imposition of linear time' (McCarthy 2011: 36). The lyric form is the vehicle by which Burnside seeks to anatomize the process of the unfolding moment in which oftentimes the solitary (and unidentified) speaker is, in Burnside's words, 'exposed, aware, at risk, untrammelled,' and able to expose themselves to a range of other conceptions of time: 'the rhythm of the earth … the presence of other animals, the elements, sidereal time' – a list to which one might add that of the spectral other, a rupture which makes time permeable, displacing the present and replacing *chronos* with *kairos* (Burnside 2006b: 101). Even the grammatical constructions Burnside employs to depict the process of this emergent moment confound linear time. Reviewing *The Hunt in the Forest*, David Wheatley picks up perceptively on Burnside's use of tenses, setting many of his poems in 'versions of the past continuous ("It seems they might still be there/if we found the place")' (Wheatley 2009). Cutting across time and notions of experiential 'reality', Burnside's lyrics gesture at the fragility and provisionality of individual experience. Indeed, Scott Brewster (2011) declares that a key feature of the lyric is that it 'stands at a critical crossing-point, poised between security and threat, spontaneity and reiteration, immediacy and posterity' (Brewster 2011: 51).

This is surely a space of haunting. The figure of the spectre is spontaneous but recursive, immediate yet historical, but these are also the features shared by the poetic speakers Burnside uses to populate his verse. Across Burnside's poetic output, we find persistent similarities in situation (a lone speaker), season and the weather (autumn/winter, frost and snow) as well as descriptive motifs which summon the onset of uncertain experience. In 'Deer', the speaker tells us: 'Sometimes I have waited at the edge/of darkness for a glimpse of something wild/and mutable' (Burnside 2002: 10), while in 'Via Negativa' from *The Good Neighbour*, we are confronted with a description of how 'something/opened:/something like a gaze//as if the middle-ground/I could not see/were watching' (Burnside 2005a: 55). In *Gift Songs* (2007), a presence emerges, 'conjured up out of the dark/between the near field and the kitchen door' (Burnside 2007: 60), while in *Black Cat Bone* (2011), the speaker in 'Amnesia' informs us that 'for a while,/at least,/I forget/what I wanted to see/from my kitchen door' (Burnside 2011: 54). These repetitions and similarities are intertextual hauntings, which make being a reader of Burnside an unsettling occupation. One's reading is frequently subject to recalled memory of earlier lyrics, settings and images, where uncanny ruptures appear which contest the linear reading experience and seemingly undermine the cohesion of freestanding poems and sequences because these already contain past presences. Gérard Genette has written of intertextual exchange in terms of 'a relation or copresence between two texts ... eidetically and typically as the actual presence of one text within another' (Genette 1997: 12). Intertextuality is a form of haunting, which reminds us that the singular, the apparently autotelic, text is actually part of a wider and richer realm of cultural codes and intergenerational evolution of ideas, insights and knowledge.

John Burnside's poetry is a lyrical means of attempting to document the unfolding moment, challenging traditional conceptions of one's inhabitation of the present and advocating a more inclusive and less boundaried sense of the individual's relationship to time, to spectres of the past and the future. Derrida reminds us that the spectre must be confronted, 'even if it is in oneself, in the other, in the other in oneself'. He continues: 'they are always *there*, specters, even if they do not exist, even if they are no longer, even if they are not yet' (Derrida 1994: 221). While Burnside's speakers frequently confront specters, however, they are of a characteristically ambiguous sort. They are emblematic of the impulse to capture 'the missed world' and 'the missed self' (Burnside 2005b: 60) that can contribute to a world of greater possibilities. They are simultaneously thematic repetitions across the breadth of Burnside's work – repetitive revenants – and the similarity of scenarios and phraseology that we find across collections also suggests that while moments of *kairos* might be summoned, they cannot be sustained and must therefore be repeated. The ecology of one's belonging to the world must, in Burnside's terms, involve both 'the meagre dead,/touched with the salt of distance' and also 'the still unborn,/the scent of a world to come' (Burnside 2007: 70). His work is haunted by possibilities: entrapped between the *no longer* and the *not yet*.

Chapter Eight: 'A Kindred Shape': Hauntings, Spectres and the Poetics of Return, David Borthwick

Andersson, D. T. (2000), '" ... Only the Other Versions of Myself": Images of the Other in the Poetry of John Burnside,' *Chapman*, 96: 35–9.
Boundas, C. V. (2009), 'Gilles Deleuze and the Problem of Freedom', in E. W. Holland, D. W. Smith, and C. J. Stivale (eds), *Gilles Deleuze: Image and Text*, 221–47, London: Continuum.
Brewster, S. (2011), '*Hern*: The Catastrophe of Lyric in John Burnside,' in A. Karhio, S. Crosson, and C. I. Armstrong (eds), *Crisis and Contemporary Poetry*, 50–8, Basingstoke and New York: Palgrave Macmillan.
Burnside, J. (1994), *The Myth of the Twin*, London: Jonathan Cape.
Burnside, J. (1997), *A Normal Skin*, London: Jonathan Cape.
Burnside, J. (2000), *The Asylum Dance*, London: Jonathan Cape.
Burnside, J. (2002), *The Light Trap*, London: Jonathan Cape.
Burnside, J. (2005a), *The Good Neighbour*, London: Jonathan Cape.
Burnside, J. (2005b), 'Travelling into the Quotidian: Some Notes on Allison Funk's "Heartland" Poems,' *Poetry Review*, 95 (2): 59–70.
Burnside, J. (2006a), *A Lie about My Father*, London: Jonathan Cape.
Burnside, J. (2006b), 'A Science of Belonging: Poetry as Ecology,' in R. Crawford (ed.), *Contemporary Poetry and Contemporary Science*, 91–106, Oxford: Oxford University Press.
Burnside, J. (2006c), 'Mind the Gap: On Reading American Poetry', *Poetry Review*, 96 (3): 56–67.
Burnside, J. (2007), *Gift Songs*, London: Jonathan Cape.
Burnside, J. (2008), '"The Wonder of Daylight": In Search of a Delicate Balance', *Poetry Review*, 98 (1): 52–60.
Burnside, J. (2009a), *The Hunt in the Forest*, London: Jonathan Cape.
Burnside, J. (2009b), 'In Praise of Madness,' *The Sunday Herald*, 7 September. Available online: http://www.sundayherald.com/display.var.2529309.0.0.0.php?utag=26349 (accessed 7 September 2009).
Burnside, J. (2011), *Black Cat Bone*, London: Jonathan Cape.
Burnside, J. (2017), *Still Life with Feeding Snake*, London: Jonathan Cape.
Davis, C. (2005), 'Hauntology, Spectres and Phantoms', *French Studies*, 59 (3): 373–9.
Derrida, J. (1994), *Specters of Marx*, trans. P. Kamuf, London: Routledge.
Finucane, R. C. (1984), *Appearances of the Dead: A Cultural History of Ghosts*, Buffalo, NY: Prometheus Books.
Fisher, M. (2014), *Ghosts of My Life: Writings on Depression, Hauntology and Lost Futures*, Winchester: Zero Books.

Genette, G. (1997), *Palimpsests: Literature in the Second Degree*, trans. C. Newman and C. Doubinsky, Lincoln: University of Nebraska Press.
Hardy, T. (1930), *Collected Poems*, London: Macmillan.
Maitreyabandhu (2011), 'Near-Belonging,' *Agenda*, 45 (4)–46 (1), supplementary essays: http://www.agendapoetry.co.uk/supplements-essays.php (accessed 23 June 2011).
McCarthy, P. (2011), 'Interview: John Burnside', *Agenda*, 45 (4)–46 (1): 22–40.
Private Passions (2008), [Radio programme] BBC Radio 3, 5 October.
Stevenson, R. L. (1998), *The Strange Case of Dr Jekyll and Mr Hyde, and Weir of Hermiston*, ed. E. Letley, Oxford: Oxford World's Classics.
Wheatley, D. (2009), '*The Hunt in the Forest* by John Burnside', *The Guardian*, 5 September. Available online: https://www.theguardian.com/books/2009/sep/05/hunt-forest-burnside-review (accessed 9 November 2018).
Wylie, J. (2007), 'The Spectral Geographies of W.G. Sebald', *Cultural Geographies*, 14 (2): 171–88.

9

'It Was Suddenly Hard Winter': John Burnside's Crossings

Julian Wolfreys

First, an index; or consider this perhaps, a somewhat sketchy and as yet undelineated map, marks for a topography still to be plotted:

To cross out, cross over; to become cross; a cross breed, a cross to bear, a right cross; a mark comprising two intersecting lines, a mark to indicate an incorrect response, a sideways movement or pass; to cross off the list or delete, to draw a line through; two paths cross the field; he attempted to cross the border; at cross purposes; to cross one's fingers, to cross the floor; it crossed my mind; to get one's wires crossed; to get to the crux of the matter; our paths crossed; X marks the spot; crosswords, rather than cross words; to cross swords; a particular point of difficulty (crux; cruces); cross my heart and ... ; to get one's point across. Have I done this?

Second, a quotation:

Not quite autumn, perhaps, but sweet, nevertheless, sweet and soft, almost transparent, like molten butter. Now, as I left, crossing the next field by way of a footpath that skimmed the hedged, plowed space, it was suddenly hard winter. It must have been late afternoon, but the horizon and the spaces between the trees and hedges were already beginning to darken; overhead, the flat, celadon sky was cloudless. I walked on quickly up the long gentle slope of the field that would take me, according to my best guess, to within ten miles of the coast ... The deer bolted, as if they had picked up my mood, or perhaps they had sensed something that I had not, some shadow, some scent, some rumour crossing the field toward them, or toward me, some rushing, predatory thing that, as I turned, seemed almost upon me, a swift, merciless presence sweeping into my face. For a moment I was lost; for a moment, I did what I had always wanted to do: I thought of nothing ... total abandonment. It was the finger of a god scraping the inside of my skull. (Burnside 2007: 200–1)

Have you ever noticed, no, has it ever *crossed* your mind the extent to which, in trying to get something across to you, John Burnside marks his writing with the motions of a cross, of crossings? If you have not, this is probably a tribute to his ability to put something across, under the radar as it were, to smuggle in, through a door, at a window, across a border, or to traverse some ill-defined liminal space between text and reader, in that act of crossing called writing, and with that, its sibling, reading. Burnside comes across as someone who expresses himself directly, without guile, without affectation, in order to get his tale, his images across. It is, though, when you come to realize the extent to which you have become inhabited, that you perceive belatedly how something has crossed the threshold between yourself and the world of John Burnside's writing and settled in as a hitherto unnoticed guest. Burnside crosses over, getting underneath your skin, infiltrating your perceptions, your apprehensions. To begin to read John Burnside – I will not say 'to have read John Burnside', as I do not believe anyone can claim to have read John Burnside, finally, definitively – is to undertake an act of traversal. It is to gather yourself for a passage, in which you are transported across the borders that hedge convention, habit and an everyday perspective on the world, to find yourself having crossed, in a moment and almost imperceptibly, over into a world that, though not dissimilar to your own, nevertheless is transformed. To begin to read John Burnside is to begin to travel, to begin a travail, a work of crossing, to a place where, suddenly, there is 'hard winter' as that beautifully stark line from *The Devil's Footprints* (2007) has it, and this is where you find yourself. Here, Burnside's writing seems to say, is winter. You may look across the border just crossed to see Spring, to see Summer or Autumn, 'soft, almost transparent, like molten butter', but you will find that, having crossed, you will always see the more generous, less austere seasons and their worlds from the side of winter.

To begin to read John Burnside, again and again, I always find that sense of having to cross over, if only so as to realize where I have been all along, and it took Burnside to hold up a mirror, to show me what I have left behind, when looking back through the mirror from its other side. It is not that I am looking in a mirror, though this may be the case of course, for in reading Burnside, I do not see the author but find myself occupying the place of 'I', uncannily; no, it is that a transport has been effected, a boundary stepped beyond. But always a boundary that has to be crossed repeatedly. For having stepped, I find I have not gone anywhere; it is merely – merely! – a matter of perceptions having been 'translated'. So a step, and no step at all.

Let's begin again.

Has it ever crossed your mind how much John Burnside's writing is informed, cross-hatched if you will, with figures of crosses, and crossing, of lines being crossed, and necessarily of borders, boundaries, liminal sites, horizons, apertures, thresholds, frames and so forth? As the good reader will have noticed, turning to traverse once more the passage of the narrating subject in *The Devil's Footprint*, there is no perception, no apperception, no reflection and therefore knowledge of Being-in-the-world without an act of crossing. Or rather, say *acts*: for the subject crosses in more than one fashion in any given moment, experience or event. There are different, and differing, modalities of crossing. There are, and there are given – *il y a, es gibt* – crossings that are physical, phenomenological, geographical, temporal and so forth. At the same time, and yet, within that time a counter-time, disruptive, deconstructive of its condition as the illusion of a continuity.

At the same time, though the act or modality of a crossing in Burnside's writing may be deliberate, chosen, a conscious motion on the part of the subject, as in the passage from *The Devil's Footprint*, crossing brings change. There is no crossing without transformation or 'translation', though what that may be is, perhaps inescapably as part of a very human condition, simply a matter of chance, that which the Greeks call '*Tukhé*': events that happen as a question either of luck or of fate. It is a defining condition of what it means to be human. Whatever befalls us happens because we have engaged in crossing from one place to another, literally or metaphorically, thus:

> Not quite autumn, perhaps, but sweet, nevertheless, sweet and soft, almost transparent, like molten butter. Now, as I left, crossing the next field by way of a footpath that skimmed the hedged, plowed space, it was suddenly hard winter. It must have been late afternoon, but the horizon and the spaces between the trees and hedges were already beginning to darken.

Autumn is almost transparent. Membranous, diaphanous, its qualities are of touch and taste, not sight. In travelling with the narrator, we have already crossed the senses, moving over into another mode of perception. Taken up in a crossing, having crossed over, the reader is caught up in the transformation. This is not all, though, for the narrator moves through physical space even as his perceptions of the world mark and remark the instant of crossing.

He crosses the 'next field', taking a footpath that acts as a passageway and a border, a marker of crossing's passage, which gives access to traversal around, across the 'hedged, plowed space'. And with this, by chance or by fate, 'it was suddenly hard winter'. Temporally there is a crossing here also, for though the narrator knows or feels at least that 'it must have been late afternoon', the spaces 'were already beginning to darken'. The passage continues, a criss-cross of movements, observations and perceptions of movements, in a constant to and fro of physical motion, bodily effort, the material world and the actions of the subject within that, perceptions of the manner of the world's becoming translated within itself and, as a result, the subject's being enfolded within, in close proximity to, the various drifts, fluctuations and activities that surround and define the subject, even as that subject perceives and so defines. The inner and outer, phenomenal and physical worlds are not here adjacent so much as they are coterminous and co-existent. The one is merely the image of the other. As we read we move across inner to outer, outer to inner.

Burnside gives us to realize how the act of narration, and with that the act of reading, enables the very perception of this phenomenological crossing of which I am speaking, a modality that is always already in play, underway, whether or not we realize it. While it may be true that all writing engages us thus, what appears particularly acute in the novelist and poet's writing is the degree to which the traversal and its travail, its labour and translation is as foregrounded as it is restless. An ebb and flow takes place. In taking place, it constructs for the reader the place that one reads, and so gives place to event, action, perception and so forth. This is not merely the formal condition of writing and neither, as Jacques Derrida has it of Plato, is 'this mere play or artifice in the crossed reconciliation [*rapprochement croisé*]' (1972: 145), at least not in the work of John Burnside. It is also to be read as being very much the point, that here is the human condition, into the secret of which he allows us access, opening a door into this condition, if we are careful enough to read in such a way as to be able to cross over ourselves. John Burnside allows us across the border into a perceptive self-awareness of Being, doing so by foregrounding, without the obvious tricks of the so-called 'postmodern' play, the work of writing itself. Burnside's writing does not describe. It is constantly performative. His trace, in tracing the motion of the narrating subject, who, in turn, traces the motion of crossing, enacts the very movements of which it speaks. The reader is already inside the act, even as Burnside's writing acts on us.

But surely, someone will say, as they cut across the path on which I have set myself going, surely such criss-cross, mazy motions are there to be discerned in any act of writing? Why Burnside in particular? Perhaps a small part of an answer is to be found in the following passage from *Glister* (2008):

'The dead fascinated him [Morrison] by the way they lived on, alone in their names, each one separate from the others, and he wanted to erase any trace that he, or his family, might leave in their solitary domain' (14). Morrison is someone who wants, who desires, to cross over, to be 'invisible, he wants, more than anything, to disappear' (9) despite his visibility being a 'function' of his being (9). Defined by the one, he craves the other, longs for the self to become an other and thus to live on, to survive as a mere trace, a writing if you will. Which, of course, is what he does, or rather this is the gift of the text, to write the self as other, thereby giving it its survival. But what makes Morrison interesting, what Burnside gives us to see, is his character's awareness of that which crosses over, that which comes to pass. Survival is in the name. It signals in itself the wholly other, distinct from every other. The trace maintains the other in having survived. Morrison's perception is an apperception of the manner in which one is not simply one side of a divide, awaiting the crossing. The subject crosses and recrosses in the apprehension of the manner of one's own expropriation: 'one expropriates oneself without knowing exactly who is being entrusted with what is left behind' (Derrida 2007: 33). To disappear would mean to abandon the anxiety of one's anticipated expropriation, given realization, appearance in the phenomenon of the proper name, that survival that one can imagine before one has vanished and so begin the process of standing before, without having crossed, the future anterior of a final crossing. The thought crosses Morrison's mind, repeatedly. It is as if he has written the statement, 'I will have survived after I die' (13). In this mode of apperception, Morrison, recollecting a kiss in the graveyard with Gwen, remembers how 'he had hesitated, probably' (13). Note that perfect uncertainty; memory struggles to define and is undercut in its own action: 'That was why he had hesitated, probably' (14). But the passage continues: 'the truth was that, at first, he hadn't wanted to go on, with the dead all around him, watching from their separate resting places across the cemetery' (14). The self is expropriated by the other. Not merely any other, each and every other intimated in the cemetery, their alterity signalled in their 'separate resting places'. Instead, the completely and wholly other. Morrison thus is the place, if you will, on which is inscribed the coming to consciousness of what Jacques Derrida describes as the 'structural' absence of the author (2007: 32), which is 'not contingent upon the actual death of the author'. For the author's 'disappearance or death is implied in the trace whether he or she is already dead or still living' (Brault and Naas 2007: 56).

Whether on the subject of knowing oneself to be haunted by the other, in the structural anticipation and reminder of one's own inescapable absence, an absence which, as I have been exploring at length in a number of places, is also loss – not *a* loss, but loss itself, at the heart of Being, as that which is Being's ownmost alterity – or in the apparently ordinary act of passage – from one field to another, one season to another – there is to be discerned in the text of John Burnside a motion that is also an awareness of what can be determined provisionally under the heading of 'crossing'. As Morrison grasps through his apperception in the singular instances of the 'glister', this inescapable condition of Being, so too does Burnside give us to read the ineluctable condition of becoming that we suffer passively. For we 'become [in the consciousness, in the appearance that crosses our minds], appearing-disappearing, like that uneducable specter who will never have learned how to live. The trace', which Burnside maps, making manifest its work, 'signifies to me at once my death, either to come or already come upon me ... It is impossible to escape this structure, it is the unchanging form of ... life' (2007: 32). As my two examples indicate, there is no one definition for crossing. There are crossings. What they can be discerned as sharing, though, is an irrevocability in a performative consciousness of the act that is, *too*, the act itself. It is the unveiling of a certain 'flaw in the sway of the world', if you will, 'where mastery fails/and a hinge in the mind swings open', as Burnside has it in the poem, 'At My Father's Funeral', first published in the *London Review of Books*:

like that flaw in the sway of the world
where mastery fails
and a hinge in the mind swings open – grief
or terror coming loose
and drifting, like a leaf,
into the flames. (2012: 18)

The writer recognizes how one lives one's 'death in writing' (Derrida 2007: 33), in bearing witness to the acts of crossing and thus the revenance of the other. More than this, though, there is the taking place of a singular event, in this case an apperception of the possibility that something – the other – can always come, can always return crossing over, effecting a crossing. This is perhaps a desire, in the poem in question, but it is more than that. In order for this apperception to take place, the subject has to become open to the other, allowing the other's crossing as a possibility, however impossible. In this, the subject's consciousness assumes a radical reorientation – again an opening, tracked in that moment where 'mastery fails', and 'like that flaw in the sway of the world', there arrives the event of the crossing, as a result of which 'a hinge in the mind swings open'.

This is, I would argue, at once wholly singular – particular to this poem and apprehensible only in the iterable trace of its singularity – and yet, tropically, as if the trope were by analogy available to us in forms and manifestations wholly dissimilar, typical, if not exemplary, of the work of crossing in the text of John

Burnside and what it comes to reveal to the reader, as well as the subject: which is, that there is for the subject in the phenomenological apprehension of the other's arrival that no mastery can dictate, predict, programme or be prepared for, a temporal suspension; the revelation, in short, of an *epoché*. Winter is there, suddenly, the dead are glimpsed indirectly, there – *there* in a space that is other than the space occupied by the subject and yet part of a continuum between the 'in here' of the subject and the 'out there' of the world, speaking phenomenologically – or the dead reveal themselves in the very impossible possibility of their revenance, a return-to-come. In each of the textual extracts considered briefly thus far, an epochal suspension takes place. In that suspension of any normative narrative or subjective temporality, there arrives a transformation of the habitual, or conventional modes of perception and understanding, as the subject, touched by what he comes to apprehend, receives as it were the gift of the other. Thus, Burnside's subjects suffer passively awaiting the arrival of a trace, a difference, a glister if you will. But what marks such moments of unveiling as significant – significant in that in each of these the very condition of one's Being is announced – is that the subject is not only observing, from the outside. The very nature of the epochal experience places the subject at the heart of that experience: I am watching this event; I am of and in the event. The 'I' reveals itself to itself in that suspension. There takes place therefore a generation of perception born out of the suspension of the habitual, as the subject's connection to place generates intuitive associations and responses dictated by the other, glimpsed perhaps through a process of heightened awareness, and with that the crossing over of an enduring language of Being. This in turn comes to appear through writing that excavates, erases, retraces and layers, to make available to the reader the common ground of Being.

What I am calling 'crossing' therefore in John Burnside's text is just this process of phenomenological apprehension embedded in narrative as a 'poetic' (for want of a better word) interruption of conventional and assumed narrative temporalities. Against the mimetic and straightforwardly representational modes of production by which narrative so often functions, even today, there occurs from within, as if surreptitiously yet always in plain sight, what Edmund Husserl describes as a 'first-awakened manner of appearance' that makes possible an '*assimilative apperception*' by which the subject apprehends its corporeality 'in the mode "There"', and thus as an other, as a bodily supplement, an object in and of the 'surrounding world' (1999: 151), analogous and coexisting with the subject. The subject in Burnside always apprehends his Being-there, his Being-in-the-world, this inescapable materiality and temporality because the subject 'crosses' over into that 'first-awakened' apprehension: winter, the dead, the resonance of place, all serve to give to the subject in narrative a suspension from the narrative motion and thus a form of border crossing, if you will, on the part of the subject into the opening of his singular 'sphere of ownness', a 'primordial ownness' as Husserl has it (1999: 151). And it is primordial inasmuch as every revelation, whether in novel or poem, because Burnside presents and enacts the unveiling *as if for a first time every time; as if* every event of consciousness does not merely present but enacts as a performative speech act a phenomenal-originary *epoché*, such is the stark poetic force of the revelation that I read. It is as if there were two John Burnsides at least. There is, on the one hand, John Burnside the novelist. On the other hand, there is John Burnside the poet. And if one hand doesn't know what the other hand is doing, this is because the other hand very much does not wish the one hand to realize what is taking place. For there is the sense that nothing crosses the border quite so much as the poet within the novelist, taking narrative hostage in its poetic arrest, bringing the reader up short, to a halt, in the name of the other.

In order to consider such modes of crossing by which the self is seen, and apprehends himself as inseparable from world, place or other a little further, I wish to turn in a moment and all too briefly to a few fragments from Burnside's poems and the conclusion of *Glister*. For the moment, however, it is necessary to go back over the ground a little. In Burnside's writing, the crossing that takes effect erases the distinction between physical and psychical reality in the epochal disclosure, as the subject finds itself presenting and performing simultaneously a particular orientation – however disorienting to the reader. The orientation assumes the form of a disclosure, which is, at the same time, what Heidegger calls an 'En-owning' of Being. The self 'owns' what is ownmost in its Being, thereby opening itself and projecting its self into the opening, thereby stepping into a space, an opening as clearing within which Being is fully realized and announces itself authentically (Heidegger 1999: 39). At the head of the poem already cited, 'At My Father's Funeral', there is a citation from J. A. MacCulloch's *The Religion of the Ancient Celts*, which recapitulates the idea 'that the body as well as the soul was immortal'. In the desire to prevent the body from returning, there comes to be articulated the strife between self and other. The desire to disown the other – 'and didn't we think, for a moment,/of crushing his feet/so he couldn't return to the house' (2012: 18) – is undone in that instant of imagining the face of the other, standing at the window, 'smoking and peering in, the look on his face'. The look is one of grief 'or terror coming loose/and drifting, like a leaf/into the flames'. I want to ask a deliberately naïve question, in order to promote what might be considered a strong reading of these lines. To whom does the terror belong? Is it merely that of the one who returns or the subject who speaks also? Is the face of the other-to-come an anticipation for the subject of his own terror? Is it an echo already returning as the possibility that the subject must own? Which is to say, is this, the possibility of the face of the other, nothing other than a figure for the primordial opening of Being that crosses from the invisible to the visible, as the echo of Being itself (Heidegger 1999: 75)? And is this not what takes place, to call a halt, and bring us up short, in every act of crossing in the text of John Burnside?

These are, I think, questions of perspective as well as of perception. The perception of the other in the poem requires, for its becoming visible not only that there is the perspective of the speaking subject but that the subject withdraws, becoming invisible in the act of sketching that perspective. In this there is an apparent paradox, as Jean-Luc Marion observes. For, the 'paradox attests to the visible, while at the same time ... it constitutes ... a counter-appearance' (2004: 1), in this case a human face that bears witness for the subject, within the 'structures of the human' (Char 1983: 140). 'What enters [and so crosses over] into visibility', Marion continues, 'is that which one should not have encountered there ... the paradox is born from the intervention of the invisible in the visible, whatever that might be' (2004: 2). This is what we are given to see in the other passages quoted, and elsewhere also, if we pause long enough to adjust our focus. And 'from this arises the necessary effect ..., in thought but also in the sensible: it dazzles, taking the mind by surprise and shocking the gaze ... in such a way that, far from fulfilling or satiating ... its very excess of visibility injures' (Marion 2004: 2). Hence the force of Burnside's writing, its power to make visible, with an excess of bruising visibility, the 'apparently straightforward encounter' revealing, as Paul Batchelor has remarked in a review of *The Hunt in the Forest*, 'unexpected dimensions' that direct 'us away from stock responses' (Batchelor np). Of the poem 'Old Man Swimming' from Burnside's eleventh collection, Batchelor observes how what begins as a 'simple recollection' of a man observed at the swimming pool during childhood shifts suddenly as memory of the other is caused to echo through 'the blue-grey of the park', which brings to mind the swimmer's eye colour. For Batchelor, this grounds the moment while at the same time leaving in place the 'meditative silence that lies behind language; by the structures of our memories; and by colour' (Batchelor np). As elsewhere, something crosses over, and we are 'regularly surprised by moments of intense beauty' (Bracke 2014: 421).

One such moment emerges from the contemplation of a painting that provides the title of the poem, 'Pieter Brueghel: Winter Landscape with Skaters and Bird Trap, 1565' (2011: 59–60). In the poem, Burnside suggests that 'we have to imagine' the everyday world being left behind, in an 'escape from/hardship' for Brueghel's subjects. These subjects retain, however, 'his private hurt, her secret dread'. Admittedly, 'it seems a fable and perhaps it is'. They – these unknown figures behind the representation of whom lies drudgery, unhappiness, abuse, casual moments of domestic violence, the absence of love – are seen in what 'seems a fable and perhaps it is'. Yet for the poet, there is that moment of response to a call, a recognition in the activity of the nameless others, so that their lives and ours echo with a shared sense of Being. We are grounded in recalling ourselves in them. For 'we live in peril, die in happenstance', the ice at once all too real and a powerful trope for all that might, or can, befall us at any moment, such is the precarious condition of Being. Yet from out this, there appears 'still a chance'

> a man might slide towards an old
> belonging, momentarily involved
> in nothing but the present, skating out
> towards a white
> horizon, fair
> and gifted with grace
> to skate forever, slithering as he goes
> but hazarding a guess that someone else
> is close beside him, other to his other. (2011: 60)

So, he skates, and the narrator of *Glister* observes that

> I am stepping forward into this vast, impossibly brilliant light. I step forward with the feeling that I'm going to fall, or be swallowed up, and instead I am standing right in the middle of that unbearable light ... everything I know is gone, and all that remains is ... the slow insistent motion of the waters ... turning on the shore and in my mind. (255)

So, the subject crosses over, stepping out from the invisible to become visible momentarily, only to disappear, to retreat. But the reader is left with this echo, this revelation of Being. For as the 'I' disappears, so the skater skates out of a forever present, into our consciousness, revealing to us ourselves as 'other to his other'.

Chapter Nine: 'It Was Suddenly Hard Winter': John Burnside's Crossings, Julian Wolfreys

Batchelor, P. 'Review of John Burnside, *The Hunt in the Forest*'. Available online: http://paulbatchelor.co.uk/wp-content/uploads/2012/06/burnside.pdf (accessed 21 October 2014).

Bracke, A. (2014), 'Solitaries, Outcasts and Doubles: The Fictional Oeuvre of John Burnside', *English Studies*, 95 (4): 421–40.

Brault, P-A. and M. Naas (2007), 'Translators' Note', in Jacques Derrida (ed.), *Learning to Live Finally: The Last Interview*, trans. P-A. Brault and M. Naas, 55–8, Hoboken, NJ: Melville House Publishing.
Burnside, J. (2007), *The Devil's Footprints*, London: Jonathan Cape.
Burnside, J. (2008), *Glister*, London: Jonathan Cape.
Burnside, J. (2011), *Black Cat Bone*, London: Jonathan Cape.
Burnside, J. (2012), 'At My Father's Funeral', *London Review of Books*, 34 (2), 26 January: 18.
Char, R. (1983), *Oeuvres complètes*, Paris: Gallimard.
Derrida, J. (1972), *La Dissémination*, Paris: Seuil.
Derrida, J. (2007), *Learning to Live Finally: The Last Interview*, trans. P-A. Brault and M. Naas, Hoboken, NJ: Melville House Publishing.
Heidegger, M. (1999), *Contributions to Philosophy (From Enowning)*, trans. P. Emad and K. Maly, Bloomington & Indianapolis, IN: Indiana University Press.
Husserl, E. (1999), *The Essential Husserl: Basic Writings in Transcendental Phenomenology*, ed. D. Welton, Bloomington & Indianapolis, IN: Indiana University Press.
Marion, J-L. (2004), *The Crossing of the Visible*, trans. J. K. A. Smith. Stanford, CA: Stanford University Press.

The Space at the Back of the Mind: An Interview with John Burnside

Ben Davies

The following is an edited version of an interview between the volume editor, Ben Davies, and John Burnside that took place on Tuesday 10th April 2018 in St Andrews, Fife.

BD: I should probably start by saying that I've never interviewed a writer before. In fact, I've always been somewhat sceptical and hesitant about the idea. This largely results from a certain and still somewhat standard critical-theoretical position that one should 'focus on the text itself', given the many problems associated with intentionality, interpretive authority, etc. So, I want to address this directly at the beginning. As this is an interview with a living author…

JB: Well, only just about…

BD: … and, especially, one who's written memoirs, I thought I'd begin by asking if you have any particular thoughts about Roland Barthes' essay 'The Death of the Author' and, correlatively, what you think about the role of the author in today's society.

JB: I haven't read that since god knows how long. I wasn't particularly interested by it. I don't think much about authors, so I wouldn't say

I think of myself through that frame. As far as being an author goes, it's very easy to see that there are, at any one time in the public eye, people who *are* authors, who fit the bill somehow. But there are also wonderful writers who don't become authors in that way because of some kind of public perception and don't think of themselves as authors. I don't think anybody thinks of themselves as an author. Well, maybe some very popular writers do, or you might say, 'I'm a children's author'. But I think there's a huge difference between saying 'author' and 'writer'. If you become an author, you can go on TV and talk about whatever you like; you don't have to do a day job in some cases. That's what being an author is. Maybe that's what Barthes meant by 'the death of the author', the death of a certain kind of writer-like figure. If so, I get that. I think there's a space in our lives for both those kinds of writing. I would rather be a writer than an author, because I think a writer can walk down the street in even the most literary town and be ignored.

BD: This discussion concerning writers and authors also relates to your role as a judge, previously for both the Booker Prize and the Forward Prize. With that in mind, then, how does passing judgement on others' work sit with you as a judge who is also a writer?

JB: It's horrible. I mean, it was lovely, and my fellow judges were just lovely people. But towards the end, when you're whittling it down to the last one, I just suddenly felt a kind of grief for a book. There was one book in particular where I thought, it's got flaws and I understand that, but this has got something else, a quality about it that dismisses all the other things you can say about it. It had a heart, basically. It's hard to say that when you're discussing it with somebody, because people will say to you, 'Oh look at the mess of this page' or 'Look at the dialogue here'. A lot of books just felt like people knew exactly what to do, which is different from having a heart. I believe that two or three of my books actually have heart. I think *Glister* is a good book. As an environmentalist's book, as an ecocritical book, I thought *Glister* was worth something. When one prize was being judged, I remember somebody had put up a big fight, somebody I respected, for that book. And I thought knowing that is better than a lot of things. If it were just for the kudos, I just wouldn't care, and I don't really care that much about money. But money buys you time to do the next book properly. If I look back, I'd say the one disappointment I have is that I've never written a book properly. I've always written a book in coffee breaks, in little short residencies, trying to pull things together. One book [*Waking up in Toytown*] I pulled together in a six-week residency. It was the place where they have the Malt Whisky Writers' Retreat on the Isle of Jura. This was the intense kind of hot housing thing. Yet, strangely enough, during the days when I was writing, I did all of the things that I don't do here, like go for long walks. And I realized how much I compose in my head while walking, even prose. I thought it was just poetry, but a lot of things come out of walking, for prose as well.

BD: Interestingly, this relates to another question I want to ask. In *A Lie about My Father*, you briefly write about 'somewhere, at the back of my mind, where stories unfold according to their own logic'. Now, this may be an impossible question to answer, but what is that space or place of creation? How would you describe it?

JB: It's not entirely internal. I say 'the back of my mind' because I don't like terms like 'subconscious' or 'unconscious'. I think what's in the subconscious mostly stays there. Whereas, at the back of your mind, you've got a big pool and you drop lines down into it and then fish things out of the subconscious. You've also got a kind of big headland or something behind the back of your head, which goes out the back of your head, and into the world, and so forth, and into memory, and history, into the woods, in a sense. And that's your own private wilderness, your own private territory. I think we all have it, different kinds. Mine seems to have quite a lot of different features that don't go together, and it seems to have a harbour, but not a fishing harbour anymore. It's like an old harbour that's no longer fishing. Mostly deserted, except for birds. But at the same time, it's got deep forests. I think forests and orchards are the things that matter most, and meadows. If you could map that back of your mind space ... it isn't just my head, as it were, it's whatever that drops back into, in terms of folk memory, or members of a tribe ... I think there are lots of orchards and forests, deep dark forests, and lots of fairy tale creatures. I'm sure Marina Warner would have fun there, put it that way, with that kind of landscape.

BD: Do you see writing as a sort of externalization of what's going on in there, to put it rather simplistically?

JB: Yes, simplistically, though I always back off when things start to sound deliberate, because the one thing I don't know is how to write deliberately. There's a book of unknown fairy tales that belongs to everybody, everyone's got their own, and I actually write mine; I bring them out. One is drawing upon all kinds of things. There's family history, which is probably the dominant thing in terms of characters, rather than one's self, as it were. But for me, the land itself is most of it. I feel as though if there were one poet that I had a kind of kinship with, on a personal level, it would be Dylan Thomas, for the sense of a kind of hinterland, of land itself. My mythology is a land. Intellectually, I'd probably feel much more in the realms of Marianne Moore. But at a kind of gut level, even though sometimes I can't stand Dylan Thomas, I feel in that way. Maybe W. S. Graham sometimes, as well. But Dylan Thomas is the one who has that landscape. It's different from my landscape in some ways. I guess his is more oak wood and mossy than mine. But in general, there's a feeling of the land, a sense of the land. But the sense of the land isn't from a person who lives on, or who lived on, the land. I kind of live in the land, but not on it. I'm a bit escaped into it. Like Dylan Thomas – I'm not looking for other comparisons – there's that sense that you run to the end of the street and then you're in a different world. I think, maybe, when a poem comes, it's a bit like running to the end of the street and getting to that different world.

BD: The other question, which has been in the background since the discussion about authors and writers, concerns form and genre, because you are somebody who's critically acclaimed for your poetry, novels and memoirs. Do you see everything as simply writing, 'mass writing', or do you see the genres separately?

JB: The end result is different, but I think they mostly depart from the same station. Sometimes they come out as a train, sometimes as a tram, or whatever. Of course, form is the guiding principle. Once the ideas begin to form, the idea … well that's not the right word, but that sort of thing, the flesh of the thing, demands a certain form. But the source of it all is the same source.

BD: So, the idea leads to the form, the form to the idea, both together?

JB: It's strangely simultaneous, yes. It's like when a new cell comes into being, and it knows what it wants to do, building new cells. But, I think genuinely there's no way of pre … I mean, if somebody gave me a commission to write a poem, and I've got an idea for a story and I shoehorn the story into the poem, it wouldn't work. I can imagine some poets or story writers doing that. But I think one of the things that we're losing is a critical culture that dares to say something isn't as good as everyone's saying it is when something is hyped. At the same time, it doesn't make enough fuss about things that are good and get overlooked. That's what critical culture should be like; people should bring their passions to the table and say, 'No!'

BD: Yes, which brings up the idea of success and failure, something else I want to ask about, because you've said that the three novels after *The Dumb House* were all unsuccessful.

JB: Well, they were.

BD: I think you use the word 'failure' at one point.

JB: They're all failures.

BD: What does it mean, then, for a text to fail?

JB: A text is only as good as you can make it, under the circumstances in which you make it. With every book I've ever conceived of, as a book, or a short story, or a poem sequence, there's a certain amount of conceiving that goes on, whereas most poems, themselves, are just intuitive things that, having it on the page, you think, 'I know what this is about'. But when you start making a sequence, a novel, a memoir, you're conceiving of something that's greater than the sum of those parts. There's no doubt that that original image that you had in your head is not matched by the thing that gets put on the paper at the end. So, it's a sense of partial failure, at least, if not complete failure. Obviously, one doesn't publish some things … there's just too much failure in them.

BD: You also talk about this a little in the Henry Miller book; the preface begins with a sense of unease.

JB: Yes, and the first version of that really was dreadful. I felt under time pressure, and so I was pushing away and going forward, and I felt that unease while I was doing it. Then I stopped. I literally was almost at the end, and I was reading it through and I thought, 'This is really terrible.' I kept bits of it in terms of the research, but everything had to be rewritten. Even then, because I was still under pressure, it wasn't the kind of book that Henry Miller would have written in the same circumstances, and that's what I really wanted, I suppose, in a way.

BD: It sounds as if you saw it as a type of creative rewriting or as a form of translation in some ways, which is something else I wanted to discuss, given the number of your works that have been translated into numerous languages. For instance, does the foreknowledge of translation have any conscious effect on your writing?

JB: No, but one is grateful to have translators like Bernhard Robben and Catherine Richard. Catherine is working on *Ashland & Vine*, and she dropped me a note recently because my main character in *Ashland & Vine* is called Jean Culver. And when she would say it in French, that doesn't work! I just didn't think of that. A forward-thinking author would say, I can't call her that because when it comes to being published in France, it'll sound rude! So, no, it doesn't really affect it. But it is nice; it's especially lovely with Catherine because I can read French fluently. I can also see how well Bernhard translates. He's a very, very fine poet himself. To be translated by someone like him is just ... it's going to be good.

BD: Yes, there's an additional poetic element to it.

JB: Yes. In fact, my most recent book of poems in English was published in Argentina in facing translation. I met a young Argentinean poet, Daniel Lipara, who's very good, and he asked if he could translate some of my poems. In the end, I told him that I had a bunch of poems I was working on and that we should just do this new stuff instead. He's translated it, and it's come out in Spanish, *Aprender a Dormir*. They were having a launch, but I couldn't go, so I sent a message, and I asked them to register my opposition to what the government was doing.

BD: Which brings us on to politics and the political. You've got a talk coming up on poetry and politics, in which you discuss Auden's infamous line 'For poetry makes nothing happen'. As a poet, a writer, what do you think about this line and poetry's relationship with and to politics more generally?

JB: You have to read the poem carefully. Somebody who wrote as many poems as Auden must have felt that poetry did something. If you read the whole passage carefully, you understand what he's saying, that poetry, the essence, isn't about making something happen. The essence is about how 'it survives/In the valley of its making'. My argument is with the idea that people pick it up and say that even

Auden says poetry makes nothing happen. Of course poetry makes things happen. It's hard for someone in the English-speaking world to make any big claim, though, about what poetry does because so few people read it. A lot of people write it, but so few read it. In truth, I think that poetry doesn't do anything in the time of its own life. But it helps shape the thinking and the language and the way language is used for the next generation, or several generations, to come. Eugenio Montale, of course, realized that a certain kind of simplicity is not far from being in the service of fascism, and capitalism uses certain kinds of poetry, too. But I think poetry, a poem like A. R. Ammons' 'Corsons Inlet', little did we know it, perhaps, shapes the way in which the few who read that poem, in its day, think about things. Then they're starting to write or think about other things, informed by that. We're not the 'unacknowledged legislators of the world'. We're definitely unacknowledged, and we're not legislators! But I think in an ideal world, the poet and the scientist would stand side by side and explore the world. Not real scientists, but the scientific establishment has said, 'We don't want that; that's subjective, but this is quantifiable; this can be demonstrated'. But all the things I prize in life are neither quantifiable nor demonstrable. In fact, most of them are invisible, and, as Marianne Moore says, 'The power of the visible/is the invisible.' But the invisible you can't measure. And poets, anyone using the imagination, do that other part of it as part of their enquiry into the world. It would seem that right now, at least, we have to put those two people together, to use all our faculties. Coleridge wouldn't have thought like that. He'd be using all his faculties as one individual. Goethe certainly would have done so. In the spat between the followers of Goethe and the followers of Newton about the mathematics of the optics, Newton was right but the wrong guy won. A Goethean world view is messier, less precise in mathematical terms, non-quantifiable, in all kinds of ways that make scientists uncomfortable. But that's part of our experience, and maybe the best part of our experience. I like the messy bits, so, poetry for me – poetry's a shorthand for the arts, all our cultural activities, or *poiesis*, a use of the imagination to make something – is an essential human activity, which has been shut down. Not by scientists themselves, but by a ... I'm sorry to use the term ... 'capitalist-consumer society' that sees an advantage in elevating objectivity and science over this other kind of stuff. Because if we were all using our imaginations, as poets, or as artists, we wouldn't feel any urgency about going out and buying the latest Samsung, or whatever. We would be looking at some old Japanese bowl, or something, like the Japanese Samurai did.

BD: In 'Poetically Man Dwells', Heidegger says we have a 'curious excess of frantic measuring and calculating', and that was in the 1950s.

JB: Heidegger understood; he was very prescient. We're slaves to those machines. I don't mind if people have those devices if, when they're walking, they're listening to the birds singing, or at least watching where they're going, that they're open to the world around them. I feel as though people are being deprived ... due to deliberate policy. The more docile we are, the more we vote for these assholes who run for office. Imagine if we got ourselves together and said, 'Hang on a minute; these guys are all liars; let's not vote for anybody', like in Saramago's *Seeing*. That invalidates the whole thing. People would say, 'Oh that'll lead to chaos.' Well, look where we're heading right now.

BD: Yes. You often talk about chaos and the irrationality of things on *the other side*, as it were...

JB: Yes, I mean it from the other side, very much. Chaos is not disorder for me. No thinking person equates chaos with disorder these days, not after someone like Feynman. But there is disorder, and there's a threat. Right now, there's a threat of horrifying disorder. It's actually breathtaking. Sometimes I stop in the middle of the day and think that the people who are in charge right now could bring us to a world war, possibly a nuclear war. We need incredibly astute people. I find it scary right now.

BD: 'Right now' brings us, perhaps, towards the end, to a juncture, which is something I wish to explore, as the idea and metaphor of juncture resonate in both *Havergey* and the Henry Miller book. In the Henry Miller book, you discuss writing about him out of a sense of need. You say you are 'at a particular juncture of my own life'. What does this juncture mean for your writing life?

JB: Well, actually that juncture is historical in a sense. Ben Tate came to see me from Princeton University Press and asked who I would want to write about and I opened my mouth and ... I was going to say Marianne Moore ... but said Henry Miller. Well, how does that work, what happened there? But I was thinking about my own life in a rather painful way, I suppose. I wasn't well; I was physically under par. I felt like I was in a kind of rut. It was health; it was a sense of purpose, a sense of direction. I was also kind of critically aware that people still see me, when they think of me at all, as a poet, which is a bit upsetting in itself, since I've written so much prose.

BD: I tend to think of you as a novelist, a prose writer, first.

JB: That's interesting. Well, most people introduce me something like, 'Here's poet John Burnside.' Anyway, the state of poetry in this country had gotten really depressing for me. I was looking around, even in America, and I was seeing all this gimmick poetry and this identity poetry. Some of it is interesting; some of it's not. One thing that is going on now amongst the more interesting poets is a redefinition in relation to tradition, not so much Eliot as maybe Montale in its spirit. We all work in a tradition, but some work within a tradition – and language – that seems to belong to the enemy, to the bosses and the oppressors. As a working-class poet, one feels that in real ways, but imagine how much worse it is for a Black American, or a 'Native American', in other words, 'Indian' poet. Terrance Hayes, for instance, has a beautiful poem, 'Snow for Wallace Stevens', and he has this wonderful notion, which I really love, 'love without forgiveness'. Wallace Stevens was a casual racist, and he made little attempt to conceal it, so there's no point in pretending otherwise. And Hayes writes this poem about him. It's the response of a younger, black poet, who's writing in a specific tradition, knowing that he loves this tradition, loves this language, but has to deal with the ways they abused people like him historically, from casual daily insult to lynching. At the same time, Joy Harjo and Gloria Bird, in a great book called *Reinventing the Enemy's Language* about being Native American women writing in English, have shown how writing by 'minorities' can subvert and enrich and renew language and tradition in surprising ways.

BD: In terms of this juncture, then, do you see a change in your own writing coming about?

JB: Yes, I wanted to do more that was more engaged. I'm not sure if I've started yet. The Miller book and *Havergey* were both attempts to write about anarchist thought ... Actually, I was planning another book called *How to Be an Anarchist* [in place of *Havergey*], which my Cape editor wouldn't do, not with that title. But I suddenly went back and thought I'd turn the whole anarchist thing around because people like me are always considered to be radical because we say we're interested in anarchist stuff. But I deeply prize order; I love order,

order that's based on something real like the natural world. Or things that we intuit, or that we can feel at a gut level. I remember coming to England from Scotland and … one isn't allowed to say this … loving England and also admiring Englishness. I loved this; I loved this sense of English fair play. Winning wasn't the most important thing, playing right was the most important thing … Don't tell anybody in Scotland this.

BD: No. Maybe that's a good place to finish, then, for now at least?

JB: Yes, probably.

Notes

Introduction

1. In his interview with Crown, Burnside offers a different spatial metaphor, telling her: 'I imagine the mind as a big house. You've got the parlour where you sit and have tea, your bedroom, your kitchen, your bathroom. But actually there are endless rooms around you that you don't use, and there's one room way at the back – the furnace room, maybe – where your thoughts begin. Sometimes they walk all the way up to the parlour to find you before you even realised they were coming. That's how it feels for me. I think good ideas work like that' (2011: para. 15).
2. Some of the essays in the special issue of *Agenda* (2011) on Burnside do refer to his prose writings, but the focus is, understandably, very much on his poetry.

Chapter 1

1. Burnside worked for several years as a computer software engineer before becoming a freelance writer.
2. In interview, Burnside, who also worked for a time as a moth-study volunteer, has said: 'I was hugely aware of the Mothman Prophecies when I wrote the book' (Clay 2015).
3. A popular religion founded on the teachings of the third-century Mani, Manichaeism taught an elaborate dualistic cosmology describing the struggle between a good, spiritual world of light and an evil, material world of darkness.

Chapter 2

1. Marjorie Perloff writes that this notoriously over-quoted line from Wittgenstein 'is … the commonsense recognition that there are metaphysical and ethical aporias that no discussion, explication, rationale, or well-constructed argument can fully rationalize' (1996: 12).

2   Jakobson collects six functions of language, ranging from the 'phatic' of everyday communication to the 'poetic', by which he refers to the heightened, stylistically dense language of literature (see Jakobson 1960: 350–77).

3   In *Ghosts in the Middle Ages: The Living and the Dead in Medieval Society* (1998), Jean-Claude Schmitt writes: 'The almost complete absence of ghosts in the Bible must ... have aided the desire of the Christian culture to reject the notion of ghosts' (Schmitt 1998: 14). Schmitt also notes, via Augustine, that ghosts were treated with scepticism by Christianity because of their association with demons (17).

Chapter 3

1   The same words are employed in the introduction to *Wild Reckoning* (2004). I am suspending the concept of 'nature' through the use of quotation marks in order to signal a necessary awareness that 'the natural' itself is a concept of human thought. It is therefore problematic in any unreflective assumption of a distinct separation between 'natural' and 'built' environments or other binaries in which 'natural' is one half. To speak of the 'natural' is to re-enter the Romantic epoch and ignore the modernity of Burnside's thought.

2   In 'A Science of Belonging: Poetry as Ecology' (2006), Burnside underlines the fact that 'what we know of life' is limited to phenomenal things and that 'we need to remember above and beyond all our other concerns ... that this is the real world, this is our enduring mystery' (107).

3   Merleau-Ponty's *il y a* (*there is*) is his translation of the Heideggerian *es gibt*, which is related for Heidegger to *Dasein* (see Philipse 1998).

4   'I say: a flower! And, beyond the oblivion to which my voice banished no contour, as something other than the familiar calyces, arises musically the fragrant idea itself, the absent flower of all bouquets' (Mallarmé 2006: xvii).

5   *Umwelt* is a concept employed by Jakob von Uexküll to denote an organism's individual manner of experiencing the world depending on their perceptual faculties. The term was later used by Heidegger and Merleau-Ponty, among others.

Chapter 5

1   Burnside writes for *The Guardian* and *The New Statesman*, in which he contributes a regular column on environmental and political as well as literary and cultural topics.

2   Burnside's interviews often offer social and political critiques (see, for example, McDowell 2003) explicitly addressing the themes of his fictional and autobiographical writing (Borthwick 2009).

3   Bracke notes that *A Summer of Drowning* is indicative of a 'subtle shift' in Burnside's fiction away from his historical focus on dysfunctional and violent masculinity and that the move to a female narrator is only one symptom of this (2014: 422).
4   Working-class psycho-biography is a fascinating but fairly sparse field; writer and historian Carolyn Steedman (2002) has written eloquently about the life and damaged relationships of her own working-class single mother.

Chapter 6

1   The first three stanzas of Stevens's poem reside as the epigraph to *The Light Trap*.
2   Although aimed against Fascism and anchored in terms of anti-foundational human freedom, Benjamin's thesis takes on morality located in the realm of action ('Fate and Character', 1919) and the politics of destruction ('The Critique of Violence', 1927).
3   Burnside draws from Benjamin's penultimate sentence in 'On Language as Such and on the Language of Man' (1916) and places it as epigraph to his poem on world language, or earth song, 'On Kvaloya': 'The language of nature is to be compared to a secret password, which passes on each post the next in its own language, contents of the password' (Benjamin 1996: 74).
4   Reported extinct by the Associated Press in September 2000, having not been sighted since 1978. Elven thousand and forty-six species were listed as threatened with extinction in the International Union for Conservation and Natural Resources (IUCN 2000) report; this rose to 16,118 in 2006 and stands at more than 23,000 today. W. Scott McGraw contests the extinction of Red Colobus.
5   Burnside has indicated that this is driven by the *Tao Te Ching*, the 'one significant factor in how [he] approach[es his] work' (2002b: 12).
6   For Blair and others in her co-edited collection (2015), it is clear that pastoral literature exerts itself as an intellectual space partly conditioned by a dialogic relationship with other genres; however, contemporary pastoral offers an altogether darker mode of consciousness, imbuing character and scene with a particular politics of dispossession, waste and suffering.

Chapter 7

1   The interweaving of creativity, ecology and politics has been a staple of Burnside's mediations on the nature of his craft across the breadth of his career (see, for example, Burnside 2000: 259; 2006: 99).
2   Other novels Macdonald includes in this cluster are Alasdair Gray's *Lanark* (1981), James Kelman's *How Late It Was, How Late* (1994) and *Translated Accounts* (2001), John Burnside's *Living Nowhere* (2003) and *Glister* (2008),

as well as particular narrative strands within works by Irvine Welsh, A. L. Kennedy, Alan Warner, Ian Banks and Ken MacLeod (Macdonald 2012: 227).

3. Broadly comparable condemnations of environmental incrementalist have become increasingly prevalent, from a range of theoretical perspectives. As well as Guattari's work, more recent articulations include Slavoj Žižek's *Living in the End Times* (2010) and Antonio Negri and Michael Hardt's *Commonwealth* (2009).

4. For Deleuze and Guattari, a rhizome is a non-hierarchical arrangement of material within which lines of confluence can be drawn between any two given points in a particular set or plane of consistency – a means of ordering that stands in opposition to linear, arboreal understandings, which are arranged and presented according to a given hierarchical rationale (see Deleuze and Guattari 2004: 3–28).

Chapter 8

1. 'Hasard objectif', which can be translated as 'objective chance encounters', is a theory outlined by André Breton in his novel *Nadja* (1928). Constantin V. Boundas describes a playfulness advocated by the Surrealists in seeking coincidences and chance encounters as 'an attractive alternative to the suffocating sedimentations of common and good sense' (2009: 241).

Further Reading

Works by John Burnside

Novels

(1997), *The Dumb House: A Chamber Novel*, London: Jonathan Cape.
(1999), *The Mercy Boys*, London: Jonathan Cape.
(2001), *The Locust Room*, London: Jonathan Cape.
(2003), *Living Nowhere*, London: Jonathan Cape.
(2007), *The Devil's Footprints: A Romance*, London: Jonathan Cape.
(2008), *Glister*, London: Jonathan Cape.
(2011), *A Summer of Drowning*, London: Jonathan Cape.
(2017), *Ashland & Vine*, London: Jonathan Cape.
(2017), *Havergey*, Dorchester: Little Toller.

Short Story Collections

(2000), *Burning Elvis*, London: Jonathan Cape.
(2013), *Something Like Happy*, London: Jonathan Cape.

Memoirs/Life Writing

(2006), *A Lie about My Father*, London: Jonathan Cape.
(2010), *Waking up in Toytown*, London: Jonathan Cape.
(2014), *I Put a Spell on You: Several Digressions on Love and Glamour*, London: Jonathan Cape.

Poetry

(1988), *The Hoop*, Manchester: Carcanet.
(1991), *Common Knowledge*, London: Secker & Warburg.
(1992), *Feast Days*, London: Secker & Warburg.
(1994), *The Myth of the Twin*, London: Jonathan Cape.
(1995), *Swimming in the Flood*, London: Jonathan Cape.
(1997), *A Normal Skin*, London: Jonathan Cape.
(2000), *The Asylum Dance*, London: Jonathan Cape.
(2002), *The Light Trap*, London: Jonathan Cape.

(2005), *The Good Neighbour*, London: Jonathan Cape.
(2006), *Selected Poems*, London: Jonathan Cape.
(2007), *Gift Songs*, London: Jonathan Cape.
(2009), *The Hunt in the Forest*, London: Jonathan Cape.
(2011), *Black Cat Bone*, London: Jonathan Cape.
(2011), with Andy Brown, *Goose Music*, Cromer: Salt.
(2014), *All One Breath*, London: Jonathan Cape.
(2014), with Will Maclean (images), *A Catechism of the Laws of the Storms*, London: Art First.
(2017), *Still Life with Feeding Snake*, London: Jonathan Cape.

Plays/Film/TV

(2001), with A. L. Kennedy, *Dice*, Canada: Cité Amérique.

Critical Monographs

(2018), *On Henry Miller: Or, How to Be an Anarchist*, Princeton and Oxford: Princeton University Press.
(2019), *The Music of Time: Poetry in the Twentieth Century*, London: Profile.

Editing

(2000), *Love for Love: An Anthology of Love Poems*, J. Burnside and A. Finlay (eds), Edinburgh: Polygon and Morning Star.
(2004), *Wild Reckoning: An Anthology Provoked by Rachel Carson's Silent Spring*, J. Burnside and M. Riordan (eds), London: Calouste Gulbenkian Foundation.
(2008), *Wallace Stevens: Poems Selected by John Burnside*, J. Burnside (ed.), London: Faber and Faber.

Selected Contributions

(2009), 'Mither Tongue', *New Poems Chiefly in the Scottish Dialect*, R. Crawford (ed.), Edinburgh: Polygon.
(2016), 'Sons and Mothers', *Treasure Palaces: Great Writers Visit Great Museums*, M. Fergusson (ed.), London: Profile.

Selected Introductions and Forewords

(1999), *The Sea, The Sea*, by Iris Murdoch, London: Vintage.
(2006), *Betrayal*, by Marquis de Sade, London: Hesperus Press.
(2008), *Lady into Fox*, by David Garnett, London: Hesperus Press.
(2009), *From Unknown to Unknown: An Anthology of Poetry by Manual Rivas*, Sofia: Small Stations Press.
(2015), *Waterland*, by Graham Swift, London: Picador.

FURTHER READING

Selected Essays, Journalism, Other Writing and Radio

(1998), 'Poetry and a Sense of Place', *Nordlit*, 1 (1): 201–22.
(2000), 'Strong Words', in W. N. Herbert and M. Hollis (eds), *Strong Words: Modern Poets on Modern Poetry*, 259–61, Tarset: Bloodaxe.
(2001), 'Bunkered by Mr Big', *The Guardian*, 28 July. Available online: https://www.theguardian.com/education/2001/jul/28/highereducation.news1
(2002), 'Reluctant Crusader', *The Guardian*, 18 May. Available online: https://www.theguardian.com/environment/2002/may/18/climatechange.physicalsciences
(2003), *Otro Mundo Es Posible: Poetry, Dissidence and Reality TV*, Edinburgh: Scottish Book Trust, Dundee Contemporary Arts and the Scottish Poetry Library.
(2003), 'Standards of Belief', *The Guardian*, 25 January. Available online: https://www.theguardian.com/books/2003/jan/25/politics
(2004), and M. Riordan, 'Introduction', in J. Burnside and M. Riordan (eds), *Wild Reckoning: An Anthology Provoked by Rachel Carson's Silent Spring*, 13–21, London: Calouste Gulbenkian Foundation.
(2005), 'The Modern Master', *The Guardian*, 6 April. Available online: https://www.theguardian.com/books/2005/apr/06/fiction.saulbellow1
(2005), 'Travelling into the Quotidian: Some Notes on Allison Funk's "Heartland" Poems', *Poetry Review*, 95 (2): 59–70.
(2006), 'A Different Kind of Truth', *The Guardian*, 28 September. Available online: https://www.theguardian.com/commentisfree/2006/sep/28/comment.bookscomment
(2006), 'Mind the Gap: On Reading American Poetry', *Poetry Review*, 96 (3): 56–67.
(2006), 'A Science of Belonging: Poetry as Ecology', in R. Crawford (ed.), *Contemporary Poetry and Contemporary Science*, 91–106, Oxford: Oxford University Press.
(2006), 'A Swansong for Cellardyke', *The Guardian*, 15 April. Available online: https://www.theguardian.com/books/2006/apr/15/featuresreviews.guardianreview1
(2008), 'Adrian Mitchell – A Poet Who Made Things Happen', *The Guardian*, 23 December. Available online: https://www.theguardian.com/books/booksblog/2008/dec/23/adrian-mitchell-john-burnside
(2008), '"The Wonder of Daylight": In Search of a Delicate Balance', *Poetry Review*, 98 (1): 52–60.
(2009), 'Ghosts of Subarctic Norway', *The Guardian*, 31 October. Available online: https://www.theguardian.com/travel/2009/oct/31/norway-subarctic-beach-tromso-andenes
(2011), 'Walk the Tightrope', *New Humanist*, 7 December. Available online: http://newhumanist.org.uk/2701/walk-the-tightrope
(2012), 'Alone', *London Review of Books*, 34 (3), 9 February. Available online: https://www.lrb.co.uk/v34/n03/john-burnside/alone
(2012), 'How Poetry Can Change Lives', *The Telegraph*, 17 January. Available online: https://www.telegraph.co.uk/culture/books/poetryandplaybookreviews/9020436/How-poetry-can-change-lives.html
(2012), 'The Hyena Is My Favourite – My Totem – Animal', *The Guardian*, 20 January. Available online: https://www.theguardian.com/books/2012/jan/20/author-author-john-burnside

(2012), 'The Visitor', *Aeon*, 19 October. Available online: https://aeon.co/essays/the-allure-and-danger-of-the-solitary-life
(2013), 'A Winter Mind', *London Review of Books*, 35 (8), 25 April. Available online: https://www.lrb.co.uk/v35/n08/john-burnside/a-winter-mind
(2014), 'Diary', *London Review of Books*, 36 (24), 18 December. Available online: https://www.lrb.co.uk/v36/n24/john-burnside/diary
Burnside, J. et al. (2014), 'Scottish Writers on the Referendum – Independence Day?', *The Guardian*, 19 July. Available online: https://www.theguardian.com/books/2014/jul/19/scottish-referendum-independence-uk-how-writers-vote
(2015), 'Dreamscapes: Imagining the Perfect Scottish Town', *The Herald*, 31 May. Available online: http://www.heraldscotland.com/opinion/13217829.Essay_of_the_week__Dreamscapes__imagining_the_perfect_Scottish_town/
(2015), 'John Clare and the New Varieties of Enclosure: A Polemic', in S. Kövesi and S. McEathron (eds), *New Essays on John Clare: Poetry, Culture and Community*, 79–96, Cambridge: Cambridge University Press.
(2017), 'My Working Day: "Writing Is What I Steal from the Usual Flow of Things"', *The Guardian*, 4 February: 4. Available online: https://www.theguardian.com/books/2017/feb/04/john-burnside-writing-day-ashland-and-vine
(2017), '"Soliloquies of Suffering and Consolation": Fiction as Elegy and Refusal', *Journal of the British Academy*, 5. Available online: https://doi.org/10.5871/jba/005.251
(2018), 'Diary', *London Review of Books*, 40 (18), 27 September: 42–3. Available online: https://www.lrb.co.uk/v40/n18/john-burnside/diary
(2018), 'He Was a True Wildcat', *The New Statesman*, 147 (5427), 13–19 July: 57.
(2018), 'Nixon Helped Save the Bald Eagle – But What Will Trump Do for America's Patriotic Emblem?', *The New Statesman*, 147 (5432), 17–23 August: 57.
(2018), 'Samiland: The Finnmarksvidda', in M. Smalley (ed.), *Cornerstones: Subterranean Writings – From Dartmoor to the Arctic Circle*, 22–8, Toller Fratrum: Little Toller Books.

Critical Material

Book Chapters

Borthwick, D. (2009), 'The Sustainable Male: Masculine Ecology in the Poetry of John Burnside', in H. Ellis and J. Meyer (eds), *Masculinity and the Other: Historical Perspectives*, 63–85, Newcastle: Cambridge Scholars Publishing.
Brewster, S. (2006), 'Beating, Retreating: Violence and Withdrawal in Iain Banks and John Burnside', in J. McGonigal and K. Stirling (eds), *Ethically Speaking: Voice and Values in Modern Scottish Writing*, 179–98, Amsterdam: Rodopi.
Brewster, S. (2011), '*Hern*: The Catastrophe of Lyric in John Burnside', in A. Karhio, S. Crosson, and C. I. Armstrong (eds), *Crisis and Contemporary Poetry*, 50–8, Basingstoke and New York: Palgrave Macmillan.
Brewster, S. (2013), 'John Burnside: Poetry as the Space of Withdrawal', in N. Alexander and D. Cooper (eds), *Poetry and Geography: Space and Place in Post-War Poetry*, 178–89, Liverpool: Liverpool University Press.

Fazzini, M. (2009), 'Kenneth White and John Burnside', in M. McGuire and C. Nicholson (eds), *The Edinburgh Companion to Contemporary Scottish Poetry*, 111–25, Edinburgh: Edinburgh University Press.

Germanà, M. (2016), 'Community Spirit? Haunting Secrets and Displaced Selves in Contemporary Scottish Fiction', in S. Lyall (ed.), *Community in Modern Scottish Literature*, 235–53, Leiden and Boston: Brill Rodopi.

Griem, J. (2015), John Burnside's Seascapes, in U. Kluwick and V. Richter (eds), *The Beach in Anglophone Literatures and Cultures: Reading Littoral Space*, 87–106, Farnham and Burlington: Ashgate.

Horton, E. (2014), 'The Postapocalyptic Sublime: A Gothic Response to Contemporary Environmental Crisis in John Burnside's *Glister* (2008)', in M. Germanà and A. Mousoutzanis (eds), *Apocalyptic Discourse in Contemporary Culture: Post-Millennial Perspectives on the End of the World*, 73–87, New York and London: Routledge.

Hyvärinen, M. (2016), 'Mind Reading, Mind Guessing, or Mental-State Attribution? The Puzzle of John Burnside's *A Summer of Drowning*', in M. Hatavara et al. (eds), *Narrative Theory, Literature, and New Media: Narrative Minds and Virtual Worlds*, 223–39, New York and Oxford: Routledge.

McGonigal, J. (2006), 'Translating God: Negative Theology and Two Scottish Poets', in J. McGonigal and K. Stirling (eds), *Ethically Speaking: Voice and Values in Modern Scottish Writing*, 223–48, Amsterdam and New York: Rodopi.

Menn, R. (2018), 'Unpicked and Remade: Creative Imperatives in John Burnside's Autofictions', in H. Dix (ed.), *Autofiction in English*, 163–77, Basingstoke and New York: Palgrave Macmillan.

Nicholson, C. (2009), 'Nomadic Subjects in Recent Poetry', in C. Nicholson and M. MGuire (eds), *The Edinburgh Companion to Contemporary Scottish Poetry*, 80–96, Edinburgh: Edinburgh University Press.

Niedlich, F. (2013), 'Finding the Right Kind of Attention: Dystopia and Transcendence in John Burnside's Glister', in S. Adiseshiah and R. Hildyard (eds), *Twenty-First Century Fiction: What Happens Now*, 212–23, Basingstoke and New York: Palgrave Macmillan.

Szuba, M. (2015), '"I Think of Them as Guests": John Burnside's Encounters with Nature', in P. Laplace (ed.), *Environmental and Ecological Readings: Nature, Human and Posthuman Dimensions in Scottish Literature and Arts (XVIII–XXI C.)*, 201–16, Besançon: Presses universitaires de Franche-Comté.

Szuba, M. (2017), 'Peering into the Dark Machinery': Modernity, Perception and the Self in John Burnside's Poetry', in J. Wolfreys (ed.), *New Critical Thinking: Criticism to Come*, 23–35, Edinburgh: Edinburgh University Press.

Journal Articles

Aldhafeeri, H. and Termizi, A. A. (2016), 'The Place of Memory in John Burnside's the Locust Room', *Pertanika Journal of Social Sciences and Humanities*, 24 (4): 1699–712.

Andersson, Dag T. (2000), '"… Only the Other Versions of Myself": Images of the Other in the Poetry of John Burnside', *Chapman: Scotland's Quality Literary Magazine*, 96: 35–9.

Baker, T. C. (2013), 'Northern Stories: The Arctic in Contemporary Scottish Gothic', *C21 Literature: Journal of 21st-Century Writings*, 2 (1): 21–36.
Borthwick, D. (2011), '"The Tilt from One Parish/into Another": Estrangement, Continuity and Connection in the Poetry of John Burnside, Kathleen Jamie And Robin Robertson', *Scottish Literary Review*, 3 (2): 133–48.
Borthwick, D. (2011), 'To Comfort Me with Nothing: John Burnside's Dissident Poetics', *Agenda*, 45 (4)–46 (1): 91–100.
Bracke, A. (2014), 'Solitaries, Outcasts and Doubles: The Fictional Oeuvre of John Burnside', *English Studies*, 95 (4): 421–40.
Brewster, S. (2005), 'Borderline Experience: Madness, Mimicry and Scottish Gothic', *Gothic Studies*, 7 (1): 79–86.
Brigley, Z. (2011), 'The Potential of Silence: Re-Reading John Burnside's Early Poems after A Lie about My Father', *Agenda*, 45 (4)–46 (1): 40–4.
Bristow, T. (2009), 'Negative Poetics and Immanence: Reading John Burnside's "Homage to Henri Bergson"', *Green Letters: Studies in Ecocriticism*, 10 (1): 50–69.
Bristow, T. (2010), 'Phenomenology, History, Biosemiosis: Heideggerian and Batesonian Poetics in John Burnside's Post-Romantic Process Ecology', *Green Letters: Studies in Ecocriticism*, 13 (1): 74–94.
Bristow, T. (2011), 'Environment, History, Literature: Materialism as Cultural Ecology in John Burnside's "Four Quartets"', *Scottish Literary Review*, 3 (2): 149–70.
Bristow, T. (2012), 'Ideas of Dwelling: Residence and Transport in Scottish Geography, German Folk Culture and the American Post-Romantic Hinterland of John Burnside's "Epithalamium"', *Australian Folklore: A Yearly Journal of Folklore Studies*, 27: 108–20.
Brown, A. (2011), 'Finding "the Lit Space": Reality, Imagination, and the Commonplace, in the Poetry of John Burnside', *Agenda*, 45 (4)–46 (1): 101–11.
Cain, R. (2011), '"Imperfectly Incarnate": Father Absence, Law and Lies in Brett Easton Ellis and John Burnside', *Journal of Law, Culture, and Humanities*, 8 (2): 1–25.
Campbell, A. (2016), 'Being, Dwelling, Tracing: John Burnside's Creaturely Cartographies', *Anglistik*, 27 (2): 95–109.
Galbraith, I. (2002), 'Eclipsing Binaries: Self and Other in John Burnside's Fiction', *Etudes Ecossaises*, 8: 147–64.
He, N. (2016), 'On John Burnside's Poetry of Repentance', *Foreign Literature Studies*, 38 (3): 65–72.
James, D. (2012), 'John Burnside's Ecologies of Solace; Regional Environmentalism and the Consolations of Description', *Modern Fiction Studies*, 58 (3): 600–15.
Klaus, H. G. (2013), 'John Burnside's *Living Nowhere* as Industrial Fiction', *Scottish Literary Review*, 5 (1): 111–27.
McCarthy, P. (2014), 'Choir Singers: Don Paterson and John Burnside', *Agenda*, 48 (1–2): 93–100.
McGonigal, J. (1993), 'Recusant Grace: The Religious Impulse in John Burnside's Verse', *Verse*, 10 (1): 65–72.
Pass, P. (2011), 'The Plight of Dwelling: "Settlements" and the Making of Home', *Agenda*, 45 (4)–46 (1): 45–9.

Pass, P. (2014), 'Desire as "Havoc in the Fabric of the Given World": Subjectivity and Text in John Burnside's *A Summer of Drowning*', *Forum for Modern Language Studies*, 50 (3): 321–31.

Ringer, L. (2018), 'Entangled States: Putting Affect Theory into Play with John Burnside's *A Summer of Drowning*', *Journal of European Popular Culture*, 9 (1): 43–57.

Roberts, A. M. (2008), 'The Visual and the Self in Contemporary Poetry', *Romanticism and Victorianism on the Net*, 51: https://id.erudit.org/iderudit/019263ar

Sampson, F. (2011), 'The Expanded Lyric: John Burnside and the Challenge to British Tradition', *Agenda*, 45 (4)–46 (1): 112–21.

Schmitt-Kilb, C. (2013), '"Poetry's a Line of Defence": Ecopoetry and Politics in the 21st Century', in U. Klawitter and V. Claus-Ulrich (eds), *Contemporary Political Poetry in Britain and Ireland*, 25–48, Heidelberg: Universitätsverlag Winter.

Smith, B. (2013), 'Beating the Bounds: Mapping the Borders of Self and Landscape in the Work of John Burnside and Tim Robinson', *Green Letters: Studies in Ecocriticism*, 17 (1): 67–76.

Szuba, M. (2017), '"The Terra Incognita of the Whole": John Burnside's Writing and the Entangled Bank of Culture'. *Litteraria Pragensia: Studies in Literature and Culture*, 27 (53): 84–100.

Volsik, P. (2007). '"Somewhere between the Presbyterian and the Tao" (Kathleen Jamie): Contemporary Scottish Poetry', *Études Anglaises*, 60 (3): 346–60.

Taylore, L. (2000), 'Comparison as the Gesture between Them: John Burnside and Jorie Graham', *Postgraduate English: A Journal and Forum for Postgraduates in English*, 2. Available online: http://community.dur.ac.uk/postgraduate.english/ojs/index.php/pgenglish/article/view/8/7

Reviews

The Hoop

Phillips, T. (1988), 'Out on the Rim', *PN Review* 65, 15 (3): 52–3.

Common Knowledge

Dooley, T. (1992), 'Incomplete Memories Friday', *The Times Literary Supplement*, 22 May: 31.

Feast Days

Dooley, T. (1992), 'Incomplete Memories Friday', *The Times Literary Supplement*, 22 May: 31.

Herbert, W. N. (1992), 'Absent Choirs', *PN Review* 86, 18 (6): 55.

Tredell, N. (1992), 'Uncertainties of the Poet', *London Review of Books*, 14 (12): 22–3.

The Myth of the Twin

Eaves, W. (1995), 'Harm's Way', *PN Review* 101, 21 (3): 59–61.
McMillan, I. (1994), 'Breathing into the Fire', *Poetry Review*, 84 (1): 77–8.
Murray, N. (1994), 'The Smell of Frost on Linen', *The Times Literary Supplement*, 8 July: 8.

Swimming in the Flood

Burt, S. (1996), 'They Found a Cardigan', *The Times Literary Supplement*, 2 February: 28.
Page, R. (1996), 'The Detriment of Influence', *PN Review* 108, 22 (4): 62–3.

A Normal Skin

Carnell, S. (1998), 'The Shiver in the Hedge', *The Times Literary Supplement*, 2 January: 21.
Henry, B. (1997), 'The Healing Darkness', *PN Review* 118, 24 (2): 75–6.
Petrucci, M. (1998), '*A Normal Skin* by John Burnside', *Ambit*, 153: 57–8.
Redmond, J. (1997), 'War against the Grown-Ups', *London Review of Books*, 19 (16): 23–5.

The Dumb House: A Chamber Novel

Baker, P. (1997), 'Experiments in Quiet', *The Times Literary Supplement*, 23 May: 20.
Redmond, J. (1997), 'War against the Grown-Ups', *London Review of Books*, 19 (16): 23–5.
Saynor, J. (1998), '*The Dumb House: A Chamber Novel*. By John Burnside', *New York Times Book Review*, 12 July. Available online: http://movies2.nytimes.com/books/98/07/12/reviews/980712.12saynort.html

The Mercy Boys

Imlah, M. (1999), 'A Connoisseur of Rain', *The Times Literary Supplement*, 7 May: 23.

The Asylum Dance

Wardle, S. (2001), 'Homing Instinct', *The Times Literary Supplement*, 9 February: 25.

FURTHER READING

Burning Elvis

McAllister, A. (2000), 'Killing off the King', *The Times Literary Supplement*, 23 June: 25.

The Locust Room

Bedford, M. (2001), '*The Locust Room* (Book Review)', *New Statesman*, 14 (658), 28 May: 57.
Crown, S. (2005), 'Burnside – Not So Hot?', *The Guardian*, 22 June. Available online: https://www.theguardian.com/culture/culturevultureblog/2005/jun/22/justfinishedj
Falconer, H. (2001), 'Inner Demons', *The Guardian*, 4 August. Available online: https://www.theguardian.com/books/2001/aug/04/fiction.reviews1
O'Brien, S. (2001), 'Doomed Liaisons', *The Times Literary Supplement*, 25 May: 21.

The Light Trap

Bate, J. (2002), 'Eco Laurels', *The Guardian*, 23 November. Available online: https://www.theguardian.com/books/2002/nov/23/featuresreviews.guardianreview8
Forster, J. (2002), 'Provisional Worlds', *PN Review* 146, 28 (6): 77.
Lomas, H. (2002), '*The Light Trap* by John Burnside', *Ambit*, 170: 49.

Living Nowhere

Flusfeder, D. (2003), 'Living in a Suburb of Hell', *The Telegraph*, 9 June. Available online: https://www.telegraph.co.uk/culture/books/3596263/Living-in-a-suburb-of-hell.html
Lichtig, T. (2003), 'Invented Places', *The Times Literary Supplement*, 11 July: 23.
Poster, J. (2003), 'Exile on Main Street', *The Guardian*, 14 June. Available online: https://www.theguardian.com/books/2003/jun/14/featuresreviews.guardianreview23
Smith, E. (2003), 'Corby, Home of the Big Themes', *The Telegraph*, 3 August. Available online: https://www.telegraph.co.uk/culture/books/3599756/Corby-home-of-the-big-themes.html

The Good Neighbour

Bainbridge, C. (2005), 'The Shape of the Wind', *The Guardian*, 9 July. Available online: https://www.theguardian.com/books/2005/jul/09/featuresreviews.guardianreview26

McAuliffe, J. (2005), 'The State of the World', *The Poetry Ireland Review*, 84: 88–93.
Roberts, T. (2006), 'Uncomfortable Consolations', *PN Review* 167, 32 (3): 90–1.
Wootten, W. (2006), 'Away at Home', *The Times Literary Supplement*, 17 February: 30.
(2005), 'Anatomists of the Unknown', *The Scotsman*, 19 February. Available online: https://www.scotsman.com/lifestyle/culture/books/anatomists-of-the-unknown-1-736708

Selected Poems

Poster, J. (2006), 'Between Heaven and Earth', *The Guardian*, 8 April. Available online: https://www.theguardian.com/books/2006/apr/08/featuresreviews.guardianreview22

A Lie about My Father

Birch, C. (2006). 'Never, and Forever', *The Times Literary Supplement*, 7 April: 25.
Jeal, T. (2006), 'Anger Passed from Father to Son' *The Telegraph*, 5 March. Available online: https://www.telegraph.co.uk/culture/books/3650695/Anger-passed-from-father-to-son.html
Mantel, H. (2006), 'What He Could Bear', *London Review of Books*, 28 (5): 3–7.
McGrath, M. (2006), 'Anti-Son on Anti-Father', *The Telegraph*, 26 March. Available online: https://www.telegraph.co.uk/culture/books/3651130/Anti-son-on-anti-father.html
Morrison, B. (2006), 'The Long Discipline of Happiness', *The Guardian*, 25 February. Available online: https://www.theguardian.com/books/2006/feb/25/featuresreviews.guardianreview

Gift Songs

Bainbridge, C. (2007), 'A Space That Nobody Owns', *The Guardian*, 28 April. Available online: https://www.theguardian.com/books/2007/apr/28/featuresreviews.guardianreview22
Lichtig, T. (2007), 'The Devil Rides Out', *The Observer*, 18 March 2007. Available online: https://www.theguardian.com/books/2007/mar/18/poetry.features
Phillips, A. (2007), 'Masters of All They Survey', *The Observer*, 28 October. Available online: https://www.theguardian.com/books/2007/oct/28/poetry.features1

The Devil's Footprints: A Romance

Enright, A. (2007), 'The Devil Inside', *The Guardian*, 17 March 2007. Available online: https://www.theguardian.com/books/2007/mar/17/featuresreviews.guardianreview17

FitzHerbert, C. (2007), 'Derangement, Deaths and Devils', *The Telegraph*, 1 March. Available online: https://www.telegraph.co.uk/culture/books/3663693/Derangement-deaths-and-devils.html

Gordon, N. (2008), 'My Bad', *The New York Times*, 13 April. Available online: https://www.nytimes.com/2008/04/13/books/review/Gordon-t.html

Griffiths, N. (2008), 'The Labyrinths of Innertown', *The Telegraph*, 10 May. Available online: https://www.telegraph.co.uk/culture/books/fictionreviews/3673251/The-labyrinths-of-Innertown.html

Lichtig, T. (2007), 'The Devil Rides Out', *The Observer*, 18 March 2007. Available online: https://www.theguardian.com/books/2007/mar/18/poetry.features

Miller, K. (2007), 'Old Nick at Work', *The Times Literary Supplement*, 2 March: 22.

Glister

Ferguson, E. (2008), 'The Landscape Artist', *The Observer*, 17 May. Available online: https://www.theguardian.com/books/2008/may/18/fiction.reviews1

Housham, J. (2009), 'The Spun Yarn', *The Guardian*, 22 May. Available online: https://www.theguardian.com/books/2009/may/23/glister-john-burnside-review

Rafferty, T. (2009), 'The Disappeared', *The New York Times*, 2 April. Available online: https://www.nytimes.com/2009/04/05/books/review/Rafferty-t.html

Thompson, S. (2008), 'Perfect Shadows', *The Times Literary Supplement*, 23 May: 20.

Welsh, I. (2008), 'Poisoned Minds', *The Guardian*, 16 May. Available online: https://www.theguardian.com/books/2008/may/17/fiction5

The Hunt in the Forest

Batchelor, P. (n.d.), 'Review of John Burnside, *The Hunt in the Forest*'. Available online: http://paulbatchelor.co.uk/wp-content/uploads/2012/06/burnside.pdf

Ferner, A. (2010), '*The Hunt in the Forest* by John Burnside', *Ambit*, 199: 62–3.

Pollard, N. (2010), 'Poetry in Brief', *The Times Literary Supplement*, 26 March: 28.

Wheatley, D. (2009), '*The Hunt in the Forest* by John Burnside', *The Guardian*, 5 September. Available online: https://www.theguardian.com/books/2009/sep/05/hunt-forest-burnside-review

Waking up in Toytown

Edemariam, A. (2010). '*Waking up in Toytown* by John Burnside', *The Guardian*, 2 January. Available online: https://www.theguardian.com/books/2010/jan/02/waking-up-in-toytown-burnside

Epstein, O. B. (2011), 'Book Review – *Waking up in Toytown* (2010) by John Burnside', *Attachment: New Directions in Psychotherapy and Relational Psychoanalysis*, 5 (3): 293–4.

Leith, W. (2010), 'Behind the Net Curtains', *The Spectator*, 13 January. Available online: https://www.spectator.co.uk/2010/01/behind-the-net-curtains/

O'Riordan, A. (2010), 'Waking up in Toytown by John Burnside: Review', *The Telegraph*, 10 January. Available online: https://www.telegraph.co.uk/culture/books/6947655/Waking-Up-in-Toytown-by-John-Burnside-review.html

Woodward, G. (2010), 'Too Sane for Surbiton', *The Times Literary Supplement*, 5 March: 24.

Black Cat Bone

Batchelor, P. (2011), 'Sweet Home', *The Times Literary Supplement*, 2 December: 26.

Binding, P. (2011), '*Black Cat Bone* by John Burnside', *Ambit*, 206: 55–6.

Lessley, S. (2016), 'Split the Lark', *West Branch*, 82: 106–16.

Thomas, M. W. (2011), 'Black Cat Bone by John Burnside – Review', *The Guardian*, 6 September. Available online: https://www.theguardian.com/books/2011/sep/06/black-cat-bone-john-burnside-poetry-review

A Summer of Drowning

Cummins, A. (2011), '*A Summer of Drowning* by John Burnside: Review', *The Telegraph*, 17 June. Available online: https://www.telegraph.co.uk/culture/books/bookreviews/8579383/A-Summer-of-Drowning-by-John-Burnside-review.html

Kavenna, J. (2011), 'A Summer of Drowning by John Burnside – Review', *The Guardian*, 22 July. Available online: https://www.theguardian.com/books/2011/jul/22/summer-of-drowning-burnside-review

Souster, T. (2011), 'On Long Light Nights', *The Times Literary Supplement*, 10 June: 19.

Something Like Happy

Drabble, M. (2013), 'The Beast in the Jungle', *The New Statesman*, 142 (5140), 11–17 January: 48.

Hanks, R. (2013), '*Something Like Happy* by John Burnside: Review', 29 January. Available online: https://www.telegraph.co.uk/culture/books/bookreviews/9823599/Something-Like-Happy-by-John-Burnside-review.html

Kelly, S. (2013), '*Something Like Happy* by John Burnside – Review', *The Guardian*, 19 January 2013. Available online: https://www.theguardian.com/books/2013/jan/19/something-like-happy-john-burnside-review

Maunsell, J. B. (2013), 'Dangerous Dreaming', *The Times Literary Supplement*, 8 February: 20.

All One Breath

Kellaway, K. (2014), '*All One Breath* by John Burnside – Review', *The Observer*, 16 February. Available online: https://www.theguardian.com/books/2014/feb/16/all-one-breath-john-burnside-review

Mackinnon, L. (2015), 'Missing', *The Times Literary Supplement*, 20 February: 22.
Sperling, M. (2014), 'Mother Tongue', *The New Statesman*, 143 (5199), 28 February–6 March: 50–1.

I Put a Spell on You: Several Digressions on Love and Glamour

Bunting, M. (2014), 'A Book for the Beach: *I Put a Spell on You* by John Burnside', *The Guardian*, 17 July. Available online: https://www.theguardian.com/books/booksblog/2014/jul/17/book-for-the-beach-john-burnside
Connolly, C. (2014), 'My Desert Island Poet: A Review of *I Put a Spell on You*', *The Spectator*, 31 May. Available online: https://www.spectator.co.uk/2014/05/i-put-a-spell-on-you-by-john-burnside-review/
Hadley, T. (2014), '*I Put a Spell on You* by John Burnside – Review', *The Guardian*, 2 May. Available online: https://www.theguardian.com/books/2014/may/02/put-a-spell-on-you-john-burnside-review
Kellaway, K. (2014), '*I Put a Spell on You* Review – John Burnside's Path Less Travelled', *The Observer*, 4 May. Available online: https://www.theguardian.com/books/2014/may/04/i-put-a-spell-on-you-john-burnside-review
Kerridge, J. (2014), '*I Put a Spell on You* by John Burnside, Review', *The Telegraph*, 2 July. Available online: https://www.telegraph.co.uk/culture/books/bookreviews/10927286/I-Put-a-Spell-on-You-by-John-Burnside-review-a-scintillating-and-insightful-ragbag.html

Still Life with Feeding Snake

Dean, P. (2017), 'Poet in Limbo', *The New Criterion*, 35 (8): 23–5.
Kellaway, K. (2017), '*Still Life with Feeding Snake* by John Burnside Review – Master of the Parallel Universe', *The Guardian*, 14 March. Available online: https://www.theguardian.com/books/2017/mar/14/john-burnside-still-life-with-feeding-snake-poetry-book-review-kate-kellaway
Mort, H. (2017), 'Subtle Apocalypse', *The Poetry Review*, 107 (2): 95–9.
Muckle, J. (2018), 'Brevity, Eternity', *PN Review* 240, 44 (4): 92–3.
Sampson, F. (2017), 'Twilight Zone', *The New Statesman*, 146 (5353), 10–16 February: 56.
Waterman, R. (2018), 'Happy Ever After', *PN Review* 242, 44 (6): 77.

Ashland & Vine

Kelly, S. (2017), 'Book Review: *Ashland & Vine* by John Burnside', *The Scotsman*, 1 February. Available online: https://www.scotsman.com/lifestyle/culture/books/book-review-ashland-vine-by-john-burnside-1-4355113
Sampson, F. (2017), 'Twilight Zone', *The New Statesman*, 146 (5353), 10–16 February: 56.
Scholes, L. (2017), '*Ashland & Vine* by John Burnside – Review', *The Observer*, 12 February. Available online: https://www.theguardian.com/books/2017/feb/12/ashland-vine-john-burnside-review

Swift, D. (2017), 'John Burnside Treads Sacred Ground in *Ashland & Vine*', *The Spectator*, 25 February. Available online: https://www.spectator.co.uk/2017/02/john-burnside-treads-sacred-ground-in-ashland-vine/

Theroux, M. (2017), '*Ashland & Vine* by John Burnside Review – The Redemptive Power of Listening', *The Guardian*, 21 January. Available online: https://www.theguardian.com/books/2017/jan/21/ashland-and-vine-by-john-burnside-review

Havergey

Cox, Roger (2017), 'Book Review: *Havergey*, by John Burnside', *The Scotsman*, 10 May. Available online: https://www.scotsman.com/lifestyle/culture/books/book-review-havergey-by-john-burnside-1-4436320

On Henry Miller: Or, How to Be an Anarchist

Fejzula, M. (2018), 'Anarchy', *The Times Literary Supplement*, 17 August: 30.

Zhou, D. (2018), 'Henry Miller – Pornographer or Prophet?', *The Spectator*, 14 April. Available online: https://www.spectator.co.uk/2018/04/henry-miller-pornographer-or-prophet/

Selected Interviews

Abrial, F. (1997), 'Rencontre Avec John Burnside', *Europe: revue littéraire mensuelle*, 817: 116–20.

Allen, R. (2011), 'John Burnside: Interview', *Granta*, 94, 16 August. Available online https://granta.com/interview-john-burnside

'Belief' (2012), [Radio programme] BBC Radio 3, 4 April. Available: https://www.bbc.co.uk/programmes/b01f68f1

Bright, R. (2018), 'Things Come as They Will: A Q&A with John Burnside', *The Quietus*, 12 August. Available online: http://thequietus.com/articles/25109-john-burnside-interview

Burnside, J. (2002), 'An Interview [with Allison Funk]', *Sou'wester*: 8–22.

Burnside, J. (2015), 'John Burnside', in M. Fazzini (ed.), *Conversations with Scottish Poets*, 111–23, Aberdeen: Aberdeen University Press.

Crown, S. (2011), 'John Burnside: A Life in Writing', *The Guardian*, 26 August. Available online: https://www.theguardian.com/culture/2011/aug/26/john-burnside-life-in-writing

Dósa, A. (2003), 'Poets and Other Animals: Interview with John Burnside', *Scottish Studies Review*, 4 (1): 9–23.

Doshi, T. (2017), 'Enrolling Fairies in the Revolution', *The Hindu*, 21 October. Available online: https://www.thehindu.com/thread/reflections/tishani-doshi-john-burnside-poets-corner-enrolling-fairies-in-the-revolution/article19895598.ece

Doyle, I. (2017), '"I'm a Human and Nothing Human Is Alien to Me": An Interview with John Burnside', *Culture Trip*, 28 February. Available online: https://

theculturetrip.com/europe/united-kingdom/scotland/articles/im-a-human-and-nothing-human-is-alien-to-me-an-interview-with-john-burnside/

Front Row (2017), [Radio programme] BBC Radio 4, 2 February. Available online: https://www.bbc.co.uk/programmes/b08byp9j

Johnstone, D. (2011), 'Tripping in the Midnight Sunshine', *The Independent*, 12 June. Available online: https://www.independent.co.uk/arts-entertainment/books/features/tripping-in-the-midnight-sunshine-2296317.html

Mackintosh, H. (1999), 'Poet's Choice', *The Guardian*, 3 June. Available online: https://www.theguardian.com/technology/1999/jun/03/onlinesupplement1

McCarthy, P. (2011), 'Interview: John Burnside', *Agenda*, 45 (4)–46 (1): 22–38.

Meo-Ehlet de, Myrtha (2015), 'Animals in and around Poetry: Interview with John Burnside', Lo Sguardo – Rivista Di Filosofia, 18 (2): 363–70.

Merritt, S. (2006), 'Dad, I Could've Killed You', *The Observer*, 26 February 2006. Available online: https://www.theguardian.com/books/2006/feb/26/biography.features1

O'Malley, J. P. (2013), 'Interview with a Writer: John Burnside', *The Spectator*, 18 January. Available online: http://blogs.spectator.co.uk/books/2013/01/interview-with-a-writer-john-burnside/

Private Passions (2008), [Radio programme] BBC Radio 3, 5 October.

Staff, H. (2012), 'Interview with John Burnside', *Poetry Foundation*, 6 March. Available online: https://www.poetryfoundation.org/harriet/2012/03/interview-with-john-burnside

Start the Week (2014), [Radio programme] BBC Radio 4, 17 November. Available online: https://www.bbc.co.uk/programmes/b04p604k

Steinmetz, M. (2014), 'John Burnside: From Software Engineering to Top Writer', *The British Council*, 14 October. Available online: https://www.britishcouncil.org/voices-magazine/john-burnside-software-engineering-top-writer

Yates, E. (2001), 'Five Minutes with John Burnside', *The Guardian*, 23 January. Available online: https://www.theguardian.com/books/2001/jan/23/whitbreadbookawards2000.costabookaward

Index

alchemy 8, 14, 17, 19–20, 23
Allen, Rachael 70
Alpers, Paul 81
Andersson, Dag T. 33–4, 36, 116
Atwood, Margaret
  Oryx and Crake 73

Bachelard, Gaston 50
Bakan, Joel 73
Baker, Timothy, C. 92
Banks, Iain, *Wasp Factory, The* 73
Barthes, Roland, Death of the Author, The 133
Batchelor, Paul 129
Bate, Jonathan 89
  Song of the Earth 81
Beardsley, Aubrey 6
Benjamin, Walter 33, 84–6, 89
Borges, Jorge Luis 31
Borthwick, David 10–11, 21, 53–4, 73, 102, 105, 109–19
Bracke, Astrid 2, 53, 55, 71, 129
Brault, Pascale-Anne 125
Brewster, Scott 53, 68, 75–8, 117
Bristow, Tom 10, 81–94, 97, 102
Brown, Eric. C. 42, 48
Brueghel, Pieter 31
Burning Elvis 9, 54–9
Burnside, John
  Authorised Version, notion of 68–71, 73, 76–8
  Bible citations (*see* religious collections)
  class and gender, views on 9–10
  Davies's interview 133–42
  on death/dead 31–4
  dwelling and *being-in-the-world*, concept 4, 8–10
  ecological thoughts 8–10
  failure, notion of 2–3
  forms of writing 1–11
  Freudian concept of uncanny 74
  gnostic and alchemical ideas 14–15
  prizes and accolades 2
  self-assessment 2
  on space and storytelling 7
  temporal and spatial metaphors 7–8
  thrawn, concepts of 3, 70–2, 74, 78
  on truth and falsehood 5–6
  on ways of being and thinking 3–4
  writings (*see also specific concepts*)
    'Essay Concerning Time, An' 31, 112
    Ashland & Vine 7
    Asylum Dance, The 2, 40–2
    Black Cat Bone 2, 9, 11
    Burning Elvis 9
    Common Knowledge 2, 29
    Devil's Footprints, The 11
    Dumb House, The 2, 7–8, 14–16
    Feast Days 2
    Glister 10–11, 15
    On Henry Miller 2–3, 7
    Hoop and *Common Knowledge, The* 2
    Hunt in the Forest, The 11, 32
    'Iona: A Quest for the Pagan' (essay) 13
    I Put a Spell on You 2, 9
    Lie about My Father, A 2, 4–6
    Light Trap, The 9–10
    Living Nowhere 2
    Locust Room, The 2, 16
    Mercy Boys, The 2
    Myth of the Twin, The 10
    Normal Skin, A 110
    'Poetry and a Sense of Place' 117

INDEX

'Samiland: The Finnmarksvidda' (essay) 4
'Slut's Hair' 1, 61, 63
Something Like Happy 9
Still Life with Feeding Snake 9–10
'Strong Words' (essay) 3, 14
Summer of Drowning, A 1, 15, 76
Swimming in the Flood 9
Waking up in Toytown 3–5, 13, 16, 32
'Walk the Tightrope' (essay) 97, 99, 102, 104
Butler, J. 58

Cain, Ruth 9, 67–79
Campbell, Alexandra 9, 53–64
Carse, James P. 42
Char, René 129
Childs, Peter 8, 13–23, 75
Clark, Timothy 60
class and gender 9, 67–8
    Authorised Version, notion of 68–71, 73, 76–8
    femininity 71–2, 76–7 (*see also specific writings*)
    masculinity 54, 56, 59, 62, 67–9, 72–4
    working-class women 72, 77, 145 n.4
Conrad, Klaus 13
Corine International Literature 2
Crawford, Robert 44

Dada (short story) 59
Davies, Ben 1–11, 133–42
Davis, Colin 110, 113, 115
Decency (short story) 56–7
Derrida, Jacques 50, 111–13, 115–16, 118, 124–6
    in *Specters of Marx* 111
Dickinson, Emily 36
Dolar, Mladen 75
Donne, John 26, 55
    'No man is an island' 55
Dósa, Attila 44
dwelling-and *being-in-the-world*
    'Appleseed' 49

Asylum Dance, The 40–2
'De Anima' 49
ecological concerns 41, 44, 50
Feast Days 48
'Fields' 41
'Kith' 45
Light Trap, The 48
'Place by the Sea, A' 41
poetic language 39–40, 42–9
'Ports' 41
'Roads' 41
'Sense Data' 45
'Settlements' 41, 43
'Steinar undir Steinahlíthum' 42
'Taxonomy' 45–6
'Travelling South, Scotland, August 2012' 43
world's natural elements 44–5

ecological concerns
    Devil's Footprints, The 100
    Glister 100–5, 107
    Living Nowhere 100
    Summer of Drowning, A 100
    'Walk the Tightrope' (essay) 97, 99, 102, 104
Eeckhart, Bart 83
Eliot, T. S. 2, 27, 46
Elulard, Paul 113
Empson, William 81, 94
Encore Award 2
Engelmann, Paul 25

femininity analysis
    Black Cat Bone 72
    Dumb House, The 76
    I Put a Spell on You 71, 77
    Mercy Boys, The 72, 76–7
    Something Like Happy 71
    Summer of Drowning, A 72, 76–7
    Waking up in Toytown 71–2
Finucane, Ronald.C., *Cultural History of Ghosts* 110
Fisher, Mark 68, 70, 115–16
Forward Poetry Prize 2
Foucault, Michel 6
Franke, William 34
Freud, Sigmund 75
Frosh, Stephen 69

INDEX

Genette, Gérard 118
Geoffrey Faber Memorial Prize 2
ghosts
   Asylum Dance, The 113
   Black Cat Bone 118
   Good Neighbour, The 110, 118
   Hunt in the Forest, The 112, 117
   Lie about My Father, A 109
   Light Trap, The 111
   Myth of the Twin, The 109, 116
   Normal Skin, A 110
   Still Life with Feeding Snake 116
Gilson, Erinn 58–9
gnostic and alchemical ideas
   'Angel Eyes' from *The Myth of the Twin* 21
   Devil's Footprints, The 18
   Feast Days 20
   Living Nowhere 18–21
   Locust Room, The 20
   Summer of Drowning, A 20
Godwit (short story) 61–3
Graham, Jorie 91–3
   Dream of the Unified Field 91
Griem, Julika 57
Guattari, Félix 99
   Three Ecologies, The 99, 105, 107

Hanssen, Beatrice 85
Hardy, Thomas, 'Spectres that Grieve' 110
Heaney, Seamus
   District and Circle 81
   Electric Light 81
Heidegger, Martin 39–40, 43–4, 46, 49, 58, 82–7, 90–1, 93, 98
   Antlits 85
   'Building Dwelling Thinking' 40
   'Language' 44
   'Origin of the Work of Art, The' 90
   'What Are Poets For?' 85
Herbert, George 26
Hopkins, Gerard Manley 26
Hughes, Ted, *Hawk in the Rain* 81
Husserl, Edmund 127–8

Jakobson, Roman 25

Lacan, Jacques 69, 70, 75–6
language and lyricism
   Lie about My Father, A 22
   Living Nowhere 22
Larkin, Philip, *Less Deceived, The* 30
Lawrence, David Herbert
   Plumed Serpent, The 16
   Woman who Rode Away, The 16
literary ecology and history. See pastoral ideology
Longley, Michael 81
Lowell, Robert, *Life Studies* 81

MacCulloch, J. A., *Religion of the Ancient Celts, The* 128
Macdonald, Graeme 100
Maitreyabandhu 114
male psychopaths
   Dumb House, The 74–5
   Lie about My Father, A 74–5
   Locust Room, The 75
   Mercy Boys, The 75
   Myth of the Twin, The 76
male sociopaths
   Dumb House, The 73
   Lie about My Father, A 73–4
   Locust Room, The 73–4
   Mercy Boys, The 74
   Swimming in the Flood 72
Mallarmé, Stéphane 49
   'Crisis of Verse' 47
Marion, Jean-Luc 129
Martin, Sean 18–19
McCarthy, Patricia 67–8, 70, 72–3, 117
McDowell, Lesley 69
McEwan, Ian 2
McGonigal, James 74–5, 78
McKay, Don 81
Melville, Herman, *Moby Dick* 32
Merleau-Ponty, Maurice 42, 46, 91
metaphysics 22–3
Michaux, Henri, 'Sur étrave': 'Pas de port. Ports inconnus' 41
Mitchell, Juliet 76
Murphy, Ann 59

Naas, Michael 125
'new beginning,' themes
   Light Trap, The 77

INDEX

Locust Room, The 78
Mercy Boys, The 78
Nietzsche, Friedrich
    Beyond Good and Evil 16
    'On Truth and Lying in a Non-Moral Sense' 5

Oliver, Mary 81
O'Malley, Jonathan Powell 71, 77
Otto, Rudolf 34–5
    Idea of the Holy, The 26

Pagels, Elaine 23
Pass, Phill 10, 97–107
pastoral ideology
    Asylum Dance, The 81, 83, 86
    Good Neighbour, The 83
    Hoop, The 81
    Light Trap, The 81–5, 87, 89–94
Paz, Octavio 85
    'A Tale of Two Gardens' 41
Petrarca-Preis 2
Pick, Anat 61, 64
Poirier, Richard 93
Priest, Stephen 91
Private Passions (2008, Radio programme) 109
Prix Litteraire Europeen Madeleine Zepter 2

Rae, Patricia 89
Ramazani, Jahan 93
religious collections
    'Black Cat Bone' 27, 32–3, 36
    Common Knowledge 29, 31–2, 36
    Gift Songs 27
    Summer of Drowning, A 33
Rilke, Rainer Maria 83–6, 88–90, 93
Riordan, Maurice 4
Roccolo (short story) 61–3
Rose, Jacqueline 76
Royal Society of Edinburgh 2
Royal Society of Literature 2
Rushdie, Salman, *Grimus* 19

Sacks, Peter, M 93
Saltire Society Scottish Book of the Year Award 2
Scigaj, Leonard 90
Scottish Arts Council Book Award 2

Shepard, Paul 84, 89–90
short story collection. *See Burning Elvis*; *Something Like Happy*
Simic, Charles 92
Slovic, Scott 94
Slut's Hair (short story) 1, 61, 63
Smith, Zadie 2
Snyder, Gary 41
Something Like Happy 9, 54, 60–4, 71
Spargo, R. Clifton 93
spiritual fictions
    Devil's Footprints, The 17
    Dumb House, The 14, 16
    Glister 15, 17
    Locust Room, The 16
    Mercy Boys, The 16
    Summer of Drowning, A 15
    'Waking up in Toytown' 16
Spycher: Leuk Literturpreis 2
Stevens, Wallace 30, 83–4, 88, 90–1
    Auroras of Autumn, The 15
    'Thirteen Ways of Looking at a Blackbird' 83
Stevenson, Robert Louis 109
subjectivity
    Being, conditions of 123–30
    Devil's Footprint, The 123
    Glister 124, 130
    Hunt in the Forest, The 129
    'At My Father's Funeral' 126
    phenomenological apprehension in 127–8
Sundial/SAC Non-Fiction Book of the Year Award 2
Suttie, Ian Dishart 43
Szuba, Monika 9, 39–51

themes and divisions. *See also* pastoral ideology
    animals 85–6
    blackbird 92–3
    erasure 91
    form of destruction 83–4
    lament 83, 85, 89–91, 93
    melancholia 84–5
    mourning 86–9
Thomas, M. Wynn 91
Thomson, Jeffrey 87
Twiddy, Iain 82

Verdi, Giuseppe, *Requiem* 27
violence
    Burning Elvis 54–9
    female victimhood 54–5, 57
    Living Nowhere 72
    Locust Room, The 72
    masculinity and 54–7, 59–60, 62
    Something Like Happy 54, 60–4

Weil, Simone 86, 91–2
Wheatley, David 117
Whitbread Poetry Award 2
Wilm, Jan 8–9, 25–37
Wimsatt, William K. 6
Wittgenstein, Ludwig 25
Wolfreys, Julian 11, 121–30
working-class
    childhood 76
    masculinity 68–9
    Waking up in Toytown 72
    women 72, 77, 145 n.4
Wylie, John 111, 113

www.ingramcontent.com/pod-product-compliance
Lightning Source LLC
Chambersburg PA
CBHW052047300426
44117CB00012B/2005